FIRE
from
HEAVEN

ALSO BY HARVEY COX

Many Mansions

Religion in the Secular City

The Seduction of the Spirit

Turning East

The Secular City

Feast of Fools

The Silencing of Leonardo Boff

Just as I Am

God's Revelation and Man's Responsibility

On Not Leaving It to the Snake

FIRE
from
HEAVEN

**The Rise of Pentecostal
Spirituality and the
Reshaping of Religion in
the Twenty-first Century**

HARVEY COX

DA CAPO PRESS
A Member of the Perseus Books Group

Lyrics from Sting's "If I Ever Lose My Faith in You" used by permission:
Illegal Songs, Inc./Reggatta Music Ltd. (BMI)

Cataloging-in-Publication data for this book is available from the Library of Congress.

First Da Capo Press edition 2001
ISBN 0-306-81049-2

Published by Da Capo Press
A Member of the Perseus Books Group
http://www.dacapopress.com

Da Capo Press books are available at special discounts for bulk purchases in the U.S. by corporations, institutions, and other organizations. For more information, please contact the Special Markets Department at the Perseus Books Group, 11 Cambridge Center, Cambridge, MA 02142, or call (617) 252-5298.

THIS BOOK IS DEDICATED TO

Nina Tumarkin
Nicholas Tumarkin Cox
Maximilian Davis Marshall
and
Sara Cox Keleman

ACKNOWLEDGMENTS

*I*T WAS MY OLD friend Brady Tyson who first encouraged me to write this book, and who personally introduced me to some of the pentecostals who appear in it, sometimes under pseudonyms because I did not want to embarrass or inconvenience them. Another old friend, Eldin Villafañe, was my principal pentecostal conversation partner during the writing, especially through our joint teaching ventures. Carl Oglesby read original drafts and urged me to keep going. The Reverend Eugene Rivers, minister of the Azusa Christian Community in Boston responded to early drafts and helped me avoid some mistakes. Jane Redmont and Dr. Grant Wacker both read the entire manuscript and offered splendid suggestions. Kathryn Tiede, Katie Crane, Julia Lieblich, and Richard Hughes Seager generously allowed me to draw on unpublished material they have written. Alberto Moisés Mendez, Pamela Lowe, Greg Supriano, Hilary Grubb, Patricia Simpson, Tricia Lyons, Carl Lindeman, Dale Gadsden, David Kim, and the other engaging students in my seminar on Theology and Culture read and discussed the book while it was still in the making and will find many of their ideas incorporated in it. Another student, Vincent Castellani, who is a pentecostal pastor, was especially helpful with his sympathetic suggestions. Dongsoo Kim offered advice on the chapter on Korea. I was very gratified to receive encouragement to explore this subject from the recognized dean of pentecostal studies, Walter Hollenweger. Other pentecostal scholars such as Frank D. Macchia and Vinson Synan continued to send me invaluable material. Wayne Warner of the rich Assemblies of God Archives in Springfield, Missouri, helped me select the photographs. My research assistant Kate Moschandreas deftly searched out hard-to-find sources. My faculty assistant, Margaret Studier, tirelessly saw the book through many print-outs. The most helpful advice I got, including the suggestion that I knock off now and then when I became too obsessed, came from my wife, Dr. Nina Tumarkin, who is chairman of the History Department at Wellesley College and who was completing her own book, *The Living and the Dead: The Rise and Fall of the Cult of World War II in Russia*, while I was writing this one. Most of all, however, I am thankful to the countless good-spirited pentecostal people in innumerable congregations in many places in the world who patiently responded to so many questions from someone they no doubt hoped would join their ranks but never did, at least not in the way they expected.

Harvey Cox
Cambridge, Massachusetts
May 23, 1994

CONTENTS

PREFACE

*A*FEW YEARS AGO the editor of a national magazine called to ask if I wanted to make a comment for an article they were preparing on the anniversary of *Time* magazine's famous "Is God Dead?" cover story. He told me that he and his colleagues were puzzled. Why did Presbyterians, Methodists, and Episcopalians seem be to losing members—down 20 to 40 percent in the twenty-five years since that cover hit the stands—while certain other churches, mainly pentecostal ones, had doubled or tripled their memberships in the same period. He had also seen reports that pentecostalism was growing very quickly in Latin America, Africa, and parts of Asia. Was there something ominous, he wanted to know, about all this? And furthermore what did I think of the rumor that President Bill Clinton used to play his saxophone at pentecostal revival services in Redfield, Arkansas? He sounded a little worried.

I thought I knew why he was calling me. Nearly three decades ago I wrote a book, *The Secular City*, in which I tried to work out a theology for the "postreligious" age that many sociologists had confidently assured us was coming. Since then, however, religion—or at least some religions—seems to have gained a new lease on life. Today it is secularity, not spirituality, that may be headed for extinction. I thought, perhaps the editor wanted me to eat a little crow in public. Instead I thanked him for the call and told him I was probably not the right person to ask. But his questions were thought-provoking. I had read some of the same amazing statistics, including the estimate that pentecostal churches are growing at the rate of 20 million new members a year and that their worldwide membership had now reached some 410 million. I had wondered myself why they have such an appeal, but the phone call pushed me into a more active inquiry. I decided to find out what I could about pentecostals, not just by reading about them but by visiting their churches wherever I could and by talking with both their ministers and with ordinary members. My project eventually took me to four different continents, to a score of conferences and conventions of pentecostal leaders, and to more congregations than I can enumerate.

Even before I started my journey through the world of pentecostalism it had become obvious that instead of the "death of God" some theologians pronounced not many years ago, or the waning of religion that sociologists had extrapolated, something quite different has taken place. Perhaps I was too young and impressionable when the scholars made those sobering projections. In any case I had swallowed them all too easily and had tried to think about what their theological consequences might be. But it had now become clear that the predictions themselves had been wrong. The prognosticators had written that the technological pace and urban bustle of the twentieth century would increasingly shove religion to the margin where, deprived of roots, it would shrivel. They allowed that faith might well survive as a valued heirloom, perhaps in ethnic enclaves or family customs, but insisted that religion's days as a shaper of culture and history were over.

This did not happen. Instead, before the academic forecasters could even begin to draw their pensions, a religious renaissance of sorts is under way all over the globe. Religions that some theologians thought had been stunted by western materialism or suffocated by totalitarian repression have regained a whole new vigor. Buddhism and Hinduism, Christianity and Judaism, Islam and Shinto, and many smaller sects are once again alive and well. For many people, however, it is not always good news that religions that were once thought to be safely moribund or at most peripheral have again become controversial players on the world stage. We may or may not be entering a new "age of the Spirit" as some more sanguine observers hope. But we are definitely in a period of renewed religious vitality, another "great awakening" if you will, with all the promise and peril religious revivals always bring with them, but this time on a world scale. But why were the predictors so wrong? Why has this unanticipated resurgence of religion occurred?

As I began work on this book I was aware that pentecostalism is only one particularly dramatic example of this wider religious revival, of what the French writer Gilles Kepel calls "the revenge of God." Still, I gradually became convinced that if I could somehow decipher pentecostalism's inner meaning and discern the source of its enormous appeal, this would provide an essential clue to understanding the larger religious upsurge of which it is a part. So, it became important for me to try to fathom exactly what pentecostalism is and what about it is so attractive to such a wide variety of people around the world.

It was not clear to me at first that I was up to the task. I am not myself a pentecostal, and I wondered if those inside the movement might view me with suspicion. I would need to explore where pentecostalism came from to appreciate the contours of its development. But I had never learned anything about the movement either in seminary or in graduate school. Perhaps my teachers felt it was not worth mentioning. However, as I started on my project I quickly discovered that I took to it with remarkable ease. First, I rarely had any trouble getting pentecostals to tell me about their faith. They talk about it at the slightest provocation. If there was a problem sometimes it was how I could delicately end the conversation. Also I never once felt any snubbing or suspicion. Wherever I went pentecostal people welcomed me to their churches and invariably invited me to come back. Part of what made my work so easy and enjoyable is that pentecostals tend to be very happy about their faith and they want you to share that happiness. It also turned out, however, that a peculiar combination of family ancestry and personal history had provided me with the right mixture of empathy and curiosity, of critical appreciation and sympathetic distance, which is needed in order to understand this complex and fascinating spiritual child of our time.

It is my hope that this book will help people who have heard about the pentecostal movement and may be curious about it to learn something from one who is neither an insider bent on painting the most attractive picture nor an outsider determined to write an exposé. I hope that the pentecostals who read it will recognize themselves, and will find that I have been accurate in my portrayal, generous in my commendations, and fair in my criticisms. I also hope that other thoughtful people who wonder what shape religion will take in the coming century will appreciate my speculations on that question as well as my intuition that a careful consideration of the pentecostal movement yields some valuable hints to its answer.

PART
I

The Little Church and the Big City

When the day of Pentecost had come, they were all together in one place. And suddenly a sound came from heaven like the rush of a mighty wind, and it filled all the house where they were sitting. And there appeared to them tongues as of fire, distributed and resting on each one of them.

The Acts of the Apostles, 2:1–3

THE PEOPLE who call themselves "pentecostals" today take their name from a story recounted in chapter two of the Acts of the Apostles. The plot describes how the confused followers of the recently crucified rabbi they believed was the messiah gathered in Jerusalem to mark the Jewish holiday called Pentecost that occurs fifty days after Passover. Suddenly there came a sound from on high "like the rush of a mighty wind." The Holy Spirit filled them, tongues "as of fire" crowned their heads, and to their amazement each began to understand what the other was saying even though they came from "every nation under heaven" and spoke many different languages. It seemed that the ancient curse of Babel—the confounding of languages—had been reversed and that God was creating a new inclusive human community in which "Parthians and Medes and Elamites and residents of Mesopotamia" could all live together.

The story then takes an unexpectedly comic twist. Passersby, the text says, were annoyed by the ruckus and thought a drinking spree was under way. It would not be the last time that people filled with the pentecostal spirit would be dismissed as inebriated. But the Apostle Peter, rising to his feet, assured the neighbors that his companions were not soused. What was happening, he said, was no less than the fulfillment of ancient prophecy. The Spirit was being poured out in anticipation of the Last Days. Soon this present world age would come to an end, the wicked would be punished, the just rewarded, and the visible Kingdom of Christ would be established on earth.

As months, then years, then centuries passed, however, this final consummation never seemed to come. Christianity, which began as an apocalyptic sect, gradually had to adjust to the long haul. Theologians gallantly tried to redefine what the Kingdom was and when it would materialize. Some decided that the Church was the Kingdom, and since it was obviously already here, there was no need to look forward to any big changes. Others taught that the Kingdom is the eternity that begins when life on this plane is over. Most Christians seemed to adjust to the new situation. But throughout the centuries there were always some who read those early prophecies, noted certain portents and omens in their own eras, and declared that this time the End was indeed near at hand. Christianity has never completely shed the millennial hopes with which it came to birth, and the conviction that the climax of history is imminent has reappeared time and time again, especially during wrenching social dislocation and cultural collapse. It also seems to come back regularly during the final years of centuries and millennia. We are once again at such a juncture, and when I started to write this book the most popular play on Broadway was one called "Millennium Approaches."

The story of the first Pentecost has always served as an inspiration for people who are discontented with the way religion or the world in general is going. They turn to it because it is packed with promise. It seems to presage a big change; and when people believe that the future will be different it transforms the way they feel about the present. Some like the story of Pentecost for other reasons. It is about the experience of God, not about abstract religious ideas, and it depicts a God who does not remain aloof but reaches down through the power of the Spirit to touch human hearts in the midst of life's turmoil. It should come as no surprise, therefore, that in our present time of social and cultural disarray, and with another century—indeed a new millennium—about to begin, pentecostalism is burgeoning nearly everywhere in the world.

Because pentecostalism is so widespread, I did not have to travel very far to begin my odyssey. I started by visiting three churches located within a twenty-minute drive of my home in Cambridge, Massachusetts. On a clear night in November, I attended the midweek gathering at a black church affiliated with the Church of God in Christ in the Dorchester section of Boston. The congregation was meeting in a former synagogue which still bore a Hebrew inscription over the doors. On the following Sunday morning I found my way to a small, mainly white and Asian, Assemblies of God congregation meeting in a rented hall in a changing neighborhood in downtown Boston. Then, on Sunday evening, I dropped in on about 400 Puerto Ricans and Central American immigrants at a rousing service in an independent Spanish-speaking pentecostal church that had taken over an abandoned Lutheran edifice in the South End.

What first struck me about all three of these lively congregations was how young the worshippers were. At the black church, for instance, though women made up the majority, young black men in baggy pants, hair clipped in the latest style, sang and clapped. The youth choir was twice as big as the young adult choir, and there was a Gospel choir and children's choir as well. At the downtown church a young white woman with honey-colored hair down to her waist, wearing a floor-length peasant-style skirt, played a guitar and led the songs while an Asian woman in a white jumpsuit sang along with her and two young men with shoulder-length manes manned the drums and the keyboard. At the Latino church four young women in tasteful multicolored frocks stood at four microphones, snapped their fingers, and moved their shoulders as they led the singing, accompanied by triple fortissimo chords from an amplified guitar and an electric keyboard.

In each of the churches the worship followed the pattern I have now learned to expect in pentecostal churches: high-amperage music, voluble praise, bodily movement including clapping and swaying, personal testimonies, sometimes prayers "in the Spirit," a sermon full of stories and anecdotes, announcements, lots of humorous banter, a period of intense prayers for healing, and a parting song. At the coffee, punch, and cookie hours after the services I met medical secretaries, computer programmers, insurance salesmen, graduate students in microbiology, and actors and police officers, as well as people who were out of work and down on their luck. It was clear that the worshippers were not simply curios, survivors of a vanishing religious age, but modern city-dwellers, who were obviously relishing one of the rare occasions in which they could engage in some personal give-and-take in a setting not stifled by some specialized technical idiom. I was beginning to see already why pentecostalism is growing with particular rapidity in cities, and since I like cities, I was beginning to feel at home very quickly. It was then that I recognized the combination of ancestral and personal history that without my knowing it had prepared me for my errand.

My ancestors fled England for the new settlement in Pennsylvania in the early years of the eighteenth century. They left because they belonged to an unpopular religion whose members were derided both for their lack of respect for established civil and ecclesiastical authorities and for the unseemly intensity of their worship. They refused to bow or take off their hats for bishops or even for kings, and they sometimes shook with fervor when they prayed. Derisively, people dubbed them "Quakers." They seem to have borne up patiently in the face of insults, but when ridicule hardened into persecution and imprisonment they set off for another continent rather than yield to further humiliation. The original epithet stuck. Though they would never have chosen the name "Quaker" themselves, they learned to carry it with pride.

The early Quakers were an ecstatic sect if there ever was one. A contemporary observer described them as "froathing at the mouth, and scrieching with a horrible noise" as they awaited the descent of the Spirit. They were so persuaded of the urgency of their message that they sometimes interrupted other people's church services. There is no doubt that they were quite fervent, intense, and more than a little intrusive. They were undoubtedly more like today's pentecostals than today's sedate Quakers like to think.

The man who led this band of eighteenth-century holy rollers to the new world, William Penn, was also a social visionary. Like many such prophets before and after him, he longed to build a colony that would, as far as possible, replicate the heavenly Jerusalem here below. When he founded Philadelphia, "the city of brotherly love"—a name he chose from the biblical book of Revelation—he made it clear that he wanted it to serve as a haven of the religious freedom and friendly persuasion the Quakers taught. It was to be an earthly version of the City of God.

By the time I was growing up in a small town in Pennsylvania some thirty miles from where Penn and his fellow refugees had landed more than 200 years earlier, the Quakers had lost most of their ardor and impertinence. They were no longer disrespectful of authority, and their worship was anything but emotionally fervent. There was no more "froathing" or "scrieching." They, or at least the Quakers who lived in our town, had become paragons of propriety. At their services they sat quietly, eyes lowered and hands folded, waiting for the Spirit to prompt someone to speak. The Spirit usually tapped the same distinguished elders, the ones who always sat on the facing bench, and the message did not vary much from week to week.

The Quakers did not seem very interested in building the New Jerusalem either. They had become the pedigreed aristocrats of the little town we lived in, Malvern, and had generally done rather well financially. They believed, as the town gossips put it, "in God and 6 percent interest." The "city of brotherly love" was a place to do their Christmas shopping but otherwise it was best to stay away. With a growing black and European immigrant population, and dirty streets, Philadelphia, in their minds at least, was no longer the shining example of God's will for the world, but a sinkhole of vice and corruption. What they were building was not an ideal city but prudent investment portfolios.

My parents had no portfolios, but they shared the prevailing local opinion of the city William Penn had hoped would be a beacon of virtue: they thought it was a good place to avoid. If we had to drive down Chestnut Street to cross the Delaware River bridge on our way to Cape May, New Jersey, they hurried through the city, even running yellow lights. If we went in to shop at Gimbels or Wanamakers, they would buy what they wanted quickly, in order to get out before nightfall. But already as a small boy I could detect that it was not just our safety that worried them. There was something about the city they did not want me to know about. I can still remember my fascination as I stared through the streaked windows of our 1936 Chevrolet at the forbidden sights we raced past. And I recall tugging at my father's hand as he pulled me along Market Street on the way to the train station while I gaped at the exotic-looking people and flamboyant window displays we were passing. With a child's unerring instinct, I sensed that if it was prohibited, then it must be interesting. I quickly learned to associate the city with exciting disorder and taboo pleasure, not exactly, I fear, what William Penn had in mind.

I was only an occasional visitor to Quaker meetings in our little town. My paternal grandfather had been lured away from the Quakers as a young man when he married a Baptist, and since my own parents preferred to sleep in on Sundays, my grandparents assumed responsibility for my spiritual upbringing. It took place, for the most part, in the First Baptist Church, where there was a junior choir and lots of hearty congregational singing. But no one quaked or screeched. A certain amount of emotion was fine, but there were, after all, sensible limits. Mostly I enjoyed it. But sometimes it got terribly dull, and I remember counting the diamond-shaped figures on the brown wallpaper over and over again during what seemed like interminable sermons.

There was one church in Malvern, however, where things were never dull. It was a tiny stucco and cinder-block edifice located on Ruthland Avenue, the street that marked the edge of town. Right behind it stood the rusting red tanks of the local heating oil company and the scrubby pine trees surrounding the water pumping station. It was known to the townspeople simply as the "little church." I don't think I ever knew its denominational affiliation or whether it even had one. It probably belonged to that family of churches designated with the term "Holiness" in which fervency in prayer, a strict moral code, and the presence of Christ within every believer were emphasized. It was certainly the closest thing in our town to what I later learned was pentecostal worship. People would say, "Well, I drove by the little church the other night and they sure was hollerin'," and someone else would reply, "Yeah, Doris said last Sunday you could hear 'em singin' as far as Woodland Avenue." Once in a while people referred to those who attended the little church as "holy rollers" and said they sometimes got down and rolled in the aisles. No wonder my curiosity was aroused. But it took some time before I found out for myself what they were like.

As a teenager, I began attending the little church occasionally when Lois, a girl with creamy skin and beautiful straight black hair, who was in my high school class, invited me to go with her. Frankly, I went at first since it seemed to be the only way I could spend any time with Lois. Because of her religion she could not attend dances, movies, or parties. So accompanying her to prayer meeting or the evening service was my only opportunity to be with her. My parents were not overjoyed by this. I think they harbored a few doubts, both about Lois *and* about what went on in the "little church." At first, I had some reservations too, at least about the little church, but I very quickly came to look forward to my visits.

I always had a wonderful time when we went, and not just because I was with Lois. People sang with gusto. They murmured and nodded when they prayed. Sometimes they sobbed and wept. The pianist threw in chords and runs I never heard at the Baptist church. Lois's wide brown eyes lit up as we sang "Love Divine, All Love Excelling," while she pressed my hand. Some of the members moved and clapped or did a little two-step to the music. Sometimes people went forward and kneeled at the altar while the pastor and the deacons placed their hands on their heads and prayed. I never saw anyone roll in the aisles.

But I remember having this one problem at the little church: the preacher. He was riveting, I have to admit; his sermons were masterpieces of suspense and melodrama, replete with vivid images from Revelation and Daniel of beasts and dragons and vials of fire—high-octane material our more reserved Baptist minister usually steered away from. He also hopped and bounced around a lot, and he sometimes acted out two sides of a conversation between, for example, God and the devil, or David and Saul, mimicking their different voices. Frequently he slid out from behind the pulpit and sauntered along the aisle as he spoke. It was dramaturgy at its best: I almost always liked the *way* he said things, but I often had serious questions about *what* he was saying, and I wanted to discuss it. Even at that age I was already fascinated by the similarities and contrasts among the various churches and denominations. But no one at the little church seemed very interested in the fine points of theology.

My romance with Lois did not survive our high school graduation, but I am grateful to her for several insights I picked up by going to church with her, ideas that have influenced me in ways I could not have foreseen then. One is that eros and agape, the erotic and the spiritual energies of life, may not be as distinct as some theologians would have us believe. Whenever I think of that little church I think of Lois, and how, even though she never wore a trace of rouge or lipstick, when she prayed, eyes closed, her head tilted back and her hands raised, the way all the people in her church prayed, I thought she was the most beautiful girl I had ever seen. But there was also something frankly physical about the congregation itself. People hugged each other, and on summer nights when they lifted their arms in praise, long streaks of perspiration reached down toward their waists. They wore their clothes in a less trussed-up way, and the men's collars always seemed to turn up at the points. They were the kind of people who sometimes put their hands on your shoulders and thrust their faces up close to you when they talked.

I learned something else at the little church too, though at the time I am sure I understood it only in the most inchoate way. I learned that the imagery, mood, and tempo of a religious service are not just add-ons. They are not superfluous. Human beings are physical as well as mental creatures, and therefore these more tactile elements are part of the substance of worship. And since life itself is so full of conflict and craving, of wild hopes and dashed expectations, any religion that does not resonate with the full range of these feelings, and provide ways of wrestling with them is not worth much. Whatever else you might say about the little church, it imparted to its people not just an idiom replete with lakes of fire and a city without tears, but the jubilant gestures and heart-rending wails to go with it.

My occasional visits to both the little church and the big city remain in my memory as exhilarating episodes in a happy but uneventful boyhood. Over the years, however, these two distinct experiences have blended together in my mind. I think I know why. Both exuded the allure of the forbidden; both could scare you; both also gave off a slightly seductive, mildly wanton scent. Both conveyed an unmistakable impression of a just-barely-controlled chaos. I often had the feeling that at any given moment something could happen without advance warning. Consequently, I was strongly drawn to both, but never entirely at ease in either. I remembered this later when during my study of pentecostalism I learned it is mainly an *urban* religion, the faith of choice for tens of millions of city-dwellers on five continents.

By the time I left my hometown after high school, my lifelong fascination with cities and with experiential religion was already firmly in place. Luckily, the university I went to allowed me to gratify both. Since there was not enough money for tuition at any of the colleges I had hoped for, my parents sent me to the University of Pennsylvania where I had a state senatorial scholarship. At first I was disappointed, but that did not last long. The university was in Philadelphia. Now, at seventeen, I could gambol in the forbidden delights of Elysium with no one tugging at my hand. The movies, the stage shows, the jazz spots, the political rallies, even the "Troc"—the fly-specked old burlesque house at 10th and Arch—were now all mine for a small admission fee and a streetcar fare.

I also quickly found out that the city was full of churches. I attended a different one each week—Catholic, Methodist, Apostolic, Pentecostal, and even some Baptist churches, black and white. Some of the services were wearisome, but others made even the worship at the "little church" seem subdued by comparison. In short, as a city buff and a religion junkie I had a splendid time during my undergraduate years.

When, decades later, I read James Boswell's *London Journals*, jotted down while he was about the age I was then, recording his coffee house conversations, his incessant church going and his constant amorous affairs, I felt I had discovered a soul mate. It was only the amorous affairs that were missing in my case. My fascination with the religion of the heart continued throughout those years, but so did my problem with it. Pascal once said that the mind builds walls that the heart jumps over, but somehow that did not satisfy me. Why did the mind and the heart have to be such antagonists, the one trying to fence the other in?

Looking back at my boyhood in the small Baptist church my grandparents took me to I have to admit that, tedious as it was at times, it had done a pretty good job of holding belief and experience—and head and heart—together. One evening in particular stands out from all the rest, and thinking about it now helps me understand why the themes of this book are so essential to me. It happened when I was thirteen, and the time had come for me, along with the other boys in my Sunday School class, to "make my decision" to be baptized and join the church. To do so, however, we had to be examined by the board of deacons. It was an intimidating prospect, and I arrived at the deacons' meeting with considerable anxiety. But the kindly elders who questioned me, along with the other four equally nervous candidates, asked only a couple of questions about my beliefs. Mainly they wanted to know whether I had *experienced* the love of God and the grace of Christ in my own life. They asked nothing about the inerrancy of the Bible or the doctrine of the Trinity or when I expected the

Second Coming. Rather, with simple directness and genuine concern, they wanted to know what God meant to me. Not to someone else, but to me.

I do not recall what I said to them. I do remember that one of the other boys got the giggles during the prayer the presiding deacon offered, but he was accepted for baptism anyway. But what stays with me with complete clarity is that these serious older men were genuinely interested in *me*. Naturally they wanted to find out what I knew about the Ten Commandments and the Sermon on the Mount. But mainly, they wanted to know what I, at the deepest level of my bumbling preadolescent being, felt about what—even then—I sensed were the deepest things anyone could think or feel about. They wanted to be sure that, however I stammered about it, God was real for me. Whatever I said must have satisfied them, for a few weeks later, on a clear Easter Sunday morning, I waded into the baptismal pool behind the pulpit and was immersed.

In college, and later as a doctoral student in religion, I gradually discarded or put on hold some of my church's beliefs. But I never rebelled or resigned, never felt that I had been brainwashed or coerced. Somehow I recognized that whatever the empirical improbability of some of those stories and lessons might be, the real point was something different. For me they continued to constitute what theologians call the "master narrative" that gives my life coherence. They have stayed with me not just as ideas and values but as a cluster of deep and ineradicable affective traces: feelings of joy, terror, awe, mystery, and well-being.

As I got older, my fascination with what I had once found in the "little church" kept coming back. I am a professor of theology, and that is both my delight and my dilemma. When you teach religion in a university, or even in a seminary today, you mainly investigate other people's ideas and other people's experiences. You study the history of religions, comparative religion, the scriptures of the world, maybe the psychology of religion. This is perhaps as it should be. Few seminaries and hardly any universities are equipped to help students enter into a mystical quest or spiritual journey. Also, in order to avoid myopia and provincialism, one must be familiar with how God has been envisioned in past ages and by other peoples, both in one's own religious tradition and in others. But there is a genuine risk involved. As Ralph Waldo Emerson eloquently warned an audience at Harvard Divinity School in 1838, the danger of a steady diet of other people's religion is that it can dry up one's own resources. Studying *about* religion inevitably means studying ideas. But ideas can be very derivative, and they can take the place of experience, which must in some way be personal.

I have sensed this peril acutely during my years as a teacher and—perhaps as a consequence—have always felt drawn to those religions which major in what Jonathan Edwards once called the "religious affections" rather than in doctrines. I find myself constantly asking what experience, what encounter with the numinous, lies behind and beneath this or that theology? All in all, it was probably inevitable that one day I would—figuratively—retrace my steps across town to the "little church." After all, pentecostalism is the most experiential branch of Christianity, a movement that first arose at the turn of the century as a protest against "man-made creeds" and the "coldness" of traditional worship. This contrast may be why the telephone call from the puzzled editor rekindled my interest.

One of the first things I discovered as I began to study the history of the pentecostal movement was that I would have to do it mainly on my own. Universities do not generally offer courses on the subject, and their libraries do not condescend to stock pentecostals' often fiery tracts. At Harvard, for example, where I teach, a student can take courses in Sufism or Tibetan Buddhism. There is even a class on Hindu Goddesses. But, until I introduced a small research seminar three years ago, there were no offerings on pentecostalism.

As I delved into the history of pentecostalism and began visiting all the pentecostal churches I could, some discoveries surprised me. The first was how *many* pentecostals there are. David Barrett, a leading expert in religious statistics, estimates that pentecostalism in all its varied forms already encompasses over 400 million people. It is by far the largest non-Catholic grouping, accounting for one in every four Christians. It is also the fastest growing Christian movement on earth, increasing more rapidly than either militant Islam or the Christian fundamentalist sects with which it is sometimes confused. In Africa, pentecostal congregations, usually called "African independent churches," are quickly becoming the main expression of Christianity. Several Latin American countries are now approaching pentecostal majorities on a continent that had been dominated by Roman Catholicism for five centuries. The movement is also growing in Korea and China.

Second, I was interested to find that the pentecostal movement worldwide is principally an urban phenomenon, and not a rustic or "hillbilly religion," as some people still believe. It is proliferating most rapidly today in the gigantic megacities of the third world such as São Paulo, Seoul, and Lusaka. Sometimes the only thriving human communities in the vast seas of tar-paper shanties and cardboard huts that surround many of these cities are the pentecostal congregations. In effect pentecostalism is a kind of communitarian counterforce within these bloated conurbations as they continue to swell and become progressively less livable.

I also learned that it is a serious mistake to equate pentecostals with fundamentalists. They are not the same. Fundamentalists attach such unique authority to the letter of the verbally inspired Scripture that they are suspicious of the pentecostals' stress on the immediate experience of the Spirit of God. This should not be surprising. Text-oriented believers in any religion tend to be wary of mystics. However, this does not mean that pentecostalism does not embody a complex of religious ideas and insights. It does. The difference is that while the beliefs of the fundamentalists, and of many other religous groups, are enshrined in formal theological systems, those of pentecostalism are imbedded in testimonies, ecstatic speech, and bodily movement. But it *is* a theology, a full-blown religious cosmos, an intricate system of symbols that respond to the perennial questions of human meaning and value. The difference is that, historically, pentecostals have felt more at home singing their theology, or putting it in pamphlets for distribution on street corners. Only recently have they begun writing books about it.

I was also in for another surprise. As I sang and prayed with pentecostals in various parts of the world I discovered that their worship constitutes a kind of compendium of patterns and practices from virtually every Christian tradition I had ever known. It would have been startling, and maybe upsetting, to the members of St. Patrick's Church, or the Quaker meeting, or the African Methodist Episcopal church in my home town, for example, to know that much of what went on in the "little church" was derived more or less directly from their traditions. Pentecostalism, while it looks to many like a narrow cult, is actually a kind of ecumenical movement, an original—and highly successful—synthesis of elements from a number of other sources, and not all of them Christian.

As I neared the end of my personal pilgrimage through the pentecostal world I found that my original ambivalence about it had not disappeared. I am still intrigued by its drama and fascinated by its ideas. I know a lot more now about why so many different kinds of people find it so appealing. But I also find myself distressed by certain features of the movement, especially the political alliances some of its members have recently entered. I still want to argue and to differ. Maybe I am still looking for the conversation I never got—despite those debates between God and the devil—at the little church. But I now harbor—paradoxically—both more hopes and more misgivings than I did so long ago in the stucco and cinder-block building on Ruthland Avenue. Maybe it is because I can see that the stakes are now higher.

When I first became acquainted with the pentecostal movement forty years ago, it was little more than a small sect. Today it is a major, worldwide religious movement. When I went to church with Lois, she was not allowed to go to the movies because they were "worldly." Today, at least in America, many pentecostals have become terribly comfortable with "this world." They started out in a faith that brought hope to society's losers and rejects. Today some of their most visible representatives have become ostentatiously rich, and some even preach a gospel of wealth. When I attended Lois's church no one asked me to sign any creeds. Indeed, pentecostalism began as a rebellion against creeds.

But today many of their preachers cling tenaciously to such recently invented dogmas as the verbal inerrancy of the Bible. Pentecostals also started out teaching that the signs and wonders that took place in their congregations were not some kind of spectacle but harbingers of God's new day. But today, some pentecostal preachers seem so obsessed with the techniques of rapture that they have forgotten the original message.

There have been other changes. Pentecostals began as rebellious antagonists of the status quo, refusing to serve in the armies of this fallen age, but many have now become impassioned superpatriots, easy marks for the high rollers of the religious right. They started out as a radically inclusive spiritual fellowship in which race and gender discrimination virtually disappeared. That is hardly the case, at least in most white pentecostal churches, today. In short, as I came to know the pentecostal movement in its present incarnation I discovered that the pentecostals themselves are facing a dilemma they may not survive. At least they may not be able to survive it and still remain true to their origins.

The pages that follow chart my peregrinations through the engrossing world of pentecostalism. They begin at the beginning, with the spiritual mood of America at the turn of the last century, and with the birth of the pentecostal movement in a former livery stable on Azusa Street in Los Angeles. Subsequent chapters describe the ethos of this new upsurge of primal spirituality with its celebration of mysticism, ecstatic praise, and radical hope. Later sections track the movement's rapid spread around the planet and the special role that music and the work of women played, and still play, as pentecostalism continues to expand in Latin America, Europe, Asia, and Africa. I close with some of my fond hopes and some of my grave misgivings about the current state of pentecostalism in the United States, and with some suggestions about what the movement's saga can tell us about the overall religious profile of the twenty-first century.

CHAPTER 1

Millennium Approaches

I saw an angel coming down from heaven
With the key to the abyss and a great
Chain in his hand. He seized the dragon
And chained him up for a thousand years
So that he might not seduce the nations
Until the thousand years were over.

Revelation 20:1–3

*F*ed by broken packing cases and discarded wrapping paper the fire quickly spread from the boarded-up Casino to the empty Music Hall. From there sparks flew through the arctic night to the roofs of the exposition pavilions that had recently housed the magnificent manufacturing and liberal arts exhibitions. Then the wind off the lake rose and carried burning embers over the reflecting pool to what had been the great fair's crown jewel, a colonnaded Triumphal Arch, surmounted by a heroic statue of Christopher Columbus standing in a Roman chariot drawn by four stallions. The flames licked the horses' haunches, then the entire vault collapsed with a roar, carrying the great explorer and his steeds with it. The towering, gilded replica of the Goddess of Liberty was the next to go. For a moment she stood enveloped in smoke, "with both arms uplifted as though appealing for help" as an eyewitness later wrote. Then she too fell, first lurching sideways, then crumpling over as the inferno raced on to yet another building, and then another.

The planners of the Great Columbian Exposition of 1893 had dubbed it the "White City" because the temporary jute and plaster material that encased the iron frames of its 200 Beaux-Arts-style palaces had glistened with such a lustrous sheen throughout those balmy summer months. Some described it as a fairyland or a magic city. But others saw it in a more sublime light. They called it the "New Jerusalem," and they claimed it had enabled the millions of visitors who came to Chicago for this massive commemoration of the arrival of Columbus to catch a glimpse of the Heavenly City the Apostle John had beheld in his vision on the isle of Patmos.

One of the principal events that took place at the Exposition was "The World's Parliament of Religions." It was the first attempt in history to assemble representatives of all the major faiths in order to seek a common spiritual basis for global unity. The meetings ran for seventeen days, and thousands of enthusiastic guests lined up every evening to attend the open sessions. The parliament was the religious counterpart of the White City, and some did not hesitate to call it a "new Pentecost," a modern-day miracle that brought back together the diverse tongues and tribes that had been scattered when the Old Testament Tower of Babel toppled.

The whole fair was seen as a kind of sacred event. For the millions who entered into its spell, the resplendent White City, with its exotic "Midway Plaisance," and Buffalo Bill's Wild West Show became the modern equivalent of a pilgrimage site, a holy place, an axis mundi. To recognize that this was an event with a transcendental resonance and no mere commercial enterprise, the visitor had only to stand before the great central arch that covered the lakeside entrance and gaze upward at the words of Jesus Christ inscribed along its cornice, "You Shall Know The Truth And The Truth Shall Make You Free." The fair inspired awe and pride and reverence. And no one could doubt that its classical parapets and fluted columns, its patriotic statuary and its scriptural assurances, represented the glorious promise of a Christian America. Over the past century the republic had successfully tamed the savage forces of the frontier, and now the ship of state was poised to sail confidently toward the new century.

But instead, the New Jerusalem was burning. When the fair closed its gates in October, the thousands of Chicagoans who had sold the tickets, dispensed the lemonade, and swept the grounds all summer suddenly found themselves jobless in the midst of a brutal economic downturn. Some had no place to live, so they found their way back *to the deserted fair buildings in search of temporary shelter. Soon hundreds were camping out in the empty Casino and the closed exhibit halls where they kindled small fires to keep warm. When the blaze started on January 8, 1894, thousands of Chicago residents, alerted by the livid glare on the horizon, left their homes and raced to the forsaken fairground to witness the catastrophe. All night long, as they looked on in horror, one spire after another first turned brass, then sulphurous yellow in a cruel caricature of their legendary whiteness. By morning the most sublime pavilions of the New Jerusalem were gone. As a cold winter sun rose, here and there thin columns of blue smoke floated up from the blackened debris and, borne by a freshening breeze coming in from the lake, drifted out over the city and disappeared.*

*A*MERICANS HAVE always had a stronger than average dose of millennialism in their veins. From the puritans who landed in New England and from the revival preachers who traveled the midwest on horseback, they kept hearing that the last act of history was beginning and that their own nation would play a special role in the grand finale. As the nineteenth turned into the twentieth century in America, prophecies and speculations about a new Pentecost and a New Jerusalem were in the air again. The old epoch was ending. What kind of world would the new one bring? What sort of nation would America become? Often the two questions merged into one because, as they prepared to leave the 1800s behind, Americans were confident that whatever the new age would bring, the United States would lead it.

Some forecasts were piercingly foreboding: Jesus would come again soon to establish his kingdom on the earth and to cast the unrighteous into the lake of fire. Other less vivid predictions foresaw progress and democracy spreading out across the continents from its American homeland until they illuminated the whole world. Conjectures issued forth from every field and occupation. Architects and evangelists, novelists and philosophers, songsmiths and tycoons, all promoted their favorite scenarios for the American future. But whatever the dream, whether spiritual or terrestrial, political or poetic, the two metaphors that appeared most often in the speeches, sermons, ballads, and essays were drawn from the Bible. The vision of the New Jerusalem pictured America as a glorified world capital where the one true God would be worshipped and served. The dream of a second Pentecost anticipated the gathering of hostile tribes and confounded tongues into a peaceable commonwealth of peoples.

Among the many prefigurations of the future to appear at the turn of the last century, two in particular stand out. One was the great World's Columbian Exposition, which drew millions of people to Chicago in the summer of 1893. It was the inspired creation of a company of gifted architects, canny financiers, and cosmopolitan religious leaders. The second was the lesser known Azusa Street revival which took place a decade later in Los Angeles among a cluster of down-at-the-heels hymn singers and itinerant evangelists, but which marked the birth of the worldwide pentecostal movement. Even though the main actors in these two separate events came from widely different social strata, they had much in common. Both drew sustenance from the same blend of biblical metaphors and American folk piety. Both were intoxicated by the realization that a whole new century was about to begin. Both of their visions were intensely religious in their pursuit of the Kingdom of God in America.

The World's Columbian Exposition held in Chicago in 1893 was the consummate symbol of America's pride in its brief past and confidence in its limitless future. For many, this outsized jamboree became both a new Pentecost and a New Jerusalem rolled into one. Intended to commemorate the achievement of the intrepid Genoese sailor Columbus, but also to celebrate the promise of American power and prowess, the great Chicago Fair had at its center a stunning complex of buildings which was quickly nicknamed the "White City." Nothing quite like it had ever been seen before. As amply demonstrated by the eloquent tributes lavished on it, this gleaming summertime Xanadu came to exemplify for many people all that was best and most forward looking about America. But it did more than that: it linked heaven and earth by demonstrating what the benevolent deity, who had guided the destiny of America thus far, intended for the whole world. It provided, as one commentator said, "a glimpse of the New Jerusalem seen of John."

The crown jewel of the Columbian Exposition was what its planners called the "World's Parliament of Religions." This ambitious event brought together representatives of "the world's ten great religions" to try to discover a basis for the spiritual unity of the human race. Buddhist sages, Shinto priests, Hindu sadhus, Catholic bishops, and Baptist preachers all took part in the parliament. For many of the Christians who attended, the only precedent for such an extraordinary ingathering of the tribes was the ancient day of Pentecost, when the tongues of flame descended on the earliest Christians and the curse of Babel was reversed.

The Parliament of Religions was by far the best attended and most widely reported of the dozens of congresses held under the auspices of the great fair. Some saw it as the inner soul of the exposition while the White City was its outer embodiment. An illustration on the cover of *Cosmopolitan* magazine in March 1893 suggests just how integral the soul and body were. In the background of the picture stands the great White City stretching, it seems, into infinity. Just in front of it looms a Roman fasces with each of its bundled sticks labeled to represent a particular denomination. The packet is tied with a cord held by two arms emerging from clouds of incense, and bears a scrolled label that reads "Fatherhood of God" and "Brotherhood of Man." Instead of the customary mermaids or goddesses that normally embellished such designs at the time, this ensemble is flanked by a Salvation Army sister and a Catholic nun. The montage is sternly guarded by a fierce-eyed American eagle holding in its mighty beak a hapless, twisted ribbon inscribed with the word "Intolerance." Taken together, as the planners intended them to be, the White City and the World's Parliament of Religions demonstrated that bold fusion of the earthly and the heavenly city which has always dwelled in the American psyche.

The second turn-of-the-century harbinger was the Azusa Street revival. After two decades of preliminary stirrings, what is now called the "pentecostal movement" burst forth in 1906 amid unpromising circumstances in a run-down section of Los Angeles. Led by an African-American preacher with no theological education, its first adherents were poor domestic servants, janitors, and day workers—black and white—who had the audacity to claim that a new Pentecost was happening, the New Jerusalem was coming soon, and that they were its designated heralds and grateful first fruits.

The Azusa Street revival spoke with some of the same spiritual vocabulary heard at the World's Parliament of Religions in Chicago, but it projected a dramatically different vision of America's future. The learned and accomplished delegates to the parliament were drawn from the religious and educational elite. In keeping with the magnificent setting in which they met at the Columbian Exposition, they placed considerable confidence in the benevolence of human progress, technical accomplishment, Yankee ingenuity, and monumental physical design. They tried not to read too much symbolism into the sorry fact that a fire reduced the White City to dust and ashes a few months after its closing.

The pentecostal movement, on the other hand, erupted from among society's disenfranchised, and it envisioned a human community restored by the power of the Spirit, a Jerusalem rejoicing where Parthians, Medes, and Elamites all came together, and where weeping, injustice, and death are abolished. At least this was the vision the movement's early leaders proclaimed. As the decades went by, however, and many American pentecostals prospered, some of them lost not only the effervescence which had been their original trademark but the communitarian dream they had embodied. But even as the movement lost some of its original vigor in the land of its birth, it began growing even faster in other parts of the world.

Today the records of the Parliament of Religions molder on library shelves. But the pentecostal movement is thriving. For millions of people it offers a vital hope and an alternative vision of what the world should be; and its powerful attractiveness to the disinherited of our own time constitutes an ongoing reproach to the status-quo. Still, at the turn of the twentieth century, the White City was the perfect embodiment of its designers' idea of the spirit of America, and its soul was the World's Parliament of Religions. Both evoked millennial hopes, and both were extolled by their admirers in the biblical idiom of New Jerusalem and a new Pentecost. But both were fraught with inner tensions and contradictions, and both ended in disillusionment and frustration. The design of the White City emerged only after a strident debate between contending schools of architects; and the dramatic difference between what the confident planners of the parliament hoped it would accomplish and what it actually did signaled a deep schism in the nation's religious sensibility. As two intertwined parts of a single concept, the White City and the Parliament together stood in marked contrast to the vision of the future that would soon break forth in the pentecostal revival at the Azusa Street mission.

Remembering the White City in his later years, the great American architect Louis Sullivan wrote, "The crowds were astonished. They beheld what was for them an amazing revelation . . . a veritable Apocalypse, a message inspired from on high." Even if we knew nothing else about the White City, the evangelical tone of Sullivan's utterance would tip us off that something more than just boards and masonry was at stake in this particular exhibition, as indeed there was. America had reached a century post. The great historian Frederick Jackson Turner had just decreed the official closing of the frontier. The nation was at a critical turning point, self-consciously entering a new era. In short, the Columbian Exposition, while ostensibly organized to commemorate the arrival of Columbus in the New World, was in fact a celebration of American accomplishment and a bold announcement of the part Americans intended to play on the world stage in the next century.

But the idea of just what America's role should be was not one on which there was complete agreement, and the debate about it took place at many levels. Arguments about whether the young nation should model itself more after Rome or Athens, Paris or Jerusalem raged in every sector, and the mythologized images of these great cities of history became symbolic rallying points for contending versions of what America should now become. The planning meetings for the Exposition began two years earlier, in 1891. The distinguished architects—including Richard Morris Hunt, Stanford White, and Sullivan himself—who met to sketch the outlines for what eventually would become the "White City by the Lake" arrived with wildly contrasting ideas of how it should rehearse America's past and presage its future. On the one hand there were the "easterners," mainly from firms in New York, who favored what was then regarded as a more European or international motif. On the other hand were the "westerners," including some from Chicago, who endorsed a less grandiose, more exuberant, "democratic" design. This latter concept, one historian claims, would have been "more intimate, potent and enduring," and might have appealed more "to the popular imagination."

But it was not to be. The populist westerners lost. The easterners won. Rome triumphed, and a panorama of 200 monumental structures, copied from classic styles but constructed with large quantities of "staff," a flimsy plaster-of-Paris-like substance, rose on the 633-acre site and lined the newly built lakeside boulevards. The message was unmistakable. Whatever America's bumpkin past might have been in the eyes of the world, its future was to be one of grandeur. Americans were claiming a place in the sun. They were a nation destined to rule. It was an august statement, even if the brittle staff that covered the iron building frames was a strictly temporary material.

The White City was indeed a dazzler. A visitor named Mrs. Van Rensselaer recorded in her diary that "no such prospect had been viewed since the Rome of the emperors stood intact." Other guests typically called it the "dream city" or even the "celestial city." But its overall design also conjured the great mythic images of U.S. history and western destiny. The walls of the main Administration Building, called by some the "sovereign of the exhibit" and created by the eminent New York architect Richard M. Hunt, were adorned with inscriptions that recounted the heroic story of Columbus. Its central dome rose 260 feet above the ground, and inside at the base of the cupola, dozens of medallions recalled other explorers and adventurers—De Soto, Vespucci, Raleigh—who had followed the path of destiny across the seas.

Visitors could enter the White City either by rail or by boat on Lake Michigan. All were greeted by a splendid reflecting pool, the centerpiece around which many of the most memorable buildings were grouped. At its head soared a great fountain on which stood Columbia, a divine giantess, on the Barge of State. At the prow of her vessel, Fame, depicted as a winged figure with a long trumpet in one hand and a laurel crown in the other, announced the approach of the goddess. The boat was oared by Arts and Industry, and steered at the helm by Time, using his scythe as a rudder. The Statue of Liberty in New York harbor had been dedicated only seven years earlier, but this goddess, though smaller, was gilded in real gold.

Many of the exhibits carried heavy religious overtones, most of them suggesting that the history of Christianity had reached its culmination in America. The Art Palace, for example, managed to combine in the same building reproductions of the central portal of the Abbey Church of St. Giles from the twelfth century, the Gothic portal of the north transept of the Cathedral of Bordeaux from the fifteenth century, and the Renaissance gallery of the Cathedral of Limoges from the sixteenth century. Thanks to American money and skill, now they could all be enjoyed, as one grateful commentator wrote, without enduring the "miles of travel" that previously would have been required.

But it was the Triumphal Arch at the end of the reflecting pool that drew the most admiring exclamations. It was set in a colonnade of forty-four Corinthian columns, one for each of the states that was then part of the union. With its heroic statue of Columbus in his stallion-drawn *quadriga*, and its inscription, "You Shall Know The Truth And The Truth Shall Make You Free" (selected by President Charles W. Eliot of Harvard University from the Gospel of John), the arch combined all the patriotic and religious themes at once. The theology of the Exposition was anything but subtle. A contemporary two-volume folio of photographs, edited by Hubert Howe Bancroft, bears on its cover page another scriptural text that highlights the particular blending of piety and national pride the fair represented. From Revelation 21:26, it reads, "And they shall bring the glory and honor of the nations into it."

There can be little doubt that for many of its visitors, the Exposition was the "city set upon the hill" transposed from Governor Winthrop's Massachusetts Bay Colony to the shores of Lake Michigan. "Whether we gaze upon this spectacle by day or by night," one guest wrote, "we feel that the dream of hope has come true. The victory of Art and Soul over the moods of tempestuous Nature is bulletined by every architrave and joyously proclaimed from the mouths and the trumpets of 1000 heroes and angels." The White City was what America was; what it was meant to be; and what, God willing, it was sure to become.

Dedication day—scheduled for October 1892 even though the gala fair itself would not open for seven months—made the religious message of the White City even more explicit. Chauncey Depew, president of the New York Central Railroad, delivered the Columbian oration. His theme was singularly appropriate in a city where railroads were now linking the east coast with the west, and for a fair in which the strength of America's technical capacity and its spiritual attainments were both on universal display. Depew also drew upon biblical lore. Just as the Wise Men had once journeyed from the east to the west guided by the Star of Bethlehem, he proclaimed, so the spirit of equality of all men under God had moved westward from Calvary to America with Christopher Columbus. He described the White City as the symbol of this "transcendent miracle."

If the president of a railroad could wax so theological it is not surprising that the ministers who preached on the Sunday following the Exposition's dedication reached even greater crescendos of homiletical eloquence. At the nondenominational Central Church in Chicago, the Reverend David Swing preached on John 7:8—"Go to the Feast." It was he who told his listeners that the White City made "nature seem greater, beauty greater, men greater in genius and sentiment, republics more valuable and religion more simple and true." Another pastor christened it not just a Columbian exhibition but "a divine exposition." But it was left to

Lyman Abbott, one of the nation's most prominent preachers and theologians, to reveal the White City's promise in an America whose increasing heterogeneity had become worrisome. Where amidst all this new diversity would the necessary unity come from? The words with which Abbott answered his own question put him at almost total variance from the vision of unity that would appear a decade later in the pentecostal revival. For Abbott, it was not the oneness found in shared religious exuberance that one should hope for. Rather, the harmony could only come from what the White City exemplified, the "power of ordered, regulated and harmonized . . . styles, materials, orders, forces." The White City might be a sign of a new Pentecost and the New Jerusalem. But it was a Pentecost in which proper English would be spoken and a Jerusalem in which refinement and decorum would prevail.

Ten years later, the leader of the pentecostal revival in Los Angeles put it quite another way. While people wept and shouted with joy at the Azusa Street warehouse, and the downtown churches complained about the turmoil and disarray, a sympathetic observer wrote, "It is noticeable how free all nationalities feel. If a Mexican or German cannot speak English, he gets up and speaks in his own tongue, and the Spirit interprets through the face, and people say amen . . . God recognizes no flesh, no color, no names . . . [but] is uniting His people . . . by one Spirit in one body."

Both the White City and Azusa Street looked backward into history in order to gaze forward into the future. Both were, in their own way, restorationist. But the White City harked back to the the splendor of classical Greece and imperial Rome. Azusa Street tried to reclaim the early days of Christianity in Jerusalem. The White City was elegant, apollonian, clearly European in concept and inspiration. Azusa Street was raw, stormy, plainly American in its tactlessness and lack of refinement. The contrast reveals a fissure that has always tormented the American psyche. The architectural historian M. Christine Boyer believes that the Beaux-Arts architects who laid out the White City did everyone a calamitous disservice. Rather than embracing the real energies of the American city and then moving ahead, they created instead a halfbreed, splicing "the civic ideals and ceremonial urbanities of the European city" onto the American town. But almost the same words could be written about the American theology of the day. It was the beginning of the period of obsequious deference to German scholarship, when Georg Wilhelm Hegel and Friedrich Schleiermacher eclipsed Americans like Jonathan Edwards and Ralph Waldo Emerson in the divinity schools. These tendencies had not yet begun to fade when I attended seminary in the 1950s and we were still taught to look to Marburg and Tübingen for our inspiration. As for the real energies of the American spirit, academic theologians viewed them mainly as errors to be corrected or excesses to be tamed down. But while contingent after contingent of young seminary graduates tried to impart the latest ideas from Europe to their suspicious congregations, the pentecostal revolution, a genuinely American spiritual revolution if ever there was one, was bubbling up from underneath.

The parallels between the conflict among the fair's architects and the controversy among the preachers both about what America's future should be, and where one should look for inspiration, can be heard in Louis Sullivan's angry judgment on the White City. His words about a "message from on high" and a "revelation" were sardonic ones; what the 28 million visitors had believed to be the revelation of some divine truth was in fact "an appalling calamity." Sullivan was furious because he believed that the fair's pretentiousness, lack of originality, and replicative timidity had set American architecture back fifty years. But what is particularly noteworthy about his remarks is their explicitly theological tenor. The crowds had been taken in by a false revelation and a spurious apocalypse allegedly from "on high." They had left believing they had glimpsed the truth, but they had not. The White City had been not just an architectural but a religious disaster.

I think that Sullivan turned to this Jeremiah-like rhetoric because he saw the fate of the American spirit hanging in the balance. His language of apocalypse and revelation—though he evoked these images negatively—would not have been strange to the pentecostals. Nor was his description of what he called the "calamity" that different from theirs in tone. For Sullivan the calamity was the suppression by allegedly authoritative experts of the more spontaneous and intuitive gifts he believed resided in ordinary people. He claimed that the fair—which was inspired by the grand success of the Paris Exposition of 1889—was elitist, a victory for effete Paris and snobbish London over bumptious but virile America. The Exposition was "feudal," not democratic; it was not at all appropriate for a people who were inventing something new.

The early pentecostal preachers also inveighed against elite experts. Just as Sullivan flogged the haughty architects who looked to Europe rather than to the heart of their own homeland for inspiration, the preachers lashed out against the effete, seminary-trained ministers of the established churches, and accused them of misleading their flocks. Just as the "wolves in sheep's clothing" were betraying congregations, the snobbish urban designers were leading the populace astray. The Beaux-Arts patricians, seduced by the Left Bank, had handed a victory to Caesar, Sullivan thought, and hamstrung American architectural creativity for a generation. These were not just architectural matters, they were also spiritual concerns, and only the pungent epithets of an angry prophet could convey the full extent of the catastrophe.

One group of Americans found the White City a particularly sharp disappointment. African Americans were barred from all of the Exposition's planning committees; consequently there was no mention of their contribution to America in any of the exhibits. The only black figure anyone seemed to remember was the mannequin in a display of angling equipment, of a little boy who had fallen asleep while fishing. Blacks were angered by their treatment. Frederick Douglass, who attended one of the fair's many conventions ironically as a representative of Haiti, announced that his fellow African Americans had hoped to tell the many visitors from abroad that "progress and enlightenment had banished barbarism and race hate from the United States" and that "the souls of Negroes are held to be precious in the sight of God, as are the souls of white men." But that was not to be the case, either in America or at the fair. "Morally speaking," he said, the White City was nothing more than "a whitened sepulchre."

There can be no denying that the White City was a powerful symbol of what was right and what was not so right about turn-of-the-century America. It came, as did the pentecostal movement, just as Americans were asking themselves who they were and who they wanted to be. But unlike the pentecostal revival that would predict God's judgment on an unrighteous nation, the White City reassured Americans that even though they might not feel ready to take on imperial responsibilities, they had the stuff to do it if they tried. And it comforted them with the idea that if their real cities were falling into crime and corruption they could still raise an imaginary one, gleaming white and litter-free, on the shores of an inland lake. The fact that it was glued together with impermanent plaster, that it was constructed only for a summer, and that within a year every building but one (now the Chicago Museum of Science and Industry) would be, quite literally, dust and ashes, did not seem to bother them.

There was another gauge of the pervasive split that divided the religious spirit of America. Clearly within the fair's boundaries, but discreetly apart from the White City stood something the Exposition's managers called the "Midway Plaisance." Here a few of the rowdier features one usually finds in a real carnival were allowed to congregate. There were dancing girls in a Persian palace with real minarets, and an Oriental Hippodrome where Bedouin marksmen and daring equestrians displayed their skills. The International Dress and Costume Exhibition soon became enormously popular as forty beauties from different lands displayed their costumes—and themselves—to growing crowds of ogglers. Primal energies, it seems, found a way to gambol, if not in the pristine city itself, then at its edges.

Religions classically struggle with this same divided consciousness about order and chaos, balance and exuberance, propriety and spontaneity. If Presbyterians most often overdo the orderliness, pentecostals frequently skirt disarray. But a religion, like a world's fair, that does not recognize and make room for both, is doomed. On balance, the great majority of Christian churches have opted for symmetry and structure, consigning dissonance and ecstasy to the sects and the mystics. To their credit, pentecostals have striven to maintain both. They have not always succeeded, but they have always recognized a fundamental spiritual axiom, that God speaks in the thunder as well as in the still, small voice. The Columbian Exposition tried to have it both ways. It made a space for each but kept them quarantined from each other. Such a separate-but-equal solution never works for long. It breeds even more rudimentary turmoil, as the later history of American religion was to demonstrate.

The other ongoing dispute in American Christianity that was reflected in the White City—and its portentious destruction by fire—is the longstanding one about the nature of evil and its most effective antidote. The debate goes back to the controversy between the Deists and the Calvinists who forged the nation's constitution. It was rehearsed again in the quarrel between the sunny Emerson and the somber Herman Melville. When I was in seminary it was being fought out between the liberals and the neo-orthodox disciples of Reinhold Niebuhr. It still goes on today. The White City embodied the naive notion that if the environment is airbrushed to a spick-and-span sheen, then morality will follow along. The French Beaux-Arts vogue in which the builders were steeped was not just a philosophy of exterior design. It was linked to a conviction, strong among French thinkers of the day, that carefully contrived cities would produce useful citizens who would display the proper moral norms.

This splendid ideal, which sounds almost impossibly innocent today, nonetheless quickened the pulse, not just of the men who sketched the blueprints for the White City, but of the millions who visited the fair that summer. As Boyer correctly observes, the design of the Exposition expressed the planners' conviction that if only an orderly, sanitary, and spatially balanced outer world could be constructed, "the natural, socially responsible man would appear from beneath the vice of depravity." Needless to say, this technological messianism represented a view of human nature that the pentecostal prophets of Azusa Street would reject outright. They believed in sin. Rather than beginning from without and hoping that the newly burnished surroundings would transform the heart, they insisted on beginning from within. Or, as they would prefer to put it, beginning with the Spirit of God which transforms the world starting with the spirits and bodies of small communities of flesh and blood.

One feature of the Chicago Exposition epitomized both the parallel and the contrast between the fair's spiritual aspirations and those of the pentecostal movement more graphically than anything else: the World's Parliament of Religions. The parliament met for nearly three weeks in September 1893 and at every one of its evening sessions, which were repeated twice to accommodate the crowds, "three thousand men and women were on their feet waving handkerchiefs, clapping hands, and cheering."

There is little wonder that people clapped. It was—for its time—a daring and visionary project. The chairman of the parliament's planning committee had predicted it would be "the most important, commanding, and influential, as surely it will be the most phenomenal fact of the Columbian Exposition," and he was right. It rivaled the Midway Plaisance in exoticism if not in exuberance, and was—in its own way—a completely unprecedented event. Jewish rabbis, Roman Catholic bishops, and scores of Protestant ministers attended. But more significantly, representatives of several religions other than Christianity and Judaism, from nearly all parts of their world, also took part. Scholars of religion from Europe sent papers to be read. This was indeed a first, not just for America but for the world. Some historians date the beginning of the modern interfaith movement as well as the academic discipline of comparative religion to the energy and curiosity the parliament generated. The delegates met for seventeen days. By the end of what must have felt to at least some of them like the religious equivalent of a dance marathon, fully 216 papers had been given—by American Protestants; by American Catholics and Jews; and by Buddhists, Hindus, Taoists, Shintoists, Jains, Muslims, and Zoroastrians. A white anthropologist even gave a talk on American Indian religion. It was almost a theological hall of fame. Many of the speakers were quite prominent, or soon went on to wider glory. It was at this ambitious meeting, for example, that Swami Vivekananda, who later founded the Vedanta Society, was first introduced to America. And it was there that the redoubtable

Annie Besant who became a world leader of the Theosophy movement gave an address. Mary Baker Eddy spoke, as did Washington Gladden, Julia Ward Howe, and Francis Greenwood Peabody. The well-placed bomb of a militant atheist could have silenced most of what were then the best-known religious voices on the globe.

The atmosphere of the parliament seems to have been cordial enough as the delegates patiently sat through one another's presentations, many anticipating a newfound unity among the religions. Expectation ran very high, especially at the beginning. The Reverend George Boardman opened its first session by telling those present that

> this Congress is unparalled in its purpose . . . not to array sect against sect, or to exalt one Religion at the cost of other forms; but "to unite all religion against all irreligion." Unparalleled in its composition, save on the day of Pentecost; and it is Pentecost day again, for here are gathered devout men from every nation under heaven.

It was not only Boardman who hailed the parliament as "a new and larger Pentecost." Another speaker, drawing on the same religious cisterns that would soon spurt to the surface in pentecostalism, testified that the Asians had come because they were "driven . . . by the imperative energy of the Holy Ghost."

But it was here that the first sour note in the melodious anthem was heard. Swami Vivekananda and the other Asians politely declined to accept the idea that their coming to Chicago had been impelled by the Christian Holy Spirit. Indeed their respectful refusal to accept the implicit Christian basis for the meeting turned out to be the central dilemma, if not the fatal flaw of the parliament. The main question was never solved: if the religions of the world were now to move toward unity, under whose auspices and on what theological basis, if any, would the oneness appear? Vivekananda suggested that Hinduism was already a sublime synthesis of heterogenous religious elements and—since it was still evolving—could easily absorb what was still left out. The Buddhist teacher Anagarika Dharmapala, of what was then still called

Ceylon, claimed that the Buddhist *dharma*, not Christianity, could reconcile religion and modern science. A Catholic speaker suggested that the papacy, since it had recently been relieved of its political encumbrances by losing the papal states, was now in a favorable position to provide the necessary rallying point. The Unitarians insisted that only a reasonable religion, beyond all creeds, could supply the basis for unity. A Protestant missionary, George Candlin, wrote that the parliament had ushered in a "bright new dawn of Gospel morning for the world, for all the world." When one reads these speeches today, it almost seems that many of the participants, though seated in the same hall, and listening to the same papers, were attending a different meeting.

The difficulties that emerged at the parliament about the basis for religious unity were already foreshadowed in the discussions that led up to it. The planners' hopes were ambitious if not epochal. Four years before the Exposition itself opened, a Chicago lawyer named Charles Carroll Bonney, a Swedenborgian layman, proposed a series of international conferences to be held in conjunction with the fair that would be "more widely representative of 'peoples, races and tongues' than any assembly that has ever yet been convened." Within this sweeping project, the purpose of the Parliament of Religions itself would be "to unite all Religion against all irreligion." The delegates would be expected to "set forth their common aims and common grounds for union" and thus secure "the coming unity of mankind, in the service of God and of man." Later the planners added their conviction that "only the impregnable foundations of Theism" could make this possible.

Compared to the pentecostal revival, whose antecedents were already appearing in 1893, and which in its own way also tried to transcend "the creeds of men" and unite peoples across cultural and racial chasms, the aim of the parliament sounds lofty but very cerebral. It is obvious that no breakthrough of primal spirituality such as would happen in Los Angeles was either expected or welcomed in Chicago. Although one observer wrote later about "the tears that were mingled with the applause", the parliament sounds in retrospect not unlike the "interfaith dialogue" meetings I have attended in recent years. Each day's program opened with the recitation of the Lord's Prayer, and the parliament's whole three-week-long stint ended with the singing of the Hallelujah Chorus. But the rest of the time was filled with the reading of the 216 papers, and although many of them were eloquent, if a little flowery by our standards, they were really philosophical and theological position papers with such titles as "Spiritual Ideas of the Brahmo-Somaj," "The Law of Cause and Effect as Taught by Buddha," and "Religion Essentially Characteristic of Humanity." Today, bound in their massive heavy green covers, they provide fascinating reading for historians. But, with a few exceptions, they are not exactly rousing. It is easy to see why a demonstration of the "vital power of that universal spirit which drives men everywhere to look upward at a star" that the Chicago *Tribune* had hoped for on the opening day seems not to have appeared.

Whatever its values, and it had many, the parliament was hardly the religious revival some of its most earnest planners had anticipated. This should not be surprising. Theism is, after all, one philosophy among others. The idea that it could provide a common theological platform for everyone, to say nothing of a spiritual inspiration, quickly came to grief when it became clear that some of the delegates, among them most of the Hindus and Buddhists, were reluctant to embrace it. Behind all the theological posturing, in the end the parliament's real basis for unity was what Richard Seager has called "the religion of western civilization" which was so magnificently displayed in the White City. The parliament was, in fact, the religious corollary of the White City. And the spirit that hovered over the proceedings was that of progress and enlightenment under benevolent, liberal Protestant, and American auspices.

The fact that the parliament took place in the penumbra of the White City, with all that it symbolized about the glory that was Rome and the glory that was to be America's future, was its Achilles' heel. Its principal weakness was its very whiteness. The voices of African Americans, which would soon become so powerful in the pentecostal eruption, were nearly nonexistent at

Chicago. And those who did speak were dissident. Frederick Douglass was asked to make some off-the-cuff remarks when he happened to be in the audience on the anniversary of Emancipation Day. He told the gathering rather crisply that throughout his life he had been "studying man, not theology." He added that although he had been asked to say something about "the race problem," in his view there was no such thing. "The great problem that confronts the American people today," he said, "is a national problem—whether this great nation of ours is great enough to live up to its own convictions." Douglass was not particularly pleased that he had been forced to secure credentials as a representative of Haiti in order to attend.

A more stinging critique of American Christianity came from Benjamin William Arnett of the African Methodist Episcopal Church, and one of only two black U.S. delegates. Arnett said he fondly hoped the Parliament might "start a wave of influences that will change some of the Christians of this land." He was not at all interested in some merely spiritual unity. Recalling the religious rationales that had once been used to buttress slavery, he declared that "in the name of Christianity . . . [we] were stolen from our native land . . . chained as captives, and brought to this continent in the name of the liberty of the gospel; they bound our limbs with fetters in the name of the Nazarene." In a phrase that was echoed by Martin Luther King, Jr., seventy years later at the Lincoln Memorial, Arnett demanded that his people be judged "not by the color of our skin, nor by the texture of our hair, but by our intelligence and character."

Still, even Arnett was unable to resist the Pentecost analogy. It is not clear that everyone there at the time caught his reference since he assumed the connection, long recognized and taught in black and pentecostal—and many other—churches, between the confounding of speech at the Tower of Babel and the restoration of understanding at Pentecost. "We have met for the first time," Arnett told the delegates, "since the children of Noah were scattered on the plains of Shinar." The Shinar he was referring to is, according to the account in Genesis 11, the name of the plain where the survivors of the Great Flood vainly tried to build a tower that would "reach to the heavens." It is likely that many of the delegates missed his allusion, but Arnett used it anyway. "The parliament of Shinar" he went on, driving the analogy home, "plotted treason against the divine command . . . and their tongues were confused. . . . In fact, this is the adjourned meeting, from Shinar to Chicago."

The only other speech by an African American was delivered by Fannie Barrier Williams, a Unitarian. Apparently sensitive to current white prejudices about the "primitiveness" of African religions, an epithet the opponents of early pentecostalism would soon hurl at that revival, Williams began by assuring the assembly that as far as the American Negro was concerned, "the fetiches and crudities of the Dark Continent have long since ceased to be part of his life and character." Still, in words that those early pentecostals might have found familiar she said there was too much "church work" and not enough real "religion" and "zeal." She criticized "the tendency of creeds and doctrines to obscure religion" and said that what was needed was a "religion which ministers to the heart." She assailed the white churches for creating the conditions in which "a young colored man susceptible of spiritual enlightenment will find a readier welcome in a saloon . . . than he will in an evangelical church." She said nothing about "theism" or the need for a unified world faith. What was needed, she said, was for white Christians "to assimilate their own religion."

Despite the unwillingness of the Asians to sign on for the unity in Christ the Americans offered, and despite the suggestion by the African Americans that perhaps the more urgent issue was for the Christians to take their own religion more seriously, the parliament seems to have ended on a triumphant note with the thunderous "Amens" of Handel's "Hallelujah Chorus" sung by Chicago's 500-voice Apollo Choir. And despite what must have been the keen disappointment some of the Americans felt about its results, as their guests packed to go back to India and Japan, those same Americans could not give up their initial visionary enthusiasm. "Nought of outlook shall be sacrificed," rhapsodized Laura Ormiston Chant in a highly ornate poem read at the closing session:

For over all the creeds the face of Christ
Glows with white glory on the face of man.

One can only muse about what the Jewish and Hindu delegates made of this benediction on their work. But the upbeat,
booster verve that had brought the parliament together would not
be derailed. The huge choir sang "America" and Mendelssohn's
"Judge Me, O God." Charles Bonney, who had been chairman of
the congress, closed it with words that would not have been out
of keeping at a pentecostal mission where signs of the Last Days
were always a matter of interest. He said:

> Worshipers of God and lovers of man. . . . What many men
> deemed impossible, God has finally wrought. . . . This Congress
> of the World's religions is the most marvelous evidence yet given
> of the approaching fulfillment of the apocalyptic prophecy,
> "Behold, I make all things new."

Then George Dana Boardman, the same devout Baptist who
had opened the parliament with an allusion to the original Day
of Pentecost, closed it on the same note. Bidding the delegates a
final farewell in a speech titled "Christ the Unifier of Mankind,"
he began with a stirring salutation: "Fathers of the contemplative
East, sons of the executive West, behold how good and pleasant
it is for brethren to dwell together in unity. The New Jerusalem,
the City of God, is descending." He thanked the chairman and
the city of Chicago, praised the White City which he said "symbolizes the architectural unity of the One City of our One God."
Then he launched into one of the longest direct quotations from
the Bible to be found in any of the parliament's speeches. "Here,"
he declared, quoting directly the story of Pentecost in the second
chapter of the Acts of the Apostles, "are gathered devout men
from every nation under heaven; Parthians, and Medes, and
Elamites, and the dwellers in Mesapotamia, in Judea and
Cappadocia, in Pontus and Phrygia and Pamphylia, in Egypt and
in the parts of Libya about Cyrene." He then listed the entire catalog of nationalities registered in the New Testament account of
the pentecostal restoration of the lost unity of humanity. He went
on to extol the "coming day" of unity when "all the nations

. . . shall be turned to one pure language." He ended with a somewhat muted but clearly millennial reference, touching on a theme that would become central to the pentecostal message a few years later. The "oscillations of mankind," he asserted, "are perceptibly shortening as the time of the promised equilibrium draws near."

Commentators were hard put to find words to describe the ceremonial splendor of the final event. But John Henry Barrows, the minister at the host city's First Presbyterian Church and the chairman of the sponsoring body, did. "Such manifestations of love, fraternity, hopeful religious enthusiasm, the world has never seen before in any such assembly of the children of our common Father," he said. Then he added the ultimate plaudit. "It is quite within bounds to say that the closing session was Pentecostal."

It is a matter of great irony that the great World's Parliament of Religions ended with a flood of references to Pentecost. Not a single one of the men or women who would soon become the voices of the pentecostal upsurge was present in Chicago. They were not among the famous and the sought-after who gathered under the spell of the White City. No one knew their names. They were largely self-educated. They came from a wholly different sector of American society, and they were the wrong class and color. Yet, many of the themes sounded at Chicago would have struck a responsive chord with them. They too believed that "the time was drawing near," if not for an "equilibrium," then for a decisive new action of the Spirit. They too believed that this new movement of God would break down the barriers of creed and color and language, would reverse the curse of Babel and unite the nations in a single living body. But the way they believed all this was to come about would have been a surprise and a shock to the genteel scholars and religious celebrities at the Parliament of Religions.

On October 28, 1893, one month after the close of the World's Parliament of Religions, the Columbian Exposition in which it had played such a starring role, celebrated an event its planners called "Cities Reunion Day." It was the last of a scheduled series of special days, including some dedicated to individual states and to various ethnic groups, designed to draw more crowds to the fair.

Iowa Day, for example, had pulled in 60,000 additional guests. Fittingly, on this occasion His Honor Carter H. Harrison, the mayor of Chicago, acted as official host. In welcoming the mayors of several other major cities, he told them that although he had "stood upon the seven hills of Rome," he had never seen anything that could compare to the White City. There were already rumors that the city of Chicago was going to allow vines to grow over the buildings and permit visitors to enjoy a kind of instant classical ruin. Harrison himself did not comment on the possibility of a ready-made Acropolis. Instead he voiced the heartfelt hope that Congress would appropriate the money to keep the Exposition open for another year.

Later that same day, as the mayor returned from the chaste prototype of the city of the future to his own home in another part of Chicago, he was shot and killed by a dissatisfied office-seeker who had worked in his political campaign. The fact that the assassin was Catholic and the mayor Protestant raised doubts in some people's minds about all the high-flown rhetoric and interfaith amity invoked by the recent parliament. The murder instantly extinguished enthusiasm for the elaborate events that had been planned for the few remaining days of the Exposition. A reenactment of the landing of Columbus was canceled. The awards ceremony for foreign exhibitors was not held. The spectacular fireworks show that was to have brought the whole Exposition to a splendid conclusion never took place. Instead all the flags in the White City fluttered at half mast, and in place of the joyous ringing of chimes, all the bells remained silent or tolled sorrowfully.

Pundits tried not to read too much symbolic portent into the calamity. But now it was hard not to descry some evil omen in the murder of the host city's mayor on the very day he had bestowed his civic benediction on the White City. The following Sunday, Chicago's ministers delivered doleful eulogies, not just for the mayor but for what the White City had sought to represent. It was "a dreadful finale," lamented one. Another, Joseph Cook of the First Congregational Church, used words to which the people who gathered at Azusa Street a decade later would have responded with a loud "amen." "Only the breath of the Holy Ghost," he said, "filling the canopy of our civilization, can dispel the ghastly portent of storm." But the portents were not over. The worst was still to come.

When the Exposition closed Chicago was already in the grip of a serious economic downturn. Now thousands of workers who had manned the booths and the support services had nowhere to turn. Unemployment soared. Mortgages were foreclosed, and rents went unpaid. By the time the new year arrived hundreds of homeless and unemployed people were camping out in the abandoned palaces of the White City. Urged to remove them, police were reluctant to turn shivering people out into the polar night.

Then, on the evening of January 8, 1894, it happened. A fire, probably started in the Casino to help keep the drifters warm, got out of hand. The winter wind carried sparks to the abandoned Beaux-Arts exhibit halls nearby. Their facades, once gleaming in the light of thousands of incandescent bulbs, but recently ominously dark, were now suddenly lit up again.

The conflagration spread. Thousands of people raced to the scene. Some clambered to the roof of the Administration Building to watch. As they looked on with morbid fascination, one after another the palaces and towers of the plaster-of-Paris city that was said to surpass the glory of Rome crashed to the ground. Then, as one appalled witness later wrote, all watched aghast as the holocaust reached the Goddess of Liberty who "stood with her arms raised up as though she was appealing to heaven for help." Columbus was next. Standing proudly in his Roman carriage with its team of mighty horses, he too collapsed and disappeared. When morning came, the finest buildings of the city so many had seen as such a beacon of hope no longer existed. The fragile fantasy was gone, like the magical summer in which it had taken place. Americans now had to look elsewhere for an embodiment of their persistent hope that another Pentecost could come. But when it did, a decade later in a dingy mission on the wrong side of Los Angeles, few would notice, and among those who did, most would not like what they saw.

CHAPTER 2

The Fire Falls in Los Angeles

And in the last days it shall be,
God declares,
That I will pour out my Spirit upon
all flesh.
Acts of the Apostles 2:17–19

Pentecost has come to Los Angeles, the
American Jerusalem. Every sect, creed and
doctrine under heaven . . . as well as every
nation is represented.
Frank Bartleman, 1906

*T*he fire from heaven descended on April 9, 1906, on a small band
of black domestic servants and custodial employees gathered for
prayer in a wooden bungalow at 214 North Bonnie Brae Avenue in
Los Angeles, California. Their leader, a self-educated traveling
preacher named William Joseph Seymour, had been assuring them
for weeks that if they prayed with sufficient earnestness, God was
ready to send a new Pentecost. Like the miraculous event described
in the Acts of the Apostles, this latter-day outpouring of the Spirit
would be demonstrated with tongues of flame, healing, speaking in
strange tongues, and other signs and wonders. Many scoffed and
doubted. Because of his controversial teaching, Seymour—from
Louisiana by way of Houston—had been locked out of one church
by an irate pastor and denied access to others. But he and his tiny

company continued to meet in kitchens and parlors, praying that God would renew and purify a Christianity they believed was crippled by empty rituals, dried-up creeds, and the sin of racial bigotry.

When the fire finally did fall, shouts of joy and rapturous dancing before the Spirit resounded throughout the neighborhood. The word got out. Night after night people crowded into the little house, stood on the porch, and stopped in the street to listen and catch a glimpse. White people began to come, and Mexicans. Soon the crowds grew too large, so Seymour and his friends rented a small abandoned church on nearby Azusa Street which had recently done service as a warehouse and then as a livery stable. They swept it out and moved their daily meetings there on April 14, 1906. It was no White City, but from that nondescript storehouse where on a rainy day one could still detect the scent of horses, a spiritual fire roared forth that was to race around the world and touch hundreds of millions of people with its warmth and power.

The Azusa Street revival itself continued day after day, month after month for three years. Like the religious dignitaries who had gathered at Chicago a decade earlier, the janitors and washerwomen who huddled in the converted stable in Los Angeles also believed that they stood on the edge of a new era. They also believed God was distressed with the disunity and confusion that plagued their religion. Like many of the speakers at the World's Parliament of Religions in Chicago, they sensed that what was happening among them was like a new Pentecost, a mighty gathering together of the tribes and nations that had been scattered and confounded at the foot of the ill-fated Tower of Babel. They saw signs and omens of this new dispensation everywhere. But they also sensed something the notables at Chicago had missed: that when the flames came, they would purge and purify as well as enliven and inspire. The proud would be brought low and the humble exalted. There would be sulphur as well as balm. It would be the fearful as well as the wonderful day of the Lord.

Of course none of the people who met at Azusa Street had been to the Parliament of Religions. They were not the right color and they came from the wrong side of the tracks. Even when white people began to crowd into the Azusa Street revival, they were mainly unlettered, unrefined, and, as often as not, unemployed as well. Even when the fire fell, and when the embers began to waft across the country, and then across the seas, the scoffers continued to scorn. These "holy rollers" were either demented or demonic, or they were comical or scandalous, or they were all of these at once. What kind of buffoonish God would entrust a revival of religion to such people? But despite ridicule and opposition, the conflagration continued to expand as the sparks blew from ghetto to slum to rural hamlet, to St. Louis and New York, and then across the oceans to Europe and Asia, Africa and South America. As the world approached the cusp of a new millennium, the fire was still spreading.

*T*HE FIRST PENTECOST happened in Jerusalem somewhere around A.D. 34. According to the biblical account, the same Spirit of God that was present in Jesus had descended again to empower his followers to continue his work. The Spirit's coming was marked with tongues of fire and the creation of a new community that brought together previously divided languages and nations. But, pentecostals believe, after this original fire from heaven, something went wrong. Instead of announcing the glad news to all the nations, Christians became smug and indolent. They lapsed into writing meticulous creeds and inventing lifeless rituals. Centuries passed, and Christianity degenerated, but God did not give up. Here and there He sent a sprinkle of blessings, but promised that just before the climax of history He would pour them down in the torrents of a "latter rain," foreseen by the prophet Joel, which would surpass even the first Pentecost in its potency. There would be a worldwide resurgence of faith, and the healings and miracles that had been so evident in the first years of Christianity would happen again as a prelude to the second coming of Jesus Christ, this time to establish his visible kingdom.

During the final decades of the nineteenth century the conviction grew among many American Christians that this long-awaited new outpouring of the Spirit might soon occur. Here and there healings and instances of tongue speaking were reported.

Church newspapers and conferences began to speak more and more about "another Pentecost" and to urge people to pray earnestly for its coming. Then in April 1906, at least as pentecostals rehearse their story, at a tiny black mission in Los Angeles, a series of events took place that convinced at first hundreds, then thousands of people that the latter rain had started to fall and the revival they had been praying for had indeed begun. Those who embraced this thrilling message became convinced that it was no longer a matter of praying *for* a revival; they *were* the revival, living evidence that what everyone had been waiting for had now commenced. They went forth to tell the world, and the modern pentecostal movement was born.

The epic of how the pentecostal crusade, despite stinging condemnation from the established churches and rancorous internal bickering, continued to grow until it encircled the globe includes many players. But it is impossible to understand pentecostalism's origins without reference to the story of one particular man. William Joseph Seymour, a black preacher born in 1870 of parents who were former slaves in Centreville, Louisiana, had an inclination to the "Holiness" teachings about the indwelling Christ that were then sweeping the south. With no formal education, he had taught himself to read. But nothing in Seymour's early life would make him the natural choice of a Hollywood casting office for the role of a social visionary who would eventually introduce into the American consciousness a vision of the New Jerusalem that was so radically different from the one that had flourished for a summer, and then gone up in smoke, on the shores of Lake Michigan.

From the outset Seymour was restless, a man on the move. In his twenties he left Louisiana for Indianapolis where he worked as a waiter in a fancy hotel and attended the local Methodist Episcopal Church. Why he joined this particular church, a black congregation in a predominantly white denomination, is a matter of some speculation. It was not the closest one to his residence. Did he join because it was more sympathetic to newly circulating Holiness ideas or, as one biographer believes, because he was already looking for the more interracial kind of Christian movement his preaching would soon help to create?

By the time he was thirty, Seymour had moved on to Cincinnati. Somewhere along the line he had been "saved and sanctified" by a revivalist group called the Evening Light Saints. These believers taught that human history was approaching its dusk and that Christ would appear soon to set up his Kingdom, but that before the final denouement, God would shower fresh gifts of the Spirit on the faithful. Just as a "latter rain" would fall on the spiritually parched earth, so also a bright light would illuminate the gathering darkness. Meanwhile, however, true Christians should leave the existing denominations—both black and white—in order to become a part of the purified and racially inclusive church God was even then raising.

Seymour soon moved from Cincinnati to Houston, where he attended a black church in which he witnessed something he had never encountered before. He heard a woman pray aloud in a language, or in what seemed to be a language, that no one there could understand. Seymour was touched to the core. As a man of prayer himself, he could sense that this woman had somehow attained a depth of spiritual intensity he had long sought but never found. But he was also excited because in the popular Holiness theology of the day such "speaking in tongues" was held to be a sure sign of the imminent coming of the Last Days and the descent of the heavenly city foreseen in Revelation.

These experiences changed Seymour's life. After the meeting he asked Lucy Farrow, the woman who had spoken in the strange tongue, more about her remarkable gift. In response she introduced him to one Charles Fox Parham, a white preacher who ran a Holiness school in the same city, and for whom she had once worked as a governess in Topeka, Kansas. Eagerly, Seymour sought out Parham and begged to be admitted to the school. Parham hesitated. A Ku Klux Klan sympathizer, he did not feel ready to welcome this obviously earnest, but just as obviously black, seeker. On the other hand, to turn him away completely would seem uncharitable. So Parham compromised. He told Seymour he could listen to the lectures seated on a chair outside an open window. On rainy days he was permitted to sit inside the building, but in the hallway outside the classroom, with the door left ajar.

Seymour was not discouraged. He listened through the window and prayed ardently for the new baptism of the Spirit and the gift of tongues. But strive as he would for his own "personal pentecost," the experience somehow eluded him. Nevertheless Seymour continued to preach and testify at black missions in Houston where he eventually met a woman named Neely Terry. She told Seymour that in her home church in Los Angeles, a black Baptist congregation, a certain Sister Hutchins had recently preached at a revival and had sounded much like him. The trouble was that the deacons of that church had not approved of her urging a second "baptism of the Spirit" (as Seymour and all the Holiness preachers did), and had ushered her out along with the church members who had responded to her message. Undaunted, Sister Hutchins had rented a storefront on Santa Fe Avenue near the railroad tracks and carried on. When Neely Terry returned to Los Angeles a short while later she told Sister Hutchins about Seymour's unusual talent as a preacher, and the sister (her full name was Julia W. Hutchins) sent him an urgent invitation to come west and assist her in her labors. To Seymour, her call reminded him of the vision that had once appeared to St. Paul when a man called to him and said, "Come to Macedonia and help us." So Seymour prayed about it, then decided the Lord wanted him to go. Borrowing the train fare from Parham he set off for his own Macedonia, eager to preach the good news of the gift of tongues and the imminent coming of the glorious New Jerusalem.

Early twentieth-century Los Angeles was to prove a fertile field for the seeds Seymour would sow. It was there that the grains would take root, the plant would flourish, and the spores would blow to distant lands. This was not exactly what the city's founder had envisioned. Father Juan Crespi, the Spanish priest who, along with the explorer Gaspar de Portola, reached an Indian village in southern California in 1769, and renamed it "Nuestra Señora la Reina de los Angeles," was a faithful servant of his church. But he was not a prophet. He can be excused for not foreseeing that the settlement he founded there would one day become a testing ground where the following centuries' visions—both religious and secular ones—would wrestle with each other; a scaled-down preview of what would take place all over the world.

At first, destiny's choice of Los Angeles as the set for this mythic battle might appear to be an attempt at cosmic humor. In retrospect, however, it is clear that there were always good reasons why this city was a likely candidate. When the first permanent settlers arrived from Mexico in 1781, twelve families of forty-six persons in all, they included people of mestizo, black, and Spanish ancestry. The city's cosmopolitan coloration was there from the first day. But it was still some decades before its conquest by the United States in 1846, the discovery of gold in 1848, and the coming of the railroads in 1869 endowed Los Angeles with the zany excess we associate with it today. It quickly became an arena of clashing dreams and rival eschatologies, where utopian socialists, real estate hawkers, script writers, and revivalists hustled the same crowds. Hollywood, Forest Lawn, Angelus Temple, and Disneyland all seemed singularly appropriate additions to the overall blend.

In addition, Los Angeles has always demonstrated a remarkably high tolerance for spiritual innovators, political cranks, and religious eccentrics. After all, the city was populated by people who came from somewhere else because they were looking for something different. So the good Friar Crespi can hardly be blamed for founding the place where, only a century later, a religious movement would arise that, within decades of its birth, would become the most serious rival his church would face not only in his own Spanish-speaking realm but all over the world. Even less could Father Crespi have anticipated that some scholars would interpret this movement as one that was restoring to Christianity many of the primal religious elements—visions, signs, wonders, and healings—that were edited out during the Protestant Reformation. But this is exactly what has happened. What we now call "pentecostalism," while it had many predecessors and has subdivided countless times since, started its globe-encircling career in Los Angeles, the city of Our Lady Queen of the Angels, in 1906. Dedicated by its founder to the gentle sovereign of the celestial powers, it became the city where spectacle, consumption, and avarice achieved a zenith unparalleled in previous history. It provides the perfect starting point for the story of a religious movement that exemplifies the tangled interaction of religion and culture in the contemporary world.

By the turn of the century, Los Angeles was already a supercharged magnet. Its drawing power was supplied by one of the biggest booster campaigns ever to thump the tub for any American municipality. Only the 187th largest town by the 1880 census, and lagging far behind San Francisco, it had doubled its population twice by 1900 and was well on the way to surpassing its snooty northern rival. Its meteoric ascent defied the usual explanations. It lacked drinking water, a seaport (the San Pedro harbor was not completed until 1914), or anything else that might commend it to prospective investors. Nevertheless, real estate developers passionately promoted moving to Los Angeles as the secular equivalent of being born again. It was the place to begin life anew in a land awash with the only thing it did have in plenteous supply—sunshine. It was a city where piety and the hard sell met. As the journalist Morrow Mayo once wrote, "Los Angeles, it should be understood, is not a mere city. On the contrary, it is, and has been since 1888, a *commodity;* something to be advertised and sold to the people . . . like automobiles, cigarettes and mouth wash." And, he might have added, a special kind of secular salvation.

People came. They came by the tens and hundreds of thousands. As one historian of the city puts it, "For more than a quarter century, an unprecedented mass migration of retired farmers, small-town dentists, wealthy spinsters, tubercular schoolteachers, petty stock speculators, Iowa lawyers, and devotees of the Chautauqua circuit transferred their savings and small fortunes into Southern California real estate." Amid citrus farms and eucalyptus trees what was one day to become the megalopolis of the Pacific basin was beginning to take shape.

But Los Angeles boasted something other than sunshine. Oddly for a city that began with exclusively Indian, black, and Spanish settlers, and which had no Protestant church until 1850, by the beginning of the twentieth century it was being touted as the last citadel of Anglo-Saxon racial purity, the final remaining bulwark against the hordes of European immigrants streaming into the cities of the east coast. Before the turn of the century, Boston had already elected its first non-Brahmin mayor, and Irish American political machines were flexing their muscle in several other cities. Not so in Los Angeles, where the previous Spanish culture had been dissolved into the "mission myth" of gentle Franciscans and grateful natives, while the white Protestant majority grew larger every day. In 1907, Joseph Widney, one of the first presidents of the University of Southern California, published his *Race Life of the Aryan People*, a celebration of Los Angeles as the future world capital of Aryan supremacy, a "new Rome" whose virile sons and daughters would one day lead the world. But even as Widney and his fellow Caucasian perfectionists dreamed of their utopia, a completely different prefiguration of the future of the city, and of the world, was about to take shape.

In view of the prevailing cultural tone of the city of the angels, William Joseph Seymour, who arrived by train from Houston in 1906, could hardly have been viewed as a welcome newcomer. The vision he carried with him to Los Angeles was in some ways the opposite of Widney's. Seymour had not come to bask in the sun, to make a fortune, or to purchase one of the wildly popular mission style bungalows, inspired by Helen Hunt Jackson's romantic novel *Ramona*. He had come to preach. More pointedly, he had come to preach about the New Jerusalem and the renewed experience of Pentecost which had now become available to all who would hear and believe.

Brushing off the dust of his journey in the railway station of the city of the sun, the preacher from Louisiana must have cut a sorry figure. Contemporary accounts describe him as quiet and unassuming but sometimes disheveled in appearance. Some note that he had a "vaguely unsettling effect" on the people he met, and a mysterious manner that suggested either demonic or divine power. He was also blind in one eye, the result of a youthful bout with smallpox. A white woman named Alma White who met Seymour before he came to California wrote that after she had heard him pray, "I felt that serpents and other slimy creatures were creeping around me. After he had left the room, a number of the students said they felt he was devil possessed. . . . In my evangelistic and missionary tours I had met all kinds of religious fakirs and tramps, but I felt he excelled them all."

A photograph of Seymour, taken shortly after his arrival in Los Angeles, hardly bears out this severe description, possibly tinged with racial animus. The picture shows him as a stocky, almost rotund man. He is pictured with a group of ministers, six including himself. All the others are white. Seymour's dark face stands out dramatically. He is wearing a wrinkled black wool suit and vest. He clutches a black, leather-covered Bible with both hands. His face, with a visible smallpox scar on the right side of his forehead, is crowned by short kinky black hair with a razor cut part down the center. His chin is framed with a wispy beard. His open left eye seems to be sightless, and despite the slight smile curving his lips, he does indeed appear formidable, like a dormant volcano capable of unannounced eruption. Hardly devil-possessed, but also an unlikely recruit for the new Aryan paradise of health and wealth that Joseph Widney had in mind.

Shortly after his arrival Seymour preached his first sermon at Sister Hutchins's storefront church on Santa Fe Avenue. He was not a great success. Apparently Neely Terry had not given Sister Hutchins a comprehensive report about his theology. Indeed, the sister and the members of her little band firmly believed that whatever sanctification and the second baptism might mean, they had certainly already had them. They allowed that tongue speaking might well be one of the gifts the Spirit could bestow, but they did not make it nearly as central as Seymour did, at least at this early stage of his life. Later Seymour would come to a position similar to Sister Hutchins', but at this point the two clashed, and the result was that brother Seymour's partnership with Sister Hutchins in the Santa Fe Street church did not last long. One day when he arrived for the afternoon service, he found the doors had been locked.

Faced with a bolted door, Seymour did what thousands of pentecostal preachers have done in similar circumstances ever since. He carried on. With no money even to rent a storefront, he began organizing prayer meetings in the humble homes of black friends and sympathizers. The pattern of fissiparation and proliferation, similar to the mitosis that allows one cell to produce thousands more, and has—perhaps ironically—contributed so much to the multiplication of pentecostal congregations around the globe, was already under way.

Some of those who gathered in Seymour's tiny new flock were from Sister Hutchins's church, and nearly all who came lived in the shabby section north of Temple Street. It was a part of Los Angeles the sunshine salesmen and civic bannermen probably wished was not there at all. The street on which one of these house worship meetings took place was Bonnie Brae Avenue, a name that was obviously some land peddler's public relations concoction, meant to evoke fragrant heather and windy moors. But the neighborhood had now fallen into straitened circumstances. Seymour's congregation at first consisted largely of black domestic servants and washerwomen, hardly the stuff of Joseph Widney's Aryan utopia. But Seymour, undeterred by the inauspiciousness of the venue or the low estate of the minuscule congregation—or even by the awkward fact that he himself had still not received the gift of tongues—continued to preach.

Now more and more people came. News of Seymour's house meetings spread by word of mouth, and—as it turned out—his message did not fall on stony soil. Los Angeles was ready for such a messenger. It was ready because the artfully crafted pipe dream of the land traffickers was beginning to sour. Industrial expansion had slowed to a crawl. Jobs were harder to find. By the following year, 1907, a genuine economic panic would set in.

Other things had changed as well. For the immigrants from the American heartland, the promise of a white, Protestant new Rome had already faded. Between 1900 and 1910, 5,500 blacks, 5,000 Mexicans, 4,000 Japanese, and more than 30,000 Europeans also arrived in Los Angeles. By 1910 "non-whites" and immigrants constituted fully 22 percent of its population. Like the original one, this new Rome found itself with "barbarians" within the gates. For many, the City of the Angels was already what it would become in the scripts of the *noir* film writers two generations later, a sunset boulevard of broken dreams. The contest between rival visions of the meaning of human life was about to begin. Religiously speaking, the city—teeming with frustrated, disillusioned refugees from the south and midwest, who had brought with them their revivalist and Holiness pieties—was tinder ready to burn.

Seymour, it seems, lit the fire. Visitors—black and white—from Nazarene, Holiness, Baptist, and other congregations began to find their way to the little house of Brother and Sister Asberry at 214 North Bonnie Brae Avenue. They listened and prayed, and when they returned they brought their friends and neighbors. But still, no one had yet spoken in tongues. Then, on April 9, 1906, as Seymour was preparing to go to the meeting at Bonnie Brae, the friend at whose home he was staying, Edward Lee, a black janitor employed at the First National Bank, told him about a vision he had experienced. The Apostles, it seemed, had come to him and told him how to reclaim the gift of tongues. Both men prayed, and that night, in the modest house on North Bonnie Brae Avenue, according to pentecostal sacred history, "the power fell." Several participants began praising God in unknown tongues, and among these was William Joseph Seymour himself.

Now there was no keeping the crowds away. Some came to seek the new power, some to chuckle, others to satisfy their curiosity. Frequently the visitors were so numerous they could not fit into the house, so Seymour began preaching from the porch. More came, and it became evident that enlarged quarters were needed. Acting quickly, Seymour's friends located a vacant two-story, white-washed, wooden frame building at 312 Azusa Street which had once housed an African Methodist Episcopal church, but had been abandoned by the congregation and used first as a warehouse and then as a stable. By now it smelled of horses and had neither pews nor a pulpit. But Seymour and his friends seized the day. They rented it, cleaned it, placed timbers on upended nail kegs for benches, and piled up empty shoeboxes for a pulpit. On April 14, the first service was held.

Sometimes in religious history seemingly inconsequential happenings in obscure places turn out to have enormous repercussions. Such was the case at Azusa Street. Within days the word was out all over Los Angeles. Something was happening in the little church in the colored section of town. There is a favorite saying among pentecostalists: "The man with an experience is never at the mercy of the man with a doctrine." What was happening in the white-washed former warehouse was that people were experiencing things they had never experienced before. But what were they exactly?

Nearly a century later it is not easy to say. The outer forms of worship themselves were not all that different from what one might have found in any Nazarene or Holiness church. Certainly for the black participants there was nothing all that unfamiliar. There were songs and testimonies, spontaneous sermons and exhortations, joyous shouts and prayers punctuated by sobs and tears. There were intercessions for the sick. Even the fact that people sang and spoke in an idiom that sounded to some like foreign languages, though unusual at the time, was not entirely new.

It is also clear that people did not crowd into the mission on Azusa Street because of a skillfully crafted publicity campaign. In the city that eventually elevated press agentry to the rank of royalty and applied the terms "colossal" and "stupendous" to tiny pictures on rolls of celluloid, the little church on the other side of town used no publicity at all. There was never a printed order of service. There were no handbills or posters. For a while, the worshippers at Azusa Street resisted even putting an identifying sign on the front wall or door. If the Spirit wanted people to come that way, they reasoned, the Spirit would guide their footsteps. Meanwhile William J. Seymour presided over this gentle pandemonium with tact and an impressive capacity for personal diplomacy. The pine planks on the upended shipping boxes were placed in a square, so those who attended sat facing each other. People spoke from anywhere, but for those who felt especially anointed, the shoebox pulpit was generously open to anyone. No collections were taken, but just next to the exit a small receptacle awaited contributions to help pay the rent.

Why did people pour into the Azusa Street revival? First of all, they were hungry for a new hope. The fantasy fabricated by the land promoters had obviously fallen apart. At the end of the yellow brick road, instead of a delectable nirvana-among-the-lemon-groves they discovered a booster behind a curtain cranking out noise and lights. As Morrow Mayo wrote, Los Angeles had been exposed as an "artificial city . . . pumped up under forced draught, inflated like a balloon, stuffed with rural humanity like a goose with corn." The effervescent eschatology of sunshine and wealth had gone flat. But the displaced and disillusioned poor people of Los Angeles, like many of their fellow Americans, found it hard to live without *some* eschatology. And Seymour had one. Not drawn from a public relations kit, his picture of the future tapped into the oldest dreams of the human race. God was doing a great new thing. History was reaching its climactic moment and there were signs and wonders to prove it. The New Jerusalem was coming. Now the rich and the proud would get their just deserts. The destitute, the overlooked, and the forgotten would come into their own. Even more central for Seymour, in a segregated America, God was now assembling a new and racially inclusive people to glorify his name and to save a Jim Crow nation lost in sin.

In retrospect the interracial character of the growing congregation on Azusa Street was indeed a kind of miracle. It was, after all, 1906, a time of growing, not diminishing, racial separation everywhere else. But many visitors reported that in the Azusa Street revival blacks and whites and Asians and Mexicans sang and prayed together. Seymour was recognized as the pastor. But there were both black and white deacons, and both black and white women—including Lucy Farrow—were exhorters and healers. What seemed to impress—or disgust—visitors most, however, was not the interracial leadership but the fact that blacks and whites, men and women, embraced each other at the tiny altar as they wept and prayed. A southern white preacher later jotted in his diary that he was first offended and startled, then inspired, by the fact that, as he put it, "the color line was washed away by the blood."

Other ethnic groups also seem to have trooped to Azusa Street to soak up the new shower of blessing. Records show that a certain Abundio Lopez and his wife Rosa not only attended the revival but went on to carry the message back to San Diego. Such close physical contact and fraternizing was hardly the practice in California churches, or anywhere else for that matter. As one source puts it, "Indeed Seymour served as pastor of an anomalous congregation . . . with leadership drawn from black, white, Hispanic and other ethnic minorities." No longer the Aryan bulwark, this little piece of Los Angeles both foreshadowed and actualized another vision of the same city—albeit a tragically unfulfilled one—that would appear decades later: Los Angeles as the multiethnic world cosmopolis of the Pacific rim. For Seymour, however, it was not an earthly city at all. Nor was it the new Rome. It was the heavenly New Jerusalem, a place where the tongues of fire that had once fallen upon the waiting disciples in the upper room were descending again, this time on the faithful remnant.

Other motives brought people to Azusa Street. Inadvertently, the *Los Angeles Times* helped. A skeptical reporter heard the rumors and, notebook in hand, found his way to the black section of town. The next day his newspaper reported "wild scenes" and a "weird babble of tongues." Other papers dragged out the worn epithets. "Holy Kickers Carry on Mad Orgies," howled the *Los Angeles Record*. "Whites and Blacks Mix in a Religious Frenzy," grumbled the *Los Angeles Daily Times*. The dailies pictured Azusa Street in tones of amusement or menace. One hinted that the worshippers might soon begin sacrificing children. But the net result of the negative coverage was not what the newspapers anticipated. Even more people came. Some were intrigued. Some came to heckle. But, at least according to pentecostal legend, even the most hardened cynics found their hearts warmed. "They came to scorn and stayed to pray."

Nature did its bit as well. Four days after the opening of the Azusa Street mission, on the morning of April 18, 1906, the great San Andreas fault settled violently. San Francisco was shaken by a severe earthquake which, together with the fire that followed, almost completely destroyed the city. It was the most spectacular natural disaster the United States had ever seen, and one can well imagine the apocalyptic sentiments it evoked. For many this was the first rumble of the coming judgment, the prelude to the Big One which, in those days was not foreseen merely as a geological tremor but as the crashing down of the final curtain. Holiness preachers throughout California and elsewhere made sure people did not miss the point. They churned out tracts and pamphlets warning that not much time was left before it would be all over. The San Francisco quake was mild compared to the roar of divine judgment soon to come.

In short, all the elements—except for the unusual interracial fellowship—that visitors found at Azusa Street were familiar ones. It was the particular combination that made it unique. Set in the context of the times, the revival persuaded participants that the Last Days were indeed approaching and that they were all pivotal actors in the grand new drama that God's Spirit was preparing to enact. The worm-eaten foundations of Babylon were tottering. The old world was passing away. The glorious city was about to descend. And they, the despised and rejected of the earth, were both its beneficiaries and its heralds. No wonder people came, and no wonder they went forth to proclaim the message to the world.

The only trouble was, of course, that the Last Days did not arrive, at least not in the form that the Azusa Street congregation expected. As months dragged into years, like the first Christians who also lived in anticipation of the imminent return of Christ, they found themselves with what appeared to be the same old world on their hands. Attacks from the established denominations became more shrill, but even more painful for Seymour was an outbreak of internal dissent fueled by some of his oldest comrades. It started with a visit to Azusa Street by Charles Parham, Seymour's one-time mentor in Houston. Exhilarated by the wonderful fruits of his ministry, Seymour had invited his former teacher to come and see for himself if indeed the outpouring of blessing before the end time had not in fact begun. For his part, Parham was undoubtedly curious. He had preached for years about the need for a new dispensation of the Spirit, so when reports about Azusa Street raced across the country he wanted to see it for himself.

Parham arrived in Los Angeles in October 1906 and was affectionately welcomed by Seymour who gladly made the shoebox pulpit available to the man who had let him listen through the cracked door. But Parham clearly did not like what he saw. What actually disturbed him is not so clear. Was it what appeared to him to be emotional excess, or was it the unseemly mixing of the races that upset him? It is hard to be sure since in his published comments the two objections are often fused. "Men and women," he wrote, "whites and blacks knelt together or fell across one another; frequently a white woman, perhaps of wealth and culture, could be seen thrown back into the arms of a 'buck nigger,' and held tightly thus as she shivered and shook in freak imitation of Pentecost. Horrible, awful shame!" Azusa Street was too much like the behavior at a "darkey revival," Parham complained. Nonetheless, he did accept Seymour's invitation to preach.

Parham seized the occasion to lambast the Azusa Street worshippers. They were engaging in "animism," he told them. Later, after his acrimonious break with Seymour, he wrote that when he entered the Azusa Street meeting he found "hypnotic influences, familiar-spirit influences, mesmeric influences, and all kinds of spells, spasms, falling in trances, etc." He insisted that "any strained exertion of body, mind, or voice is not the work of the Holy Spirit." This comment seems to support the idea that Parham was upset by the agitated atmosphere. But in another obvious reference to the same occasion he also wrote that he had seen people "crowded together around the altar like hogs, blacks and whites mingling; this should be enough to bring a blush of shame to devils, let alone angels, and yet this was all charged to the Holy Spirit." Whether it was the mesmerism or the mingling, Parham did not like it one bit, and he said so.

Understandably, Seymour and the elders—both black and white—of what was now known as the Pacific Apostolic Faith Movement did not appreciate Parham's condemnation. They believed that what was going on in their midst, both in the physical signs and wonders and in the breaking down of racial barriers, was in fact the work of the Holy Spirit. They asked Parham to leave and never come back. He moved across town where he opened a rival, but largely ignored, evangelistic campaign. Finally, in December, he left Los Angeles for good, whatever claim he had once made to the leadership of the new pentecostal or "apostolic" movement forever shattered.

But Parham was not the last adversary Seymour would confront. In 1911, after the pentecostal movement had already sped across the nation and leaped the seas, one of his early white supporters, William H. Durham, also returned to Los Angeles. Seymour, of course, invited him to preach. But Durham, like Parham a few years earlier, chose the occasion to launch a polemical attack on Seymour. He argued that the "finished work of Christ on the cross" required a supplementary baptism by the Spirit, but that sanctification was not a "second work of grace." Durham's message seems to have had a certain appeal to the minority of Seymour's followers who had been raised in white Baptist and Presbyterian churches with their more Calvinistic theologies. But Seymour himself, and most of the members of the Azusa Street congregation, were devastated. Durham had undercut the entire theological rationale for the revival. It was as though a visiting preacher had spoken from Martin Luther's pulpit in Wittenberg and told his listeners that "justification by faith," the key idea of the Protestant Reformation, was not really true after all.

Now, sadly, and perhaps with a sense of irony, it was Seymour who locked the doors of the church—this time against Durham. But Durham persisted; he seemed to feel a special calling to oppose Seymour and wherever he went he fiercely pressed his case against Azusa Street. Many fledgling pentecostal congregations followed him. Seymour suspected that the dispute was as much a matter of race as it was of theology. A few years later he believed his suspicions were borne out when Durham's disciples joined others to organize a rival pentecostal denomination, the Assemblies of God, in which white ministers would not have to be led by blacks. The new, predominantly white denomination actually was formed for other reasons as well, but it did gain a large following, especially in those parts of the country where racial separation was strongest.

Seymour's altercation with Durham created a painful crisis for him. During his first years at Azusa Street, he had put central emphasis on the gift of tongues both as the clearest evidence of baptism in the Spirit and as a harbinger of the Last Days. But now he began to change his mind. Finding that some people could speak in tongues and continue to abhor their black fellow Christians convinced him that it was not tongue speaking but the dissolution of racial barriers that was the surest sign of the Spirit's pentecostal presence and the approaching New Jerusalem. The early white pentecostals disagreed. Uncomfortable under black leadership and embarrassed by the opprobrium heaped on them for "worshipping with niggers," they finally opted to reject the interracial fellowship and keep the tongues.

Faced with sharp condemnation by people he had once considered his brothers in the faith, Seymour grew tired, and apparently he showed it. Attendance at the mission began to fall off. Bickering set in. When Seymour married Jenny Moore, one of the black leaders of the church, two of the white women who had helped steer the mission through its earliest storms jumped ship. Contending, at least for public consumption, that they opposed the marriage because Christ was coming again so soon, Clara Lum and Florence Crawford not only left town but took the address list of Seymour's popular journal *The Apostolic Faith* with them to Portland, Oregon, where they started their own mission, which is still flourishing today.

Seymour soldiered on. Still, the rancor that goes with such partings of the way is never easy to bear. The defection of the two sisters, the loss of the subscription list, and then more divisions fomented by white followers who chafed under black leadership all combined to weaken his influence. It also nearly broke his heart. Stung by the hurts inflicted on him by former friends he began to teach that tongue speaking was only *one* of the gifts of the Spirit, and might not, in some cases, be a gift at all. He may have had his detractors in mind when he told his people, "If you get angry, or speak evil, or backbite, I care not how many tongues you may have, you have not the baptism with the Holy Spirit." The genuine fruits of the Spirit, he now taught, were "love, joy, peace, long suffering, gentleness, goodness, meekness, faith, temperance."

Seymour had come to believe that the breaking of the color line was a much surer sign than tongue speaking of God's blessing and of the Spirit's healing presence. But now, with the racial barriers reerected by the white defections, Azusa Street became almost entirely black, and Seymour himself became increasingly defensive. In 1915 he published a long tome, *The Doctrines and Discipline of the Azusa Street Apostolic Faith Mission of Los Angeles, Cal.*, a rambling attack on his antagonists that hardly anyone read. Then, the pastor who had been willing to welcome virtually any visiting preacher into the shoebox pulpit, and who had distrusted all forms of ecclesiastical hierarchy, consecrated himself as bishop of his now diminished church. Further, he made sure the church's constitution stipulated that any successor to his office should be a "man of color." Having slipped almost completely out of view, the man who has more right to be called the "father of pentecostalism" died with little notice from his white colleagues in 1922.

There is another old photograph of Seymour, this one obviously from the last years of his life. The earlier one had been taken outside the Azusa Street church building. This photo was made in a studio. Seymour is alone. The white fellow evangelists with whom he had posed in the earlier picture are gone. Now the man who once looked so forceful and self-possessed appears tired. His hair has begun to go gray; he is definitely portly now, and his black suit and white vest are well pressed. He holds his Bible in his right hand, head erect, against the painted background of a waterfall. But the hint of volcanic force is no longer there, maybe because his left eye now somehow appears normal. Perhaps the photographer has touched it up.

A few years back I sought out the address at 312 Azusa Street to see if I could find any traces of its importance in the history of modern Christianity. I knew that after Seymour's death, his wife Jenny had attempted to carry on the work of the mission. Later I found out that eventually the congregation dwindled and the building was abandoned once again. Now I discovered that it was finally torn down and the property sold by the city to collect back taxes. The site was purchased by a developer who turned it into a plaza to serve the "little Tokyo" district that had grown up there.

I had an eerie feeling when I learned this. In the Boston area where I live, we can still visit the Old North Church where Paul Revere is said to have hung his lanterns. In Europe tourists wander through cathedrals that are centuries old, and in India and Japan there are temples dating back thousands of years. But Los Angeles, like most of America, changes so quickly. Buildings and congregations come and go. History disappears overnight and time rushes on. Still, I wondered, does anyone ever pause at that plaza, perhaps at night when the traffic noises have subsided somewhat? If they do slow their steps, do they hear the echoes of shouts and songs? Do they harken to the glad testimonies of people whom the world had counted as nothing, but who here on this spot came to believe that God had touched them with the fire of the Spirit and had sent them forth on a mission to the world? At first I wished that someone would at least place a marker somewhere on the concrete to alert the passersby to what had happened there. But then I knew right away that this would not be appropriate. A carved plaque with an occasional bouquet of cut roses is hardly the memorial those early saints would have wanted. Instead, the Azusa Street memorial is something they could never have foreseen. It is a spiritual hurricane that has already touched nearly half a billion people, and an alternative vision of the human future whose impact may only be in its earliest stages today.

CHAPTER 3

The Fire Spreads

*This is the work of God, and cannot
be stopped. While our enemies scold,
we pray and the fire burns.*
Household of God, Nov. 1907

*T*HE FIRE THAT FELL on Azusa Street was only the beginning.
News of the extraordinary happenings in Los Angeles, and
then in other places, filled the pages of church newspapers and
resounded through camp meetings and conference grounds.
During the next few years, the pentecostal wave swirled across
the nation, vaulted the seas, and seemed to touch nearly every
outpost of human habitation. Its spread was not the accomplishment of professional media elites. As D. W. Myland, one of the
movement's early interpreters, wrote in 1910, "God sent this latter
rain to gather up all the poor and outcast, and make us love
everybody . . . He poured it out upon the little sons and daughters, and servants and handmaidens . . . God is taking the despised
things, the base things, and being glorified in them."

It was indeed the down-and-out who seemed most eager to
hear the new message. The times were uncertain, and they were
looking for something. Prosperity seemed eternally elusive. Rumors
of war were abroad. Many people were fed up with conventional
religion. For the first pentecostals, and for the many thousands
who soon joined their ranks, the period from the Azusa Street
revival until the outbreak of World War I was one of excitement,
expectation, and jubilation. And as one can see from reading

what its enthusiasts wrote about it at the time, it was also a period in which a certain amount of hyperbole and embellishment is evident. But exaggeration is not an unfamiliar device in religious writing, and the early pentecostals apparently had witnessed wonders.

Consider the following: in October, 1907, at Simpson's Bible Tabernacle in New York City, Harold Moss saw the woman who was one day to become his wife float five or six feet in the air. We have it from his direct testimony. It was during one of the hundreds of revivals that broke out all over the country following the eruption at Azusa Street. During these often hectic meetings, railway cars, rented halls, tents, and churches were transmuted into scenes straight out of apostolic days. Anything, it seemed, could happen. People prayed all night, spoke in unknown tongues, leaped in the air, shouted, and fell to the floor in trances which the pentecostals called " being slain in the Lord." Levitations were rare, but there is this remarkable diary entry about his future spouse written by Moss himself:

> People were slain everywhere under the mighty power of God including the ministers on the platform. The case of one young lady, Miss Grace Hammore (who since has become my wife), was quite remarkable. She was caught away in the Spirit and rendered wholly oblivious to anything natural. A sweet spirit of holy song came forth in notes like that of a nightingale and it filled the whole building. The power of God took hold of the physical and she was raised bodily from the floor three distinct times. She afterwards stated she had seen a vision of a golden ladder and had started to climb it.

One finds such stories time and again in Hindu mythology and Catholic folk legends, as well as in the current genre of Latin American literature sometimes called "magical realism." Miss Hammore's experience, however implausible it must seem to most readers, is only one of countless examples of healings, exorcisms, and miraculous signs that crowd the diaries and participants' descriptions of the early pentecostal meetings. Celestial glory often filled the wind-beaten canvas tents, and glowing halos appeared from heaven. The official minutes of a revival sponsored by the

Church of God records that a woman who had never had a music lesson was so touched by the power that she sprinted to the organ and played beautiful music. One exultant convert wrote something that reminded me of Dante's description of heaven in *The Divine Comedy* as the place where he heard the *riso del universo*, the laughter of the universe. This man, who probably never heard of Dante, says that when the Spirit entered him he felt as though "everything in my body was laughing with unspeakable joy."

Fire was especially in evidence. Some saw it in long luminous streaks, others in huge bright spheres. When reports began to drift back from pentecostal revivals abroad, the flaming marvels became even more spectacular. In Wales, "colored lights were often seen, like balls of fire, during the revivals there." In India, it was reported, the girls at a Christian mission school who had prayed for revival after hearing about Azusa Street became so overwhelmed when the Spirit fell that they refused to eat. Instead they collapsed into a trance and when they returned to normal consciousness told of seeing a great white throne, a resplendently robed throng, and "a glory so bright they could not bear it." Soon "the whole school was aflame" and classes had to be suspended. That night the holy fire returned again upon one of the girls who was still seeking. Her roommate, so the report goes, "seeing fire envelop her, brought a pail of water to dash upon her."

In another part of India, at a missionary orphanage for girls, pictures depicting the life of Christ appeared supernaturally on the walls. "The figures in the pictures moved and were in color. Each would last from two to ten minutes, then gradually faded away, to appear with a new scene." The chronicler who passes on this news appears to be aware that small children sometimes possess extremely creative imaginations, so he judiciously adds that these high-resolution pictorial transmissions appeared not only to the children but to "eight missionaries, native Christians living nearby, and even heathen coming to see the wonderful sight."

It goes on. One can hardly open a book of pentecostal reminiscences from the vertiginous years that followed the Azusa Street revival without signs and wonders tumbling out of the pages. At one midwest revival the "weight of glory" was so heavy the people could not even remain seated but had to sprawl full length on the floor. Even the evangelist says that he simply lay on the low platform on his face "while God ran the meetings." When it was time for the preachers to move on to the next town but the means were not at hand, train tickets appeared from nowhere. Money, like manna, was unexpectedly pressed into the hands of destitute evangelists at just the last minute, in answer to prayer but usually by people they had never met before.

I admit that when I first began to peruse these letters and testimonies I was puzzled and sometimes a little annoyed. What had gotten into these people? Did they really believe that the Spirit had enabled people like Ms. Hammore to suspend the law of gravity? Who really saw the aureoles, the incandescent halos, the miraculous moving pictures? How could they be sure the inspired organist had never had a lesson? Was this all just a matter of runaway credulity, mass hysteria, or overwrought salesmanship? What in the world was going on?

As I continued to read, however, sometimes in fading, fragile pamphlets and brittle old books that had not been taken from the library shelves for decades, a different attitude crept in. I found I was being caught up myself. Not lifted off the floor, but swept along, at least temporarily, in the heady excitement and breathless joy of this first generation of pentecostal believers. So I decided to let myself go, to take the plunge and bob along for a while in the fabulous world their writings conjure, the way one might, for example, in reading a short story by Jorge Luis Borges or one of Gabriel García Marquez's novels.

It was a satisfying change. I quickly found that my new attitude allowed me to follow the spectacular spread of pentecostalism better than either credulity or skepticism could. As I pored over these archaic accounts, it became clear to me that for those early converts, the baptism of the Spirit did not just change their religious affiliation or their way of worship. It changed everything. They literally saw the whole world in a new light. Spirit baptism was not just an initiation rite, it was a mystical encounter. That is why they sometimes sounded like Saint Teresa of Avila or

Saint John of the Cross, although they had probably never heard of either one. That is why they spoke of an "absence of fleshly effort" and "walking softly with God." Their own tingling flesh convinced them that a whole new epoch in history was beginning and they were already living in it. In the words of Paul "old things had passed away and all things had become new." As one grateful convert wrote, "It seemed as though the whole world and all the people looked a different color." Sixty years later a teenage pentecostal boy in Chile testified in nearly the same words. "When I was fifteen," he said, "a work was done in me. I experienced repentance, I began to weep, and I asked God to pardon my sin and to transform my life. And I heard a voice say to me: 'Your sins are forgiven,' and in the same instant my life completely changed . . . when I left the building I had the impression that everything had changed; the streets, the trees were different. It was a very poor neighborhood, old houses, unpaved streets. But for me, everything was new, everything was changed."

As a theologian I had grown accustomed to studying religious movements by reading what their theologians wrote and trying to grasp their central ideas and most salient doctrines. But I soon found out that with pentecostalism this approach does not help much. As one pentecostal scholar puts it, in his faith "the experience of God has absolute primacy over dogma and doctrine." Therefore the only theology that can give an account of this experience, he says, is "a narrative theology whose central expression is the testimony." I think that he is right, and it may well be that the reason for the kind of magical realism imbuing many pentecostal testimonies is the same one that pushes people toward dancing and jumping and praising in strange tongues: the experience is so total it shatters the cognitive packaging.

The lightning spread of the pentecostal movement was not like the dispersal of some new idea. It was more like the spread of a salubrious contagion. First thousands, then hundreds of thousands, then tens of millions were struck by the Spirit. However small the sparks at Azusa Street were, within a few decades, pentecostalism had become a full-fledged forest fire. One of the reasons it spread so quickly was that people were waiting and praying for it. For African Americans the period from 1890 to 1920 was what the historian Samuel Eliot Morrison calls the worst in their postemancipation history. But it was also a bad time for poor whites who also responded to the pentecostal preachers. Populists and progressives sought to turn back the growing power of the monopolies, but with limited success. America's graduation to the status of an empire with its acquisition of Puerto Rico and the Philippines did not bring much comfort to hard-pressed farmers or unemployed urban workers. The vote for Eugene V. Debs's Socialist party increased tenfold between 1900 and 1920. Furthermore, mainly among the lower classes, people had become dissatisfied with the coldness and empty formality of the churches. For decades Christians had been praying for a great revival, for a new downpouring of the Spirit: "Send us another Pentecost!" When word came that, first in Los Angeles and then in other locations, it had actually begun, they could hardly wait to hear direct testimonies from those who had actually experienced the new descent of the Spirit.

It was not just individuals who responded, but whole congregations and in some cases whole denominations. In June of 1907, leaders of the black denomination called the Church of God in Christ came to Azusa Street, stayed a few weeks, then returned to transform their whole church into what is still the largest black pentecostal denomination in the world. The historian Douglas J. Nelson believes that this church may have the best claim to being the direct descendent of the original Pentecost "insofar as both fellowships began with the disappearance of racial and other barriers between believers amid exuberant joy and glossolalic utterance." While white pentecostals, he says, almost always see tongue speaking itself as the principal distinguishing mark of their faith, blacks understand tongues to be a mark of the divine power "which brings people together in reconciliation . . . creating a new community in Christian brotherhood."

When the conversion of an entire cluster of churches was at issue the baptism of the Spirit sometimes assumed commensurately epochal proportions. A very important one took place in 1908 in Cleveland, Tennessee, when a pentecostal preacher named

G. B. Cashwell, who had also been baptized in the Spirit at Azusa Street, attended the general assembly of a recently organized white Holiness—but not yet pentecostal—sect called the Church of God. This was no ordinary church gathering. It was the annual conference at which virtually every preacher and many lay people were present, and all of them had been praying for a new Pentecost.

At the close of the conference, most of the participants attended the revival at which Cashwell was preaching at a nearby Church of God congregation. Enthusiasm was running high as rumors of a great nationwide awakening, maybe the "latter rain," circulated among the delegates. To a hushed and expectant crowd, Cashwell described the outpouring of blessings in Los Angeles and testified to his own Spirit baptism. While he spoke the congregation could see that A. J. Tomlinson, the General Overseer—the highest officer of the church—who was seated on the stage near the speaker, was listening with rapt attention. Suddenly, to everyone's amazement, Tomlinson fell out of his chair and crumpled "in a heap on the rostrum at . . . Cashwell's feet."

While he lay there Tomlinson received the pentecostal blessing and, according to his own later testimony, spoke in ten different languages. This opened the door. The entire Church of God and all its branches, with only a few congregations dissenting, became pentecostal within a few years. Tomlinson himself died in 1943, but according to a poll conducted by *Time* magazine in January 1992, the Church of God is today the fastest growing of the predominantly white denominations in America, up 183 percent since 1965.

Not everyone welcomed either the message or the messengers with such gusto. Naturally most of the more established churches were embarrassed and angered by the unseemly goings on. These holy rollers gave all the churches a bad name. But there were other reasons for their opposition as well. After people found their own "personal pentecost," either at Azusa Street or at one of its offspring congregations, and then returned to their own churches brimming with newfound enthusiasm, they were often in for a rude awakening. Their fellow church members ridiculed, shunned, or expelled them—sometimes all three. In response to this often unexpected hostility, the new converts soon took to warning their opponents that the established churches were fallen and corrupt if not minions of the Evil One. A favorite text used by the pentecostals to describe the churches that disowned them was drawn from Revelation 3:15 where it was first addressed to the congregation at Laodicea. In the unvarnished King James version, the translation that was favored by these rebuffed preachers, reads:

> I know thy works, that thou art neither hot nor cold: I would thou wert cold or hot. So then because thou art lukewarm, and neither cold nor hot, I will spue thee out of my mouth.

The early pentecostals were obviously not ecumenists, at least not in today's sense. If God was now forming a new church to replace the old, corrupt ones, then why waste time worrying about ecclesiastic unity? Most people who became pentecostals joined the new movement from other denominations, so were not eager to cooperate with them. They had left them for what they considered to be good reasons, and now they had also been rejected by them. Such churches, some of them believed, were led by wolves in sheep's clothing, craven hirelings who were misleading the flock. "Be not unequally yoked together with unbelievers," Paul had plainly said. They took him at his word, and they urged the members of other churches who dropped in on their revivals to do the same. Many did. And this did not endear the pentecostals to the other churches.

The religious press in the first decade of pentecostal history teems with blistering attacks on the new movement. But of all the coarse assaults, by far the most ferocious came from the fundamentalists. It is especially important to understand this vendetta because today many people mistakenly lump pentecostalism together with fundamentalism, in part because both emerged at about the same time, and they shared certain features. In recent years the relationship has become complex, but in the early years of each they were antagonists. Fundamentalists were obsessed with doctrinal purity. Their targets were the advocates of higher biblical criticism, modernism, Darwinism, and the Social Gospel, whereas for pentecostals the real enemy was the "coldness" of conventional religion and the remoteness of the God preached by the downtown churches. Pentecostals railed against "man-made creeds and dead rituals." In some respects, especially in their emphasis on the need for a personal experience of God, they were closer to some of the Protestant liberals of the day than they were to the fundamentalists. The difference was that while the liberals liked to talk about the importance of religious experience, the pentecostals seemed to generate it.

If the mainline churches merely disliked the pentecostals, it is not an exaggeration to say that the fundamentalists loathed them. The early attacks on the Azusa Street mission by Parham and Durham were the opening fusillades in what soon became an all-out fundamentalist war against the pentecostals. Some of the most vituperative attacks came from highly respected conservative protestant theologians. The staunch Presbyterian and unyielding fundamentalist Benjamin B. Warfield condemned the pentecostals by lumping them together with Roman Catholics and others who believed that miracles still took place today. The Lord, insisted this professor at Princeton Theological Seminary, had not performed a single miracle since the days of Peter and Paul. Another conservative theologian, H. A. Ironside, fired off the most influential antipentecostal barrage in 1912. In a book entitled *Holiness, the False and the True*, he asserted of the pentecostals that "superstition and fanaticism of the grossest character find a hotbed in their midst." Still another fundamentalist, G. Campbell Morgan, trumped all the others by declaring that pentecostalism was "the last vomit of Satan."

What clearly bothered the fundamentalists more than anything else was the same issue that has divided them from the pentecostals ever since: the question of spirit versus letter. While both parties claimed to believe that both the Bible and the Holy Spirit are sources of authority, clearly the pentecostals put much more weight on the Spirit than the fundamentalists do. In their growing emphasis on the authority of the letter, fundamentalists soon began to teach that every single word of the Bible was verbally inspired and that to differ with them on this novel view of scripture was to read oneself out of Christianity altogether.

It is important to recall the issue that underlies this early animosity because in the decades that followed, as many white pentecostals, uneasy about the interracial character of their movement, allied themselves with more socially acceptable white fundamentalists, these same issues would surface again. Pentecostal "converts" to fundamentalist theologies and worship patterns were never entirely comfortable with them, and today many pentecostals regret that they ever made the move in the first place. Recalling this history explains the effort some pentecostals are now making to cut their ties with fundamentalists and even with the more moderate evangelicals, and to restore what they believe to be the original pentecostal focus on the direct experience of God. Whether this effort is a massive defection or a return to the original roots is an issue of considerable controversy among pentecostals today.

As if they did not have enough snipers firing on them from the outside, the pentecostals could also become their own worst enemies. Even before Parham and Durham tried to subvert Seymour's ministry the new movement had begun to splinter and divide. Then, as the years went by, more disputes broke out. Arguments arose about whether sanctification was a two-stage or a three-stage process, whether the wearing of neckties was worldly, and whether building a storm cellar suggested a lack of faith in God. Some received revelations that prohibited them from drinking tea or coffee or from eating pork. One sister, Abbie C. Morrow, presaged later spiritual diet regimes by insisting that the Bible taught believers to stick exclusively to fruits, grains, vegetables, and nuts, but she did not win many followers. Some preachers accused others of undue emotionalism, and then were faulted themselves for relapsing into coldness and formalism. Within a few years the entire movement was torn apart by a debate over whether to baptize in the name of the Father, Son, and Holy Spirit (which had been traditional for centuries) or in just the name of Jesus, which some pentecostals insisted was the practice in The Acts of the Apostles (they were right) and therefore the theologically correct formulation for these Last Days.

The fractiousness seemed endless, and with no pope or presbytery to adjudicate disputes, the arguments raged on and on. The movement that had started as a reaction against dogma fell into doctrinal bickering. Newly born denominations, upholding teaching or practice that was essential to its leaders, split off from previous ones, merged and split again. The organizational chaos of all this cantankerousness can render the task of anyone who tries to make sense out of the first decades of pentecostal history very taxing. Take this excerpt from Vinson Synon's careful history *The Holiness-Pentecostal Movement in the United States*, for example. Here he describes one of the many small pentecostal denominations:

> In 1911 the group dropped the name Apostolic Faith Movement and accepted credentials from Mason's Church of God in Christ. At the same time . . . another group adopted the name "Church of God" . . . without knowledge of Tomlinson's church with headquarters in Cleveland, Tennessee. At the second meeting . . . the church changed its name to The Church of God in Christ. . . . Thus by 1911, three groups operated under the name of Mason's church.

And so on. At this point even the most elaborate flow chart can no longer help, and all but the most patient and scrupulous aficianados find their eyes tiring and patience running thin. And yet, it does not really matter, since pentecostals were always suspicious of organizations anyway. Some considered them works of the devil. Just as the growth of the movement was not caused by public-relations know-how, it was not produced by organizational wizardry either.

The most amazing thing about the runaway divisiveness in the young pentecostal movement is that while the spats and squabbles continued, so did its spread. The more the pentecostals fought, the more they multiplied. One of the most astonishing features of the movement is that it seems to thrive not only on opposition (which many religious movements have), but also on division. This is another reason for its growth. Wherever pentecostalism goes it evokes both joy and anger, gratitude and rejection, polemic and schism. In Los Angeles this spiritual conspiracy, literally from across the tracks, with its message of a new outpouring of the Holy Ghost, caused such alarm and consternation in the other churches that those who accepted it were locked out. Over the years pentecostals have gotten accustomed to exclusion and excommunication. But, as in these early years, what followed rejection was a deeper determination to move on and continue. When Seymour's early sponsor, Sister Hutchins, turned her back on the offended Baptists and betook herself and her flock to the storefront across town, and when Seymour himself walked away from the barred door of the church to start the prayer meetings on Bonnie Brae Street, they signaled a tendency that has continued ever since. Resistance from without and friction within have led not to death but to new life. "If the world hates you," the scriptures say, "fear not, for I have overcome the world." The pentecostals might add, "Where a falling out among the brothers and sisters takes place, there will be two churches instead of one, then three or four."

This pattern of division and proliferation continued apace in the pentecostal movement roughly until the outbreak of World War I. Then it slowed down, though only temporarily, between the two wars, but blazed forth again after World War II, this time finding its "fields white unto harvest" in the black ghettos of urban America and in the growing cities of Africa, Asia, and Latin America. It is time now, however, to step back from the story of the expansion of this twentieth-century reformation and to ask a very basic question. Why did this fire blaze around the world? Why did pentecostalism, in all its variants and subdivisions, so quickly become such an enormously successful religious movement?

As the nineteenth century ended, hopes for a new Pentecost—a reuniting of the tribes scattered at the Tower of Babel—gripped the American imagination. At the World's Parliament of Religions, held in Chicago at the Colombian Exposition in 1893 (whose White City is pictured here), religious scholars declared that the new Pentecost was at hand. Instead, the participants bickered and later a devastating fire destroyed the palaces of the exposition. (Courtesy of the Art Institute of Chicago)

The worldwide pentecostal movement was born in a swept-out warehouse that had been used as a livery stable on Azusa Street in Los Angeles, California, in 1906. It is pictured here in the 1920s before it was razed to make way for a shopping plaza.

The leader of the Azusa Street revival was an African-American preacher named William Joseph Seymour, shown here with four other early pentecostal preachers. Back row, left to right: "Brother Adams," F. F. Bosworth, and Tom Hezmalhalch. Seated next to Seymour is John G. Lake. Tensions soon disrupted the interracial leadership of the early movement.

News of the outbreak of pentecostal spirituality in Los Angeles in 1906 spread very quickly, in part through William Seymour's newspaper the *Apostolic Faith*. The first issue carried a headline announcing that the new Pentecost had come.

William Seymour, leader of the Azusa Street revival (seated, second from right), believed that the breaking of the color line and the exercise of spiritual gifts by women were among the signs that a new descent of the Holy Spirit was taking place.

Charles Harrison Mason founded the Church of God in Christ in 1897 and led it into the Pentecostal movement in 1907. It is now the largest predominantly black pentecostal denomination in America. It was at a church named after Mason in Memphis (Mason Temple) where Martin Luther King, Jr., gave his last sermon ("I have been to the Mountain . . . ") before his assassination in April 1968. (Courtesy of the Church of God in Christ)

During the 1920s and 1930s the best known pentecostal in America was Aimee Semple McPherson, the controversial evangelist and founder of the Church of the Foursquare Gospel, who also practiced divine healing. She is shown kneeling while praying for the sick in Denver in 1927. (Courtesy of the Denver Public Library, Western History Department)

Music has played a decisive role in pentecostal spirituality. All instruments and music styles are included. Aimee Semple McPherson believed there was nothing wrong with using certain show-business methods to get the message across. Here (in white dress, front row) she leads the band during her highly publicized tour of Britain in 1918.

These cartoon caricatures appeared in the Los Angeles Times, July 23, 1906, supposedly representing the types of Pentecostals at the First New Testament Church. The photo at the right is of Elmer Fisher, pastor of the Upper Room Mission.

Newspapers lampooned what they called the "fanaticism and unseemly contortions" allegedly going on at pentecostal revivals and were especially disturbed by the interracial character of the meetings. On July 23, 1906, the *Los Angeles Times* published these caricatures which, however, had the effect of arousing widespread curiosity and attracting even more people.

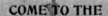

COME TO THE

Union Pentecostal

CAMP MEETING

Of the Sixteenth Inter-State Convention and Central District Council

At West Park, Findlay, O.

In Large Tent on the
Gospel School Campus

JULY
7-23

t Wm. Lambert Brant
OF CHICAGO, ILL.

cial Revivalist

y many Ministers of the Council and
ries with Soul Stirring Messages

ICES   Good Vocal and
H. and   Instrumental Music
7:30 P. M.

PENTECOSTAL
Camp Meeting

To be held at Martinsville, Indiana

During the Month of August, 1915

[D. V.]

A Full Gospel Camp Meeting will be held at this place commencing the first of August, continuing throughout the month.

God has wonderfully visited this city in power during the passed few months, and we have the prospects of a wonderful meeting in the future.

We have purchased a large tent which is situated in a beautiful location, and God has been richly blessing us.

Able workers will be with us to give out the Word, and the Gospel of our Lord and Saviour Jesus Christ will be presented in its fullness.

Rooms for light housekeeping, and furnished rooms and board can be obtained at reasonable prices.

Martinsville is located 30 miles South of Indianapolis on the I. & V. railroad, also hourly service on interurban cars. For further information, address:

Pastor Fred Vogler

590 W. Morgan Street   Martinsville, Indiana

OLD TIME

CAMP MEETING
JULY 25 to 31

ASSEMBLY OF GOD
STATE CAMP

HUNDREDS

COME ALL!

BERL DODD

As evidenced by these announcements for "camp meetings" in Ohio, Indiana, and Oklahoma, the pentecostal movement spread quickly throughout the United States during the two decades following the Azusa Street revival, often eliciting criticism and rejection from members of the more established churches who ridiculed pentecostals as "holy rollers."

The rapidly growing independent Christian churches of Africa are pentecostal in their style of worship, welcoming visions, ecstatic praise, healing, trance, and the veneration of deceased ancestors. Here, pentecostals are shown praying in Nigeria in 1990.

Latin American immigrants to the United States are leaving the Catholic Church in large numbers to join pentecostal congregations. Here, worshippers pray at the Iglesia Vida Nueva en Cristo (Church of the New Life in Christ) in Binghamton, New York.

Pentecostals have been a persecuted minority in the former Soviet Union and eastern Europe for decades. Since the fall of communism, they have made use of the new freedom to respond to the spiritual hunger of hundreds of thousands of seekers. Here, new converts are pictured being baptized in a river in Romania in 1992.

The explosive growth of pentecostalism, especially among young adults, promises to create non-Catholic majorities in some Latin American countries within the next ten to fifteen years. This 1993 photo shows young people praying at a pentecostal church in Argentina.

In recent years, pentecostalism has begun to expand with great rapidity in Asia, including mainland China. Dr. David Yonggi Cho, pictured here in 1994, leads the Yoido Full Gospel (Pentecostal) Church in Seoul, Korea. Its 800,000 members make it the largest single Christian congregation anywhere in the world.

PART
II

CHAPTER 4

Another Voice:
The Recovery of
Primal Speech

*For last year's words belong to next year's
language
And next year's words await another voice.*
T. S. Eliot, "Little Gidding"

W HEN YOU ASK pentecostals why they think their movement grew so rapidly and why it continues to expand at such speed, they have an answer: because the Spirit is in it. They may be right. But as I have pondered these questions from a more pedestrian perspective, it has occurred to me that there is also another way to think about why the movement has had such a widespread appeal. It has succeeded because it has spoken to the spiritual emptiness of our time by reaching beyond the levels of creed and ceremony into the core of human religiousness, into what might be called "primal spirituality," that largely unprocessed nucleus of the psyche in which the unending struggle for a sense of purpose and significance goes on. Classical theologians have called it the "imago dei," the image of God in every person. Maybe the pentecostals are referring to the same thing with different words. Scholars have sometimes described pentecostalism as a "restorationist" movement. My own conviction is that pentecostals have touched so many people because they have indeed restored something. But they have done it in a

·ry particular way. They have enabled countless people to recover, on a quite personal level, three dimensions of this elemental spirituality that I call "primal speech," "primal piety," and "primal hope."

The first, *primal speech*, pinpoints the spiritual import of what scholars of religion sometimes call "ecstatic utterance" or glossolalia, what the earliest pentecostals called "speaking in tongues," and what many now refer to as "praying in the Spirit." In an age of bombast, hype, and doublespeak, when ultraspecialized terminologies and contrived rhetoric seem to have emptied and pulverized language, the first pentecostals learned to speak—and their successors still speak—with another voice, a language of the heart.

A second dimension, *primal piety*, touches on the resurgence in pentecostalism of trance, vision, healing, dreams, dance, and other archetypal religious expressions. These primeval modes of praise and supplication recall what the great French sociologist Emile Durkheim once called the "elementary forms" of religious life, by which he meant the foundations of human religiosity. Perhaps they also represent a kind of universal spiritual syntax, resembling the "universal grammar" that such structural linguists as Noam Chomsky claim underlies all human languages, however diverse. In any case, the reemergence of this primal spirituality came—perhaps not surprisingly—at just the point in history when both the rationalistic assumptions of modernity and the strategies religions had used to oppose them (or to accommodate to them) were all coming unraveled.

The third, *primal hope*, points to pentecostalism's millennial outlook—its insistence that a radically new world age is about to dawn. This is the kind of hope that transcends any particular content. It is what the German philosopher Ernst Bloch once called the "principle of hope," the kernel of all utopianism, the stalwart refusal to believe that what we see is all there is or could be. It is what the Epistle to the Hebrews calls the "evidence of things not seen," and because it is more an orientation to the future than a detailed scheme, it persists despite the failure of particular hopes to materialize. Thus despite the fact that the early pentecostals' belief in the imminent and visible Second Coming of Christ seemed to be controverted at one level, the tenacity of primal hope has made their message more contemporary with every passing year.

For many thoughtful people, all three of these qualities of the pentecostal phenomenon—glossolalia, dreams and trances, and millennialism—appear at best merely bizarre and at worst downright scary. But if we think of the three, in the broader perspective of religious history, as the recovery of primal speech (ecstatic utterance), primal piety (mystical experience, trance, and healing), and primal hope (the unshakable expectation of a better future), then their contemporary reemergence becomes a little less baffling. Long before primal scream therapy, dream journals, liturgical dance, psychodrama, or futurology made their appearances at elite conference centers and expensive weekend workshops, the early pentecostals were spreading their own versions of all of them.

I believe that the unanticipated reappearance of primal spirituality in our time tells us a lot about who we human beings are as we approach the twenty-first century, and that its meaning transcends all merely social or psychological explanations. In an age that has found exclusively secular explanations of life wanting, but is also wary of dogmas and institutions, the unforeseen eruption of this spiritual lava reminds us that somewhere deep within us we all carry a *homo religiosus*. Pentecostalism is not an aberration. It is a part of the larger and longer history of human religiousness. In this and the next two chapters, devoted to primal speech, primal piety, and primal hope, I will try to show why, after a mere ninety years, what began as a despised and ridiculed sect is quickly becoming both the preferred religion of the urban poor and the powerful bearer of a radically alternative vision of what the human world might one day become. I begin with the recovery of primal speech.

The first time I ever heard anyone speak in tongues I found it strange, fascinating, and a little frightening. Glossolalia did not occur at the "little church" in my hometown, at least not when I

was there. I first witnessed the phenomenon at a huge pentecostal rally I attended as a college freshman. A friend had invited
me to go with him. He was a psychology major, had read William
James's *Varieties of Religious Experience*, and was an irrepressible
commentator on human behavior in all its many manifestations.
He told me he had heard some wild tales about the revival that
was then in progress at a huge public auditorium, sponsored by
what I later learned was an especially enthusiastic subsect of the
larger pentecostal family which called itself The New Order of
the Latter Rain. Always curious about such things myself, I readily agreed to go. It was an unforgettable evening.

We arrived a little late amid rafter-raising singing by perhaps
3,000 black and white, mostly young adults, and climbed to the
balcony where we could command a better view. The usher who
welcomed us and handed us a songsheet continued to bellow
out the tune while he directed us to seats in the front row. The
stage was crowded with at least 50 or 60 leaders, men and women,
and again both black and white. Shortly after we arrived the song
ended with applause and hallelujahs. Then one of the leaders
spoke excitedly for several minutes about how the Spirit of Jesus
in these "last and evil days" was waiting, at this very moment,
hovering expectantly over this very building, eager to pour down
a blessing into the hearts of every single one who was present.
He added that if we received the Lord that night there would
surely be "signs following."

"That means tongues," my friend said, his eyes lighting up.
"Just watch this."

At that point the speaker invited those who had already
received the Spirit to help "pray through" those who were seeking. I was not in a seeking mood that evening, nor was my friend.
So when a stout young man in a rumpled sportcoat asked us if
we would like to kneel at our seats and seek the baptism we
politely declined. He seemed to understand and did not press us.
But then, as we watched over the balcony railing, an amazing
scene opened below us. Hundreds of seekers did kneel at their
seats, with others—their guides and helpers—kneeling beside
them, hugging them, usually with one arm, while the other arm

was extended upward. People cried out, called, moaned, ̶
wept. Blacks and whites and men and women knelt together i̶n̶
an unintentional reenactment of what must have both thrilled and
upset those astonished visitors at Azusa Street. Then, individuals
would stand, extend both arms to the heavens and cry out in
phrases that sounded to me a little like Jesus's last words on the
cross, "Eli, Eli, lama sabacthani," but in a different order and with
many other syllables mixed in.

The "praying through" and speaking in tongues went on for
about a half an hour. I watched transfixed. Then one of the song
leaders tried to lead a hymn, but despite the efforts of the electric
organist and his own energetic arm waving, only a few people
joined in. The rest continued the praying through, welcoming the
newly sanctified with laughter and hugs. Then someone gave a
benediction, hardly audible over the clamor. As the leaders left
the stage and others began moving toward the exits my friend
and I glanced at each other. Then we also left. We walked to his
trolley stop without saying anything, and as he climbed on board
I just said, "Really something, eh Bill?"

"Yeah," he answered, still staring straight ahead as the trolley
pulled away. I could sense that although we had both come
mainly out of curiosity, maybe even to be entertained, we had
found ourselves in the presence of something that was more than
we had expected. It didn't seem right, somehow, to talk about it
just then.

Since that night in Philadelphia many years ago I have visited
dozens of churches and congregations in which tongue speaking
of one sort or another took place. Sometimes virtually the entire
congregation does it all at once, and the sound is like small waves
of murmurs and gentle sighs, mounting into billows of muffled
vowels and muted consonants. Sometimes it begins as a tiny
trickle, grows into a roaring cascade, then wanes again into a rus-
tle. Sometimes it is a single person who stands and, for thirty seconds or so, rarely more, speaks clearly discernible but
incomprehensible syllables. Sometimes this is followed by an interpretation by another person, sometimes not. Sometimes it happens with music, a polyphony of tones and vocables but with no

rds. Sometimes the speakers sound anxious or
⸜n they sound joyful, thankful, or serene.

have asked myself two questions about tongue
hat is really going on? And why does it continue
owerful attraction for so many people? Pentecostal
believers themselves interpret speaking in tongues in a variety of
ways. A few, like their early predecessors, still claim it is a miraculous gift, and that its recipients actually speak in languages they
have never learned. But hardly anyone I have asked about it
makes this claim today. Instead, most say it is a "prayer of the
heart" that goes beyond mere words, or that it is a spiritual language known only to God. Clearly the practice itself persists while
interpretations of it vary. But why did it spark such an outburst
in Los Angeles, and why does it continue to draw so many people today?

I think the answer is that tongue speaking responds to one of
the most glaring features of the spiritual crisis of our era, what
one writer has called "the ecstasy deficit." Whatever one may
think of the different ways people understand it, tongue speaking
is an ecstatic experience, one in which the cognitive grids and
perceptual barriers that normally prevent people from opening
themselves to deeper insights and exultant feelings, are temporarily suspended.

Ecstasy, as my late teacher, the theologian Paul Tillich, wrote,
is not an irrational state. It is a way of knowing that transcends
everyday awareness, one in which "deep speaks to deep." At
some level, if only in dreams, nearly everyone longs for such an
experience. But nearly everyone also recognizes that lowering
one's perceptual barriers is a perilous business. In order to take
such a risk, people need to feel they are in a secure setting. Both
in the Azusa Street meetings and in the spread of pentecostalism
around the world, this security was provided by a familiar *biblical* framework of stories and metaphors, one that assured people
that God loved them and had a special task for them. Also, since
most who first responded were poor, the biblical teachings about
the coming great reversal, in which the disinherited would be
blessed and the rich sent away empty made them feel not only

loved but favored. In the context of this message, it became easier to "let go and let God."

For the early pentecostals, however, tongue speaking was not
just a delightful experience. It had a clear theological purpose.
Miraculously endowing people with the capacity to speak Chinese
or Russian or Arabic, languages they had never studied, was God's
wondrous way of equipping them to make known to every tribe
and nation the urgent news that the Last Days were at hand. Some
avid believers actually set sail for Hong Kong or Jerusalem with
the firm assurance that when they arrived the Spirit would
empower them to speak in the local idiom. The Last Days were
near. The "latter rain" had begun to fall, and the Holy Spirit was
pouring out upon the faithful the gifts they would need to make
the message known. It did not take long, however, for the gift of
tongues—construed as the ability to speak foreign languages and
expected as the only infallible sign of Spirit baptism—to assume
a less commanding place in pentecostal belief. By the end of the
decade after the birth of the movement, many followers of the
new faith—both black and white—had begun to think of the gift
of tongues more in the terms Paul had used in the Epistle to the
Romans: "Likewise the Spirit helps us in our weakness; for we do
not know how to pray as we ought, but the Spirit himself intercedes for us with sighs too deep for words." (Romans 8:26).

Now tongue speaking was viewed as the Spirit mercifully providing the sounds by which a stammering soul could speak to
God. Speaking in tongues was thus detached from the Last Days
eschatology. It was understood not primarily as a supernatural
tool for world mission but as a deliverance from the iron cage of
grammar and a graceful provision to those who did not have the
strength or the fluency to pray with their own words. Thus the
practice of tongue speaking has persisted even though the interpretation has changed. It has persisted, I believe, because it represents the core of all pentecostal conviction: that the Spirit of
God needs no mediators but is available to anyone in an intense,
immediate, indeed interior way.

The word "available" is the key. Pentecostals continue to grow
today in part because they can change. In the early days when

tongue speaking was taken to be the only sure-fire "evidence" of Spirit baptism, there was no question about it. If you spoke in tongues you were baptized by the Spirit, if you did not you were not. Now, however, most pentecostals consider the gift of tongues only one gift of the Spirit among many. As for its strictly super-natural origins, there is no clear consensus on that either. Some pentecostal pastors have assured me that speaking in tongues, which they often equate with "praying in the Spirit," is a mode of praise which—whatever its ultimate sources—can be taught and learned. They still consider it a "gift," not for world mission but for the spiritual deepening of the individual believer and the upbuilding of the community. In fact I have heard more than one sermon in pentecostal churches in which the preacher exhorted the congregation not to engage in public tongue speaking in a way that would disrupt common worship or cause a distraction. However they may define it theologically, there can be little doubt that pentecostals have rediscovered a powerful and primal form of religious expression. One of the reasons they continue to attract people is that they emphasize the experience, not the interpreta-tion, and that is what an ecstasy-deficient generation seems to be looking for. But that does not begin to answer the question that first came to my mind when I heard people speak in tongues: What is going on?

During the first decades of pentecostal history most academic theologians and psychologists either ignored what they called "glossolalia" (a term most pentecostals do not like) or dismissed it out of hand. But today, with pentecostals pushing toward the half billion mark and with pentecostal practices appearing in other churches, the phenomenon is becoming harder to disre-gard. Psychologists Ann and Barry Ulanov in a book called *Primary Speech* recently observed that all of us, without excep-tion, still retain a certain capacity for what they call "primary speech," the preverbal expression of pressing needs, demanding urges, and tumultuous emotions that is so evident in infants. Babies gurgle with pleasure, scream with pain, and howl with fear. They also communicate in vigorous bodily movements and facial expressions. After we develop the ability to speak in words, these psychologists suggest, primary speech still continues as a kind of undercurrent. For obvious reasons it is never fully express-ible in words. Could it be that what we find in pentecostal and other churches is the resurfacing of this surging, ever-present undercurrent, bursting to the surface because the religious setting provides a reassuring environment where we can safely become as little children, at least temporarily?

Once the discussion began about speaking in tongues and primal speech, suddenly all the scholars who had so spectacu-larly slighted it began to argue about it. Theologians, Bible exegetes, psychiatrists, even literary critics began to talk about the crisis of language, the new spirituality, and the psychology of prayer and meditation. One of the first things the biblical investi-gators did was to look again at Paul's famous passages about "the tongues of men and angels" in the First Epistle to the Corinthians. The fact is, of course, that Paul warns against certain kinds of tongue speaking. He apparently thought the Corinthians were overdoing it. Still, in his effort to tone things down a bit he brags that he also speaks in tongues "more than you all." This text is an embarrassment to the more conservative scriptural scholars. But it is a favorite with pentecostals. They repeatedly cite it to both the fundamentalists on the one side and the religious liber-als on the other who, for completely different reasons, both reject tongue speaking. If Paul did it, pentecostals ask, even though he did not want it to get out of hand, then why shouldn't *we* do it?

Paul's backhanded endorsement, however, still requires some further explanation. Why, if tongue speaking was so important in the early Church, does it seem to have died out after a couple of centuries? For the first pentecostals the answer to this was easy. The Church had fallen away from God, and consequently God had withdrawn this gift, along with some others. He was restoring it again, they added, only because the Last Days were drawing nigh and lost souls everywhere regardless of language could hear the message and be saved. They taught that after an inundation of gifts, during the early decades of Christianity, there had come a long, long drought. But now was the time of the "latter rain" foreseen by the prophet (Joel 2:23). One ingenious pentecostal writer even investigated the rainfall patterns in Palestine and claimed that his findings corroborated this pluvial philosophy of history. The Latter Rain movement, whose revival I visited in Philadelphia with my neophyte psychologist classmate, took its name from this pre-eschatological rainfall.

Once the church historians began to pay attention, they noticed, sometimes to their chagrin, some very respectable predecessors of those who hold to the "latter rain" theory. One was none other than John Wesley (1703–1791), the revered founder of Methodism. Like the increasing number of pentecostals who study the history of Christianity today, Wesley knew that although speaking in tongues virtually disappeared as a general practice a century after Christ's death, reports of its recurrence among Christians have cropped up here and there in nearly every century. He also wanted to understand both facts. Why had it disappeared? And why did it pop up now and then?

One important instance of this recurrence of tongue speaking happened under the leadership of Montanus, the leader of a vigorous Christian movement that appeared in the latter part of the second century. Before his conversion Montanus had been a priest of the Asian religion of the Magna Mater in which ecstatic states were not uncommon. When he became a Christian teacher, he was assisted in his work by two prophetesses, Priscilla and Maximilla, who, it was said, went into trances and spoke the words of the Holy Spirit. Montanus's followers also preached that the Spirit had a higher authority than the bishops (there was as yet no agreed upon authoritative scriptural canon), and that the Last Days were at hand.

On the surface, at least, the Montanist movement bears a striking similarity to early pentecostalism which also combined women prophets with trance and tongues and End Time eschatology. The trouble is that Montanus and his disciples were eventually excommunicated, though not until he had begun to organize his own hierarchy, a fact that suggests that it might have been his growing power rather than his theology which troubled the bishops who excluded him. In any case, the movement did not die. There is evidence that it continued in some parts of Phrygia for five centuries and spawned many successors.

What Wesley wrote about Montanus is instructive, and by reading between his lines we can see that he had to tread carefully. He knew of reports about tongue speaking returning in his own day, and he apparently—like Paul—felt more than a little ambivalent about it. Nonetheless, about Montanus he is very straightforward. Wesley described him as a "real scriptural Christian" and extolled him as "one of the best men then upon the earth." The reason why tongue speaking and similar gifts had disappeared, Wesley said, in a sentence that presages the "latter rain" theory, was that "dry, formal, orthodox men" had begun to "ridicule" such gifts because they themselves did not possess them. Worse, they decried them as "either madness or imposture."

Madness or imposture. In these two words Wesley registered virtually the full range of what would eventually be said about tongue speaking right down to the present. The vast majority of psychological or sociological observers classify it either as a form of mental aberration or as calculated fakery, hysteria, or showmanship. Milder diagnoses view it as merely neurotic or as a desperate but ineffectual social coping mechanism. Theologians and preachers have condemned it as unscriptural, disorderly, syncretistic, or otherwise suspect. Or—despite everything—they continue to ignore it, something the vast class chasm between most pentecostals and most theologians makes relatively easy.

Students of comparative religion, on the other hand, have evidenced somewhat more interest in tongue speaking. They tend to locate it within the more general religious practice of "ecstatic utterance." Such vocalizations, they point out, occur in a wide variety of religions, as anyone knows who has listened to Tibetan Buddhist monks chanting their double-basso drones, or to Hindu holy men intoning in their characteristic nasal whine, or to the moans and cries and exclamations one hears in other religious settings. And here I think they have a point. If we understand speaking in tongues as an example of ecstatic utterance, as I think we should, this would provide yet another example of pentecostalism's power to tap into a deep substratum of human religiosity, and would signify another radical departure from evangelical or fundamentalist protestantism in which neither tongue speaking or links to other religions are condoned.

This comparative analysis helps us to see that both primal speech and its contemporary recovery go beyond the boundaries Christianity. But what that analysis fails to do is to plumb either the specifically *religious* meaning of ecstatic utterance or the theological significance of its spectacular reemergence in this allegedly secular century. I believe that the inner significance of speaking in tongues or praying in the spirit can be found in something virtually every spiritual tradition in human history teaches in one way or another: that the reality religious symbols strive to express ultimately defies even the most exalted human language. Virtually all the mystics of every faith have indicated that the vision they have glimpsed, though they try desperately to describe it, finally eludes them. As The Preacher in the biblical book of Ecclesiastes puts it:

> All words wear themselves out;
> a man cannot utter it;
> the eye is not satisfied with seeing,
> nor the ear with hearing.

Confronted with this verbal paralysis, what can people do? They sing, they rhapsodize, they invent metaphors; they soar into canticles and doxologies. But ultimately, words fail them and they lapse into silence. Or they speak in tongues.

It seems ironic that pentecostalism, the religion of the poor and the unlettered, should in this respect be closer to the most sublime forms of mysticism than are the more respectable denominations that sometimes look down on it. But it seems to be the case. Sometimes when I sit in a large room full of 300 or 400 people all praying in the Spirit at once, the volume is nearly ear-shattering. But in such situations I have often noticed something else, something that one writer, referring to a quality of modern poetry, calls the "furious calm." Within what sounds like cacophony I hear something that reminds me of what a philosopher of language has recently written; that religious language does not describe what is. It describes what is coming to be. Perhaps, indeed, this is a point where high culture and low culture, the intuition of the most advanced poets and the anguish of the people who have never read them or even heard of them, converge. But, though the poets may not wish to admit it, the religious vision may be the more original one.

In 1967 the novelist and critic Susan Sontag published an essay titled "The Aesthetics of Silence." Having described the various sociological reasons for our contemporary ambivalence about language, she adds that one must also recognize "something like a perennial discontent with language that has been formulated in each of the major civilizations of the Orient and the Occident, whenever thought reaches a certain high, *excruciating* order of complexity and spiritual seriousness." She points out that when it comes to a radical suspicion of the capacity of language—any language—to convey what is true and important, "the antecedents of art's dilemmas and strategies are to be found in the radical wing of the mystical tradition." This mystical suspicion of language she recalls, exists in a *variety* of religions. It is the one thing, perhaps, on which the Sufi, Hindu, Taoist, Christian, and Buddhist mystics would all readily agree. She believes, however, that in our time it is not the "timid legatees of the religious tradition," but the artists who are carrying on this protest against the tyranny of words.

Sontag is certainly right that in our time human thought has reached a point of excruciating complexity. Perhaps that is why various kinds of primal and spiritual speech are returning. She is also right about the timidity of most religions. And it is hardly surprising that she did not think of tongue speaking as a possible exception. Pentecostalism was not as widespread or visible when she wrote the essay in 1967, and in any case, because of the social crevasse that separates them, few high-culture writers ever come into contact with pentecostals. But the case could be made that it is precisely this ragtag religion from across the tracks that is now bearing the mystical torch with most vigor and carrying on the insights of some of the very same mystics Sontag discusses.

One particularly noteworthy example is the Christian mystic Jacob Boehme (1575–1624), the "cobbler of Goerlitz," whom Sontag herself mentions. Boehme drew his inspiration from the

Bible and from the Swiss physician and mystical writer Paracelsus, who died in 1521. Boehme believed that God was the great unity who contained all apparently antithetical and contradictory principles. Boehme's writings are thought to have influenced such later philosophers as Hegel and Friedrich Schelling. For those who are concerned with glossolalia, however, Boehme had a particularly intriguing view of language. He believed that Adam did not speak any of the "known" languages, not even Hebrew, but rather conversed in something he called "sensual speech." This was, he thought, a direct form of discourse that expressed the immediate perceptions of the senses and, though more complex and subtle, was closer to the speech of the animals than to the sick and distorted idiom of fallen humanity. He also sometimes called it the "natural language," and he believed that human beings would speak it once again when they reached paradise.

Today's pentecostals do not teach this elaborate theory of what their experience of speaking in tongues or praying in the Spirit means. I am glad they do not. When Boehme wrote, the Reformation was still fresh. The main issue that concerned Christians in Europe was the corruption of the established faith and the search for a simpler, perhaps more "natural" form of piety. Luther wanted to retrieve the Gospel he believed had been distorted by the rise of the papacy. The so-called radical reformers wanted to go even further back, to the Apostolic church or to the New Testament itself. It was a theology of pruning and purification, and this impulse was reflected in how they understood language. They wanted to peel away the excrescence and get back to the simple Gospel message itself.

The early twentieth-century pentecostals, on the other hand, though they were also concerned with escaping ecclesiastical corruption by reaching back to the primitive church, were more interested in the future. Their theology was radically eschatological. The Last Days were nigh. What they needed, at least in those first boisterous years, was not just a way of speaking *to* God, but a way of speaking *about* God, to carry the message to the whole world. Consequently, they interpreted the unfamiliar sounds and syllables coming from their ecstatic brothers and sisters not primarily as a return to "natural" language (as Boehme might have) but as equipment for mission and evangelism. The Lord, after all, might return tomorrow, or even tonight. There was no time for the arduous toil required to master a foreign language. If they did not hasten to the fields, untold millions of Chinese and Africans would perish in their sins with no chance for repentance. What a merciful God He must be to have such compassion on these lost ones that, before the final curtain, He was miraculously preparing the tongues of those who would bring them the message of salvation.

But as we have seen, the way pentecostals explained the meaning of tongue speaking began to change almost immediately. The explanations are still changing. Today, if pentecostals want to become missionaries, they attend a Berlitz school. They understand tongue speaking as a way for individuals within a faith community to pray without the limitations of verbal speech. They see it as a bonding device, tying people together in a beloved community. They see it as a radically democratizing practice, enabling even the least educated person and not just the trained preacher to speak out. Some see it as a form of protest, a verbal blow struck against the life-smothering power of ecclesiastical language and clerical argot. Speaking in tongues allows less educated and less articulate people to express themselves without learning the proper phraseology the priests and pastors require. But most often, pentecostals interpret tongue speaking as evidence of the wonderful nearness of the Spirit, as close as one's own larynx and vocal chords.

I have heard all these explanations of tongue speaking, and more, from pentecostals. But this contrast between *different theological interpretations* of what is at base the *same religious experience*—that of breaking through the limitations of human language—is a critical one to recognize. It illustrates clearly that tongue speaking *itself* should not be identified with any of the passing theories or the different theologies that purport to explain it. Almost all religious traditions have now, or have had at one time or another, the basic phenomenon of what might best be called "ecstatic utterance." They have explained it in a wide variety of ways and created innumerable theologies about it. Sometimes, as we have seen even in the brief—hardly a century long—history of pentecostalism, the phenomenon has persisted while the explanations have evolved. What links these religious traditions to each other, and what connects one century to another even within a single tradition, cannot lie in the theological explanations, which are notoriously ephemeral (or the psychological theories which are even more so), but is to be found in the searing realization that the reality of God utterly transcends our puny capacity to describe it. This was probably what the usually rather confident Paul had in mind when he wrote, "O the depth of the riches and wisdom and knowledge of God! How unsearchable are his judgements and how inscrutable his ways!" (Romans 11:33).

But something in glossolalia or ecstatic utterance goes beyond even this lofty, classical mystical insight. It is something with particular relevance to our own searching but skeptical generation. Not only is the ultimate mystery indescribable and its ways unsearchable. Not only is the infinite God unapproachable in mere human language. The even deeper insight of ecstatic utterance is that, despite all this, human beings can nonetheless speak to God because God makes such speech possible. Prayer itself is an act of grace. We are unable to pray, but the Spirit "maketh intercession." Our corrupt and inadequate language is transformed by God's love into the tongues of angels. What Sontag calls the "excruciating pain" of linguistic atrophy, desiccation, and banality is transfigured, if only momentarily and episodically, into free-flowing praise. No wonder the people one sees and hears "praying in the Spirit" in pentecostal congregations and elsewhere frequently appear so joyful.

This capacity of God to turn what sounds like gibberish into the prayer of the heart is well illustrated in an old rabbinic tale. Once, it seems, the great Chasidic master Levi-Yitzhak of Berditchev was leading his congregation on Rosh Hashanah, the Jewish New Year. To his great sadness, however, he noticed that even though the ram's horn had been blown with gusto, neither its shrill peals nor the prayers of the people were ascending into heaven as they should. The rabbi scanned the congregation anxiously. Finally he saw that far in the back stood a young shepherd boy with a troubled look on his face. When the rabbi asked why he was so sad, he replied that, although he had once managed to learn the *aleph-bet*, the Hebrew letters, he had never learned to pray. The rabbi thought for a moment. Then he advised the young man merely to chant the letters over and over. God, he assured him, would arrange them into words. The boy appeared skeptical, but then began to chant the *aleph-bet*, over and over again. As he did, the rabbi looked up again. Now he saw the prayers, not only of the shepherd but of the whole congregation, soaring up to heaven along with the blasts of the shofar.

CHAPTER 5

Signs and Wonders: The Recovery of Primal Piety

*And I will show portents in the sky
above, and signs on the earth below—
blood and fire and a pall of smoke.*
Acts of the Apostles 2:19

*Spiritualistic manifestations, hypnotic forces
and fleshly contortions as known in the
colored Camp Meetings in the south had broken
loose . . . in freak imitation of Pentecost.*
A contemporary critic's comment on Azusa Street

*T*HE SIGNS AND WONDERS that appeared at Azusa Street and in the global movement it loosed included far more than speaking in tongues. People danced, leaped, and laughed in the Spirit, received healings, fell into trances, and felt themselves caught up into a transcendent sphere. In retrospect we can also describe the revival as the principal point in western history at which the pulsating energy of African American spirituality, wedded by years of suffering to the Christian promise of the Kingdom of God, leaped across the racial barrier and became fused with similar motifs in the spirituality of poor white people. It marked the breaking of the barrier that western civilization had so carefully erected between the cognitive and the emotional sides of life, between rationality and symbol, between the conscious and unconscious strata of the mind. In this context, the mixing of the races was not just an early equal opportunity program. It had powerful archetypal significance as well. It presaged a new world in which both the outer and the inner divisions of humankind would be abolished, and it was the harbinger of one of the great surprises of the twentieth century, the massive and unanticipated resurgence of religion in a century many had thought would witness its withering away.

The pentecostal impulse exhibits—albeit at a more popular level—a striking kinship to many other twentieth-century cultural currents. In 1905, just a year before African American spirituality, by way of pentecostalism, was to make its most decisive impact on U.S. religion, the artists of Paris became profoundly impressed by an exhibit of African masks. Painters and sculptors began looking for inspiration in spontaneity and primitive feeling rather than in the lecture halls of traditional learning. In 1912, when trance and tongue speaking were spreading across America, the Russian artist Vassili Kandinski published a book titled *The Spiritual in Art* in which he proclaimed that the artist should henceforth forgo all mere representation but should rather put forms on canvas that would "call forth a basically similar emotion in the soul of the spectator." The French philosopher Henri Bergson, who published *Creative Evolution* in 1907, the year after pentecostalism was born, celebrated the "vital impulses" that come "gushing out unceasingly . . . from an immense reservoir of life."

But unlike the enthusiasms of these artists and philosophers, which were mainly individualistic, the pentecostal wave has an irreducibly communal dimension. The Spirit descends on groups gathered in prayer, not on an inspired painter at an easel, or on an isolated sculptor chipping a block of granite. Most importantly, for the pentecostals the purpose of the Spirit's visitation, unlike that of the muse, is not to ravish the soul of the individual but to gather up and knit together the broken human family.

There is a certain irony in all this. The very features that Parham and Durham had anathematized at Azusa Street—the trance and ecstasy of the "colored camp meeting," the interracial fellowship—were precisely what enabled pentecostalism to speak with such power to the twentieth century. Despite the criticism, seekers and pilgrims and the merely curious continued to arrive at Azusa Street. Preachers, missionaries, evangelists, and many ordinary people made the trip, received the blessing, often lodging for a few days on the second floor of the former stable, then fanned out to spread the word. They went to Seattle, Chicago, New York, Memphis, and to cities in Africa, Europe, and Asia. By 1908, the movement had spread to Egypt, South Africa, Norway, Holland, and other countries. The newspaper published at Azusa Street, *The Apostolic Faith*, was reaching 50,000 subscribers by that year, an astonishing figure even by today's standards.

Under Seymour's deft hand, long-suppressed currents of archetypal human religiousness had resurfaced in a new form and under explicitly Christian auspices. Seymour had grown up in a southern black religious culture in which an extraordinary synthesis of indigenous African elements had already been incorporated into Protestant Christian worship. Trance, ecstasy, visions, dreams, and healings were not foreign either to the slaves or to their descendants. Furthermore, they did not retain these primal practices merely as heirlooms. In keeping with the typical African respect for spiritual power wherever it is found, they adapted and transformed their African spirituality in the new environment. This extraordinary bit of what might be called "folk syncretism" accounts for the continuity in America of what the historian Albert J. Raboteau terms "a distinctively African religious consciousness."

At Azusa Street, a kind of primal spirituality that had been all but suffocated by centuries of western Christian moralism and rationality reemerged with explosive power. Along with primal speech, this newfound spirituality became the second key feature of the revival. This resurfacing of archetypal modes of worship, elements that lie close to the surface in some cultures but are buried more deeply in others, helps explain why the movement raced across the planet with such electrifying speed. Its potent combination of biblical imagery and ecstatic worship unlocked existing, but often repressed religious patterns, enabling pentecostalism to root itself in almost any culture. Not only did missionaries travel all over the globe (thirty-eight left from Azusa

Street within six months of the mission's origin), but wherever they went, the people who heard them seemed to make the message their own and fan out again. Almost instantly pentecostalism became Russian in Russia, Chilean in Chile, African in Africa. Within two years the movement had planted itself in fifty countries. It was a religion made to travel, and it seemed to lose nothing in the translation.

It need not be condescending to the early pentecostals to observe that they could hardly have been fully aware of exactly why their faith became so immensely attractive to so many people. They believed that they were living at the end of the present world age, not at what turned out to be the beginning of a new epoch. They did not think they were forging a radically new form of Christianity, but restoring the original. Confronting what they took to be a massive defection of the established churches from the true Christian faith, they believed that they were reclaiming it (or rather, that God was restoring it through them). They did not see themselves as synthesizing anything. On the contrary, they saw themselves as purifying a church that had become diluted, dehydrated, and despoiled. It is one of the great paradoxes of modern religious history that at the very moment Christianity was opening its gates to the rites and customs of myriad other peoples, those who were opening the gates saw themselves as purgers and expungers. They insisted that the explosive events occurring in their midst were the work of the Holy Spirit. They may well have been right. But it is possible that the Holy Spirit was doing something much larger and more all-encompassing than they could have imagined.

Not everyone, however, welcomes the return of primal spirituality to the modern world. Just as in the days of the Azusa Street upsurge and its aftermath, today many religious and nonreligious people are very unhappy with what is going on. Their disquietude is understandable. They want to know what this unanticipated spiritual rebirth means for them and their families, and their curiosity is mingled with unease. Even the people who suspected that the proclamation of the deity's demise at midcentury was premature, and who sensed that neither atheistic communism nor secular modernity would last forever, harbor severe misgivings: they worry that because religions are often fused with ethnic and national loyalties, their revival can also awaken old grudges and smoldering vendettas. It is true that the historic spiritual traditions have given birth, in the last half century, to an impressive array of compelling moral exemplars: Mother Teresa, Martin Luther King, Gandhi, and the Dalai Lama. But at the same time Christians, Muslims, Hindus, Sikhs, and Jews are—in various combinations and coalitions—at each other's throats. Can a crowded planet survive a dozen simultaneous new great awakenings? There is much earnest talk in America today about the need for "spiritual values," but what if the pursuit of such values sets one hallowed vision against another and transforms the whole world into a nightmare of contending zealotries? Will the current renaissance of religions lead toward some peaceful parliament of faiths, such as the one originally envisioned by the planners of the World's Columbian Exposition in Chicago one hundred years ago, or will it ignite a new outburst of jihads, crusades, and inquisitions?

Other questions crowd around the current resurgence of primal spirituality. Why were so many wise and well-qualified people—not just popular pundits but careful scholars who might have been expected to know better—so demonstrably wrong when they predicted the imminent decline of religion? If God really did die, as Nietzsche's madman proclaimed, then why have so many billions of people not gotten the message? Was there something fundamentally askew in the reigning philosophical analyses of western and world culture that caused such respected thinkers to make such a bad call? Why have Yahweh, Allah, Jesus Christ, Krishna, the Buddha, and a host of goddesses, demigods, and lesser deities all come back from their premature internment as though to mock the dirges intoned at their entombments? We will be in a better position to address these questions if we first pose a more specific one. Why is it that while many denominations are still losing members, despite the religious resurgence, the pentecostals continue to attract so many people?

Pentecostals succeed because they respond with such effectiveness not only to the religious awakening but to a tidal change

103

in what religion itself is and what it means to people. The causes for the change are vast and complex, but they are linked to the massive urbanization of the world that has occurred in this century. The continued growth of megacities, and the depletion of rural and small-town populations, means not only that there are more people than ever living in cities but that the majority of them came from somewhere else. The great dislocation and uprooting that this seismic shift entails have had at least two results. They have cut the nerve of traditional religion, which is often tied to specific geographical locations and cultural patterns. But, in addition, actually having to *live* in elephantine cities amid urban throngs has taken most of the glamour out of the vision of modernity that helped attract people to the metropolis. The culture shock caused by this harrowing trek to the big city has pushed these pioneers into a search for new forms of community and an effort to retrieve and transform old symbols and beliefs. It is precisely among these rootless pathfinders that pentecostalism is exhibiting its fastest growth.

The results this jarring change has produced are familiar to most of us. As the twentieth century progressed, large blocs of people became increasingly skeptical about inherited religious dogmas, and ecclesiastical institutions steadily lost their power to shape cultures. This is the part of the story many scholars expected, and I was one of those who accepted their appraisal. This is what gave the talk about secularization and the "death of God" a certain plausibility. But something else was happening as well. Not only were large numbers of people becoming alienated from traditional religion, they were also losing confidence in the bright promises of science and progress. And this was the part most scholars missed. What happened was actually a double-barreled disillusionment, *both* with conventional religion and its institutional expressions *and* with the pseudoreligions of technical advancement and rational enlightenment. Consequently, large numbers of these newly urbanized masses settled neither for secularization nor for the "old time religion," but struck out toward a third option. They felt a desperate need for credible values and a personal spiritual center. Intrigued by the shards and fragments of traditional religions, but suspicious of organized church hierarchies, millions of young urban nomads began to construct new spiritual identities, using bits and pieces from the old faiths but without buying the whole package of a philosophy, a religion, or an ideology.

These traumatic cultural changes created a radically new religious situation. Most churches fumbled their efforts to respond to it. Conservatives dug in and insisted that dogmas were immutable and hierarchies indispensable. Liberals tried to adjust to the times but ended up absorbing so much of the culture of technical rationality that they no longer had any spiritual appeal. But the pentecostals, almost by accident it sometimes seems, found a third way. They rebelled against creeds but retained the mystery. They abolished hierarchies but kept ecstasy. They rejected both scientism *and* traditionalism. They returned to the raw inner core of human spirituality and thus provided just the new kind of "religious space" many people needed.

In October 1993, the *New York Times* reported on its front page that in Europe, despite sharply declining church attendance, people are thronging the shrines and pilgrimage sites in record numbers. Such places as Lourdes in France; the tomb of Saint James in Santiago de Compostela in Spain; and Fatima in Portugal are receiving millions of visitors. Lourdes, which is also associated with healing, welcomed 5.5 million pilgrims in 1993, a million and a half more than came in 1983.

The *Times* reporter asked Father de Roton, a Catholic priest who serves the church associated with the Lourdes shrine, why this was happening. His answer says a lot about the cultural transformations the pentecostals are addressing. "We have no sure answers," Father de Roton replied. "Perhaps people find religious life too monotonous and want something more intense, more festive, more emotional. Perhaps the form our religion has taken today does not respond to people's needs." Another priest suggested that people seem to be turning their backs on the impersonality of formal religion as they look for an alternative to the materialism that has engulfed them but left them spiritually dissatisfied.

Pentecostals have not prospered in the twentieth century simply by blending into its cosmopolitan ethos. They succeed by criticizing that ethos and by suggesting an alternative to it. At first this message appealed mainly to the most disenfranchised; those with little stake in the status quo, people with no reason to hope that things would improve. To these wretched of the earth the pentecostals held out the possibility of a radically new order that would come about not because of the patchwork efforts of mere mortals but by the action of a loving God. This emphasis on what we might call "primal hope," a topic to which I will return in the next chapter, no doubt still speaks to the millions of outcasts and social exiles who embrace the message in the poorer parts of the world. But it is not only the outcasts who are responding. Especially after World War II, the pentecostal option also seemed to speak to millions of people whose hunger was not physical.

As the century reached its midpoint, millions of young adults in the richer countries became progressively disenchanted with the omnipresent but somehow unsatisfying consumer culture. They began casting about for an alternative. Most of the established churches, however, had little to offer; they were themselves too inextricably enmeshed in the reigning values of the times. At first, many of these young seekers turned to Asian spiritual traditions. Gurus by the score arrived by Air India and set up shop in the Western Hemisphere. But many of their young adepts soon discovered either that these imported versions of oriental religions were just as compromised to mammon as Christianity was, or that such paths were too esoteric for most westerners to traverse very far. Many grew discouraged or disenchanted and dropped out.

As the 1960s ended and the wave of neo-oriental spirituality began to decline, the seekers began to look elsewhere. The pentecostal vision of a radical spirituality—an "other" way of life—began to attract them. Some joined pentecostal congregations. Others were able to find what they were looking for in the more conventional churches, some of which by then had begun to cultivate the "charismatic movement," which incorporated certain pentecostal practices such as speaking in tongues and prayers for healing—but in a milder and more domesticated version compared to actual pentecostal services. However tame, these charismatic approaches still met severe resistance from the more cautious leadership of the established denominations. Then in

January 1974 a breakthrough occurred. A thousand people gathered in the National Cathedral in Washington, D.C., under the leadership of Francis M. Sayre for a service in which many spoke in tongues. A year later, 10,000 Roman Catholic charismatics packed St. Peter's in Rome and some prayed in unknown tongues under the benevolent gaze of Pope Paul VI. Soon Methodists, Episcopalians, and especially Lutherans began to welcome modified forms of pentecostal practice. Wherever they could uncover it, these restless explorers were looking for a spirituality that welcomed emotions as well as ideas, a piety that accepted the music and body language they were used to. Pentecostals, with their encouragement of lay participation and their enthusiastic use of rock, jazz, country, and folk musical idioms provided it.

Whether middle class or poor, by the last decades of the twentieth century more and more people in every part of the world felt uprooted and spiritually homeless. Whether it was poverty or geographical dislocation or cultural chaos that caused it, all sensed the loss of a secure place in a world where whirl was king. The desperate rural family driven off the land and into, say, Lima or Lagos; the Guatemalan or Korean immigrant in Manhattan; the deracinated computer programmer stuck in front of a flickering screen in Silicon Valley or in some faceless new suburb of Paris; all had something in common: they were looking for a supportive cohort in which to compose and recompose their personal identities, to regain some sense of orientation, to touch base with a center, or simply to make real human contact.

For many of these postindustrial wanderers, the primal quality of pentecostal worship seemed to fill the bill. The songs were sung to rollicking tunes, but the lyrics talked about Jesus and the Spirit. They kept the old biblical landmarks alive, but in a more informal and vernacular language. The sermons were stories instead of disquisitions. The practice of personal "testimony," a staple of pentecostal worship, provided an ongoing opportunity for anyone who felt the need to tell and retell his or her story and to relate it to the Big Story of human life and destiny.

Yet another feature of pentecostal and "charismatic" spirituality appealed to large numbers of people. The crowds that swarmed into the tents and missions of the early pentecostals often came because they had heard reports of miraculous healings. Even when such claims evoked skepticism and ridicule, both the sick and the curious continued to come. They sensed an underlying authenticity behind the sometimes exaggerated stories. The spiritual explorers who had tried to reunite healing and faith in the previous century, such as Mary Baker Eddy, the founder of Christian Science, had never succeeded in recruiting a mass following, and they were frequently ostracized as mesmerizers and charlatans. But the pentecostals did reach the masses, and their ability to bridge the gap between the cure of the soul and the cure of the body was—and still is—part of their appeal. Whenever primal piety reemerges, the link between health and spirituality emerges with it.

As in so many of their other practices, it now turns out that in their beliefs about healing the pentecostals were ahead of their time. They were not only ahead of the other churches, they were ahead of the medical profession as well. History shows that the norm in most of the cultures of humankind and over most of the millennia has been the *complementarity* of religion and healing, not their *separation*. It has been only very recently, and mainly in the West, that the two have been so utterly divorced. The separation began with the rise of medical faculties at European and American universities. Gradually the view of illness as a strictly biophysical defect and the application of scientific, or allegedly scientific, methods to the diagnosis and treatment of diseases forced the spiritual dimensions of healing more and more to periphery.

The unintended result of the wrenching apart of healing and spirituality, however, was that the human body came to be thought of as an object of analysis and observation. Led by the scientific community, people lost sight of the patient as self, to say nothing of the patient as spirit. Reciprocity between the healer and the healed almost disappeared as the physician became increasingly powerful and the sick person was defined as feeble and incapable. As the medical establishment tightened its monopoly on diagnosis and prescription, it also expanded the area under its control. Soon aspects of human life that had once had a personal, even moral, dimension were "medicalized." The use of alcohol and drugs, sexuality and family relations, the management and definition of death, the control of birth—all fell one by one within the ever-widening empire of the medical "experts."

But just as the monopoly had become virtually complete—even dissenting schools of medical thought, such as osteopathy, chiropractic, and homeopathy, were driven from the fold—a reaction began. Beginning with the pentecostals, brought to high visibility by the widely publicized ministry of Aimee Semple McPherson in the 1930s, then gradually spreading to the more cautious denominations, prayers for healing—often with the "laying on of hands"—reappeared. In one sense, of course, spiritual healing had never died out. Pilgrims never stopped traveling to Lourdes or Fatima, and even the most conventional churches had continued to pray for the sick. But the idea that faith might have something to do with the actual healing of bodily illnesses has reemerged as an important element in Christianity only in the past two or three decades. As it has, even the most hard-nosed medical researchers have had to concede that there is something to it. A rush of research has appeared in scientific journals on the significance of the so-called placebo effect, as the recognition dawns that the improvement patients frequently experience after they have had "nothing but" a sugar pill may stem from the trust they place in the doctor. New research points to the possibility that certain ritual acts might actually trigger human endocrine and immune systems, and evidence has revealed the vital importance of a patient's perception of being loved and cared for in his or her recovery. A few medical researchers have begun to ask whether what they call "alternative states of consciousness," or trances (what the pentecostals called being "slain in the Lord"), can help release the body's inner healing mechanisms.

The irony in all this is that just as the medical establishment has finally begun to recognize that there may be some genuine validity in what it had rejected for so many years as fakery and fraud, many middle-class pentecostal churches, especially in the United States, have begun to soft-pedal healing, as they become more "respectable." They have become a little uncomfortable about the healings their grandfathers and grandmothers testified to. But in the rest of the world, as we shall see in the following chapters, healing still holds a very central place in pentecostalism. It is an essential element of the primal piety, the archaic spirituality, that pentecostal worship brings to the surface.

Visions and ecstatic states, dancing in the Spirit and weeping for joy, healings and testimonies: the early pentecostals, recalling the descriptions in the Acts of the Apostles, called them "signs and wonders." These events were irrefutable evidence that the Last Days were near, that the Latter Rain of blessings had begun to fall, and that the long-awaited earthly reign of the Savior would soon begin. The passing of the years has cast some doubt on their timetable, but it has not disproved their conviction that God was near and that the touch of a strengthening and healing Spirit was available to all. The truth is that pentecostalism was, and is, as the sociologist David Martin says, "a potent mixture of the premodern and the postmodern, of the preliterate and the postliterate, of the fiesta and the encounter group." Little wonder that, once having fallen on the City of the Angels, the fire would spread to the cities of the earth.

CHAPTER 6

The Future Present: The Recovery of Primal Hope

Behold, I am coming soon,
Bringing my recompense,
To repay everyone for what he has done.
I am the Alpha and the Omega,
The first and the last,
The beginning and the end.

Revelation 22:12

*O*NE REASON pentecostals did not disappear when Jesus did not come upon the clouds in judgment and mercy, as they fervently thought he would, is that they believe that one can enjoy the benefits of the Kingdom even if its full arrival is delayed. You can start to live in the emerging Kingdom right here and now. People's *ideas* about what the coming new age will actually be like may change from decade to decade. But the *hope* itself persists.

One evening I attended a special service at Holy Tabernacle Church, the largest black pentecostal congregation in Boston, with about twenty guests from various other churches in the city. Our delegation included ministers and lay people from white, Latino, black, and Asian churches. This rousing evening began with the congregation singing "We're Marching to Zion," accompanied by electric organ, amplified guitar and bass, and trap drums. The minister preached a dramatic sermon on Peter's vision, recounted in the Acts of the Apostles 11, of the various animals lowered from heaven in a great cloth, clean and unclean together, while a voice urged him to eat. Pentecostals love this story and their ministers frequently preach on it, for two reasons. First, it attaches such a positive significance to visions, something to which pentecostals pay a lot of attention, unlike most other Christians. Next, the vision of Peter suggests that cultic barriers clustered around eating rules had been broken. "We should not follow the traditions of men but the leading of the Spirit" was the main point the minister drew from the text this time.

As the evening proceeded, people testified, danced in the aisles, and punctuated the preaching and prayers with shouts and affirmations. Three separate choirs sang. During one of the anthems, a handsome black woman wearing an off-white tailored suit with a violet blouse and purple corsage seemed to enter into an ecstatic state. Dancing in place with great energy, she eventually fell back into the arms of three or four sisters who had gently surrounded her so she would not hurt herself. Toward the close of the service the minister asked the visitors to stand. We did, with the keyboard still trilling runs and the regulars smiling and craning their necks to get a better view of us.

The minister surveyed our dappled delegation with its brown, white, yellow, and black faces, then beamed a toothy gold and white benediction toward us. "Yes," he said nodding, "this is the way it *ought* to be. Yes. This is the way it's *going* to be in heaven. *Yes*," he went on more vigorously, "and we don't have to *wait* for heaven because here at Holy Tabernacle tonight this is the way it is *now*." The congregation exploded with applause and hallelujahs.

Pentecostals, like many other Christians, have always talked about the Great Day that is coming. Their particular spin on the subject is that it has already begun to arrive. What the thirsty seekers who crowded into the mission on Azusa Street found was not just a new and radically egalitarian spirituality. They also found a fellowship that foreshadowed the new heaven and new earth in which the insults and indignities of this present wicked world would be abolished or maybe even reversed. At Azusa Street literally any person who came in could stand and prophesy. There were no official mediators, licensed by an ecclesiastical hierarchy or set apart by apostolic ordination. Instead, God's Spirit was present in a direct, intense, and undeniable way.

When William Seymour first heard a black sister speak in tongues in Houston, what excited him most was the realization that perhaps the long-awaited messianic era was about to come in its fullness. As a black preacher he had some very clear ideas about what this new era would be like. The African American religious subculture in which he lived was a swirling ocean of millennial preaching and speculation. Some of these ideas shared in the white theologies of the day but others had a distinctly black cast. In 1892, for example J. W. E. Bowen, the president of Gammon Theological Seminary, a black institution in Atlanta, Georgia, wrote:

> The golden age is not in the past as the heathens ignorantly taught, but it is before us in the dim tracery of the future, and possibly we have come to the edge of this new heaven. I do not believe that the age will find its characteristics so much in the material acquisitions as in the spiritual triumphs of the soul.

Other African American preachers suggested that the healing of divisions among the churches, the end of wars, the abolition of the opium traffic, and the disappearance of "slavery in every form" would be marks of the coming dispensation. R. Henri Herbert, a lay member of the African Methodist Episcopal Church, wrote in his church's journal that when the millennium came its government would be one in which "there shall be no Pagan, no Mahomedan, no Catholic, no Protestant, no Negro, no Caucasian." The black journalist John Edward Bruce put a sharper edge on the prophecy. He wrote that the nation was "standing on a volcano" and that God would soon bare his sword. "Judgement is coming!" he wrote:

> The noisome pestilence, the destruction that wasteth at noonday, the arrow that flieth by day, the Pestilence that walketh in darkness will have no terrors for the Godly, but will as surely overtake the great majority of Negro-hating white Christians.

Some black preachers taught that when the New Day dawned, not only would all the tongues and tribes be united, each bringing its distinctive gifts, but the African peoples would contribute "the heart element—the element which Christ engrafted into the religion of His day." Many, like Theophilus Gould Steward, insisted, against the popular otherworldly theologies of the day, that the heavenly Jerusalem was not on some other plane but that "the reign of peace and justice will be established on this earth for a thousand years, under the Lord Jesus."

These were the visionary dreams that churned and glittered like white-hot meteors in the supercharged religious atmosphere in which Seymour took up his preaching career. He did not have to invent a utopian alternative to the present wicked world. He heard about it and read about it wherever he went. Nor did he invent that particularly intense expression of yearning called speaking in tongues. It was already happening. What he did was to provide the setting in which the vision of the New Jerusalem, the signs of its imminent arrival, and the reality of its presence all came together.

Another theme in black millennial thinking flowed into the early pentecostal theology. It is one that is often overlooked, but it may be the most important of all, especially in helping to explain the contemporary appeal of pentecostalism to so many people. It was the idea that in the coming new age, faith and spirituality would be primarily matters not of ritual and dogma but of action and behavior. This point was made with a special acuity by James Theodore Holly in his article "The Divine Plan of Human Redemption in its Ethnological Development," published in the *A. M. E. Church Review* in October 1884. Philosophizing about the course that history would follow after that judgment, and using the terms that were familiar to him, Holly sketched out a scheme in which the "Semitic race" must be credited with having given humankind the "written thought" of God's divine plan. What he called "the Japhetic race," meaning white Gentiles, had proclaimed and preached this word. But in this final dispensation, "both alike await the forthcoming ministry of the Hamitic race [by which he meant African Americans] to reduce to practical ACTION that spoken word, that written thought."

When I read this bold prophecy made by a black American Christian over a century ago, I was reminded of another seer. In the closing years of the twelfth century an Italian Cistercian abbot named Joachim of Fiore propounded a theology of history that bears certain intriguing similarities to Holly's, though Holly never mentions Joachim. The abbot suggested that the different persons of the Trinity, although they lived in eternal mutuality, actually manifested themselves in history in a sequential fashion. Thus the Father had been the principal actor during the period of the Old Testament. The first millennium of Christian history had been the age of the Son. But in his own time, the abbot taught, humanity was about to enter its third—and final—period, the age of the Spirit.

In this dawning new age, Joachim taught, the church would no longer need a hierarchy because the luminous presence of God the Spirit would suffuse all people and all creation. Priests and bishops—even popes—would become superfluous. Sacred scriptures would no longer be necessary because the Spirit would speak directly to each person's heart. Further, with the arrival of this new age of the Spirit, the strife and hostility that had divided Christians from infidels would disappear. All clans and nations would be joined in a single harmonious body. It almost seems as though Joachim was writing the script for the pentecostal drama that would come 700 years later.

Understandably, Joachim's opinions, like those of the later pentecostal preachers, did not win much approval from the church officials and theological teachers of the day. The bishops did not take to the idea of their expendability. The promised disappearance of interreligious conflict was not greeted warmly by the Crusaders who were at that very moment engaged in bloody but sometimes quite profitable campaigns against these very infidels in Palestine and Syria. Still, Joachim of Fiore's imaginative teachings enjoyed a certain popular approval for a century or two, especially among the Spiritual Franciscans who believed that Saint Francis himself had come to introduce this new dispensation. But eventually church authorities declared Abbot Joachim's teachings heretical, and his books were burned. He died in 1202. The age of the Spirit he announced seems not to have appeared. Instead, the Crusades intensified, the most powerful pope in history—Innocent III—reigned, and a century later the Black Plague, probably carried by returning Crusaders, killed two thirds of the population of Europe.

Likewise, the hopes for a world delivered from war and racism that those domestic servants and day laborers at Azusa Street celebrated did not come about. What came instead were world wars, a Great Depression, a Holocaust, and threats of nuclear destruction. But, then as now, hope for a new era dies hard. And in our own time, as another new millennium begins, once again seers and visionaries claim that a fundamentally different world age is about to begin. I think that one of the reasons for the continuing appeal of the pentecostal message is its focus on the future, on the imminent coming of a different order of things. The early pentecostals proclaimed an "end of history," a "new age," and a "postmodern era" long before any of these currently fashionable terms were invented. They did so using the popular religious language of the day—the Second Coming of Jesus to establish his Kingdom—but it was their mood of joyful expectation even more than their words that reached the masses, and it is that hopeful note that still attracts them today.

I began to understand the continuing appeal of its message only when I realized that what we call "pentecostalism" is not a church or even a single religion at all, but a *mood*. It represents what might be called a "a millennial sensibility," a feeling in the pit of the cultural gut that a very big change is under way. This means we have to see past the image conveyed by the radio and television preachers who may turn out in the end to have been little more than an entertaining but unrepresentative fringe. Despite the publicity lavished in the 1980s on the fall of the popular television evangelists Jim and Tammy Faye Bakker, they do not help us to fathom a religious groundswell that transcends the boundaries of any single denomination. It is not just pentecostals today who believe that God can heal bodies as well as save souls, or that the Spirit can speak through ordinary people, or that hierarchies are to be distrusted, or that dreams and visions reveal truth. The people who call themselves "pentecostals" are only the visible crest of a very large wave. They know how to ride it. But they did not create it, and it is much bigger than they are.

The great scholar of religion Victor Turner once suggested that millennial movements are to a culture what rites of passage are to an individual. They signal moments of change and transition. They enable the person or the society to touch base with the past and with their deepest symbolic roots in order to be better prepared to take the next—sometimes frightening—step into the future. But the rhetoric of such movements cannot be taken literally. It needs to be interpreted both in the light of the mythic structure within which the movements are located and in relation to the environing culture. The earnest fellow with the placard warning us that the end is near may have something important to tell us, but the end may not be what he thinks it is. The pentecostal movement and the religious renaissance of which it is a part embody not just a popular protest against the reigning assumptions of our time, but also the outline of an alternative, a heavenly city to replace the earthly one.

The early pentecostals succeeded in part because they warned people who had never read Oswald Spengler about the coming decline of the west. They succeeded because they brought hope to the losers whom the march of progress had left behind. They continue to evoke a response because they tell people who don't read sophisticated journals about a big change that is coming soon and in some ways has already started. But even though the language they use is the idiom of popular religious culture, they are hardly alone anymore in their apocalyptic sensibility. Even the most detached and secular observers have begun to detect more than a mere whiff of that admixture of moral decadence and religious effervescence that permeated the later years of the Roman empire. Is this, then, "a changing of the gods" for some future Edward Gibbon to eventually trace?

There is a widespread suspicion that something is up. Take the current fascination with dire forecasts, for example. Religious millenarians have been invoking "end of history" rhetoric for centuries. But today they are not the only ones talking about impending disaster. Only a few years back, *The Bulletin of Atomic Scientists* set the hands of its so-called doomsday clock at three minutes to midnight. Recently they moved them back. But just as they did so, ecologists, epidemiologists, and alarmed demographers have taken up the cry. Today the man carrying the placard warning that the end is nigh may well be wearing a white laboratory coat.

Obviously the scenarios of these various secular millenarians differ widely from each other, but my experience as a student of religious history suggests that the most profound anxieties and the wildest hopes of a people are often most clearly pictured in eschatological beliefs, concepts of how and when the world will end. All cultures hold such beliefs implicitly, and religions make them explicit. Pentecostals specialize in eschatology. Unlike those religious conservatives who want to go back to a mythical "Christian America," the pentecostal message points ahead to the city without death or tears which God is preparing for those who hear and respond. They started as a radical millennial movement, teaching that Jesus would come again any day and that the powers of healing and prophesying that were being showered on believers were signs of the End Time. Some of the details of the prophecy have been modified but the future orientation is still there.

Since the early pentecostals announced that Jesus was coming "any day now" a century has passed. Still, I believe that they somehow sensed the coming tidal change in world culture, and they talked about it in the only language they knew, the technicolor idiom of Christian apocalyptic imagery, with conflagrations, dragons, and beasts, and a New Jerusalem descending onto the smoking ruins of a world that God had judged and purified. None of this took place literally, as they predicted, though there were surely more monsters and conflagrations than the sunnier official forecasts of the time had anticipated. More than one White City of progress has collapsed in ashes in the hundred years since the Chicago Columbian Exposition.

Pentecostalism has become a global vehicle for the restoration of primal hope. The movement started from the bottom. A partially blind, poor, black man with little or no book learning outside of the Bible heard a call. Seymour was anything but a Paul of Tarsus, trained by the leading religious scholars, or an Augustine of Hippo, schooled by the most polished Roman rhetoricians, or a Calvin or Luther educated in the original languages of scripture. He was a son of former slaves who had to listen to sermons through a window and who undoubtedly traveled to Los Angeles in the segregated section of the train. Yet under Seymour's guidance, a movement arose whose impact on Christianity, less than a century after his arrival in Los Angeles, has been compared to the Protestant Reformation.

That the Lord has tarried longer than they originally thought He would may have dampened the millennial zest of some pentecostals, especially the estimated 13 percent who live in affluence. But the other 87 percent, those who live below the world poverty line, still believe the New Jerusalem is coming soon. Rather than an embarrassment or an incumbrance, the fact that pentecostals still preach a radical hope is an essential part of their appeal and a reason for their growth. The simple fact is that belief in a Big Change whose benefits may be savored right now is good news to some people and bad news to others. Those who benefit from the way the world is now arranged do not yearn for major transformations. But the racially excluded, the economically disinherited, and the psychologically wounded certainly do. This helps explain why pentecostalism is attracting most of its membership among the impoverished majority rather than among the privileged few.

Still, no religious movement, pentecostalism included, is isolated from the rest of the culture. Having studied new religious movements for three decades and in many different countries, I have a strong hunch that they all provide an invaluable set of clues about an even more comprehensive set of changes. The religious dimension may be the tip of the iceberg, but the underlying cultural shift is the sea in which the iceberg is floating. I do not see this change as the beginning of the Last Days before the

Second Coming, but it does represent a major reconfiguration of our most fundamental values and patterns of perception, one that will ultimately alter not just the way some people pray but the ways we all think, feel, work, and govern. In the remainder of this book and especially in the concluding chapter I will describe this reconfiguration in more detail.

By way of summary of what we have seen so far, it seems evident that pentecostalism, in all its myriad forms, has become the most rapidly expanding religion of our times for three basic reasons. In the first place, the "language of the heart" that the movement has encouraged—both in the early speaking in tongues and in the more recent "praying in the Spirit"—challenges the flattened language and commercial blather of consumer society. Their rejection of "this world" meant that the early pentecostals did not accept ·its myths and values. In the first years at least, they eschewed the accumulation of worldly goods as a snare and a delusion, a distraction from the important considerations of life. Later on, many pentecostals would accept these very values in a surprisingly uncritical way. But in the beginning, and in many places still, the rejection of the seductions of the "boutique culture" is an integral part of what it means to walk in the Spirit.

Further, pentecostalism confronted chaos,. normlessness, and ennui by affirming and then transforming them. By embracing ecstatic praise, visions, healing, dreams, and joyous bodily movement, pentecostal worship lured anarchy into the sacred circle and tamed it. It tapped into a raging underground sea of raw religious feeling and turbulent emotion and gave it shape and expression. In the history of religion, beginning with the Babylonian epic of Gilgamesh, the conflict between Order and Chaos is deeper than the rift between Good and Evil. The pentecostals sensed this and boldly made that struggle a part of their liturgical life.

Finally, the pentecostal message provided despondent people with an alternative metaphor, a life vision at variance from the image of the "good life" the culture had dangled before them. In this sense theirs was the latest in a long line of Christian utopian visions; imaginative constructions of the heavenly city on earth that trace their lineage back to the prophecies of Isaiah, the book of Revelation, Thomas More, and the earlier nineteenth-century American Christian utopians of Oneida and New Harmony. Like William Penn's, theirs was a social, indeed a political, vision that—at least at its birthplace on Azusa Street—included a dream of racial harmony as radical as Martin Luther King's. It is not a vision that subsequent pentecostals have always adhered to, but neither has it been entirely lost.

In a number of different ways, the pentecostal movement created a religion that was singularly appropriate—both as partner and as antagonist—to the emerging twentieth-century urban world in which it was born. But a question still remains. If the restoration of these primal human religious emotions suggests some answer to the question of its amazing appeal, we must still ask *how* that message was carried so far so fast. As I have thought about this part of the puzzle it has become clear to me that there are two crucial factors. One is the extraordinary part that *women* have played in the spread of the movement. The other is the remarkable centrality of *music*, not just as embellishment but as the wavelength on which the message is carried. Pentecostalism is unthinkable without women. Seymour was touched in his youth by a woman with a gift, then recommended by a second woman to a third who actually provided him with a place to exercise his call. From Sister Hutchins and Aimee Semple McPherson to Kathryn Kuhlmann, the pentecostal healing evangelist of the 1960s, women have continued to play a disproportionately prominent place in the pentecostal movement. As in the racial integration discussed earlier, this is more than a matter of equal opportunity. As we shall see later on, the salience of women in this movement has resulted in a dramatically different conception of who God is, and the quiet subversion of centuries of patriarchal theology.

But if women have often been the principal agents in the spread of the pentecostal movement, music has been its principal medium. It was not just Aimee Semple McPherson who came to embody pentecostalism for a previous generation of Americans, it was Sister Aimee with her tambourine, and later backed up by a full symphony orchestra. The first thing most visitors to pentecostal churches notice is not only that the music is integral rather than peripheral, but that even the prayers and the sermons have a musical lilt. I think that this kinetic lyricism is crucial to understanding the movement's power.

CHAPTER 7

"Your Daughters Shall Prophesy"

*"And in the last days it shall be, God
declares,
that I will pour out my spirit upon
all flesh,
and your sons and your daughters
shall prophesy.*

Joel 2:23

IN 1936, AS THE thirtieth anniversary of the beginning of the Azusa Street revival approached, some of the wrinkled old black veterans of that outpouring of pentecostal fire paid a visit to the forty-six-year-old woman who, in the meantime, had become the most famous pentecostal preacher in America. Her name was Aimee Semple McPherson. Thirteen years before, in 1923, after a decade of leading revivals in rented halls and canvas tents from New York to Florida to Colorado, Sister Aimee, as everyone called her, had built her own church—Angelus Temple— in the Echo Park section of Los Angeles. It seated 5,300, accommodated two large choirs and a full orchestra, and its floors were softened by red carpets. Crowds of would-be worshippers and visitors often lined up for hours to get seats for services.

Sister Aimee was a talented thespian as well as a legendarily eloquent preacher. She had made the Angelus Temple famous (some would have said infamous) for the elaborately dramatized sermons she staged. With professional lighting, imaginative

costuming, and entertaining scripts typed out by the Sister herself, she had attracted hundreds of thousands of people to the
Temple with production values that rivaled Florenz Ziegfeld. It
was rumored that Charlie Chaplin sneaked into the back row to
enjoy Aimee's compelling stage presence. The actor Anthony
Quinn has reminisced about his playing trumpet in the pit band.
Lawsuits and rumors about McPherson's love life, conflicts with
her temperamental mother Minnie Kennedy, and the mysterious
finances of the Temple frequently put her handsome face with its
knowing smile on the front pages of the newspapers. She was a
genuine celebrity, one of the best-known women in America, and
as far as the rest of the country was concerned, she had definitely put pentecostalism on the map.

Sister Aimee's unprecedented success was due in large measure to her own vast God-given talent and tireless dedication. But
it was also because she was a pentecostal. She belonged to a
church which, despite many inner contradictions, provided a space
where gifted women could play dramatically important roles. The
scroll of honor is impressive. The same black woman, Lucy
Farrow, who had once enkindled William Seymour with her spiritual gifts, later carried the message to Norfolk, Virginia, on her
way to Africa. Marie Burgess, together with some coworkers,
started a flourishing pentecostal organization called Glad Tidings
Hall-Apostolic Faith Mission on West 42nd Street in New York
City. Florence Crawford, who had earlier quarreled with Seymour,
nevertheless went on to bring the movement to Oakland, Portland,
and Seattle. A woman of fabled eloquence, Maria Woodworth-
Etter, led massively attended revivals in Dallas, Chicago, and on
various Indian reservations.

There is a clear basis, both in the Bible and in pentecostal
belief, for this remarkable display of feminine leadership. In the
story of the first Pentecost in the Acts of the Apostles, the Old
Testament text from the prophet Joel that Peter quotes to explain
the strange goings-on in Jerusalem says that in "the last days"
God would "pour out his Spirit on *all* flesh" and that both "your
sons *and your daughters* shall prophesy." Also, since in a pentecostal worship service literally anyone can suddenly be filled with

the Spirit, pray in an unknown tongue, testify, or prophesy, there is a strong egalitarian momentum.

But pentecostalism has not always adhered to this momentum. Ever since the beginning of the modern movement, both men and women have tried to undercut the Spirit's gender impartiality. And they have met with considerable success, especially where pentecostals have drifted into theological alliances with fundamentalists who insist on enforcing the dictum from 1 Corinthians, 14:34 which says that women should be silent in church. But wherever the original pentecostal fire breaks through the flame-extinguishing literalist theology, women shine. When I began to visit pentecostal churches in Latin America, Asia, Europe, and the United States, I immediately noticed that—despite Paul's strictures—women almost always seemed to play some leading role. It was obvious that they participate fully, even in churches where the pastor is a man. They sing and testify, prophesy and heal, counsel and teach. In fact, it often appeared that the part men play in some pentecostal churches is more shadow than substance. It also became evident to me that women, far more than men, have been the principal bearers of the pentecostal gospel to the four corners of the earth. As I thought about this, two questions kept coming to mind. *How* do women justify the leadership roles they play in a church which seems to be controlled by men at the top and in which the "official" theology (at least where a literalist interpretation of the Bible obtains) seems to forbid them? *Why* are women drawn to pentecostalism in such disproportionate numbers in the first place, and why do they feel it is so urgent to carry the word to others?

My purpose in this chapter is to try to answer these two questions, starting with Aimee Semple McPherson herself, surely by far the most widely known of all the pentecostal women preachers, and then applying our questions to the lives of some lesser known female ministers.

In the case of Aimee Semple McPherson, the answers to both these questions are straightforward. As for the official theology of pentecostalism, she just never paid much attention to it. She was always serenely sure of her call from God to preach, and when both men and women questioned her ministry, she simply organized her own church and then formed her own denomination. As to why she was drawn to the movement in the first place, the story of her life shows McPherson's deep convictions about the radical core of the pentecostal message, especially its racial and gender inclusiveness.

Aimee Semple McPherson's commitment to transcending the color line was no doubt one of the main reasons why the Azusa Street pioneers had sought her out for the anniversary. From the earliest days of her barnstorming, Sister Aimee had always insisted that the coming together of the races was one of the surest signs of the presence of the Spirit. Twenty years earlier while preaching at the Pleasant Grove Camp grounds in Durant, Florida, near Tampa, she had written in her diary, "Glory! . . . All walls of prejudice are breaking down, white and colored joined hands and prayed . . . people so hungry after God that color is forgotten, even here in the Southland."

Angelus Temple in 1936 may have seemed a long way from the ramshackle Azusa Street warehouse with its white-washed walls and shoebox pulpit of 1906. But the black survivors of the revival from which the new pentecost had spread around the world knew a kindred spirit when they saw one, and they had come to ask Sister Aimee a big favor: could they work together to plan a week-long celebration marking that historic descent of the Spirit?

She immediately agreed. Not only had the Azusa Street revival long since run its course but attendance at Angelus Temple was also beginning to flag, especially when Sister Aimee herself was on one of her many road trips. Maybe an anniversary jubilee would bring some new life. It did. A revival-cum-birthday party that was originally planned for one week roared on for months. It was almost as though the Spirit had decided to honor the occasion by making a return appearance. As McPherson described it:

> Hundreds rushed to the altar in ever-recurrent waves, crying "God be merciful. . . . " No less than three altar calls marked

some of the services, especially the divine healing services. . . . Moreover hundreds of people at a time were sometimes slain under the power of God, many receiving the baptism of the Holy Ghost.

Furthermore, the revived spirit of Azusa also seemed to revive Sister Aimee. Some fund-raising projects, such as a campground near Lake Tahoe and a church-sponsored cemetery scheme (promoted by her managers with the slogan "Go up with Aimee") had gone sour. Normally bubbly and animated, she had seemed tired and overworked. There had been lawsuits, staff problems, snide editorials. But as the celebration rolled on she seemed to regain some of her characteristic vigor. And, for the first time in eighteen years, she spoke in tongues. Those who interpreted her utterances said she was warning of a terrible battle that was soon to come, a war so bitter and destructive it would make people forget the one that had ended only two decades before.

After the United States entered World War II, in December 1941, Sister Aimee led rallies to sell Victory Bonds. But mainly she continued to preach, to teach the adoring students in her Bible school, and to present her spectacular stagings of biblical plots, morality tales, and spiritual—but often intentionally comical—adaptations of stories like "The Lone Ranger," "The Trojan Horse," and "The Wizard of Oz." Sister Aimee herself—in fetching costume—always played the lead character. She was the first of what would later develop into a series of full-fledged pentecostal media stars. But she was also often a lonely person, sneered at by many male ministers, ridiculed by gossip columnists, and never able to find a husband who could give her the emotional support her mercurial nature seemed to require.

Sister Aimee died in 1944, from an accidental overdose of sleeping tablets. But she had lived long enough to found one of the major pentecostal denominations, the International Church of the Foursquare Gospel. When she died, the denomination had 410 churches, all in North America, and about 29,000 members. Now it has 25,577 affiliated churches and 1,700,000 members in 74 countries all around the world. Sister Aimee, who at this moment is probably producing showy musicals with an all-star angelic cast, must have been doing something right.

The term "foursquare" in the name of the denomination Aimee Semple McPherson founded has a double reference. It recalls the description of the New Jerusalem in Revelation 21:16: "The city lies foursquare, its length the same as its width." This allusion recalls again the persistent hope for a new city, another and more just society, which has always animated pentecostal faith. But "foursquare" also symbolizes the basic teaching of the church, the four truths: that Jesus is Savior, Sanctifier, Healer, and Coming King. This "fourfold" message, which Sister Aimee had picked up from the New York revivalist A. B. Simpson, has continued to serve as the core of doctrine for millions of pentecostals in several different denominations. The little lady from Salford, Ontario, who was the object of ceaseless gossip, mocked by sophisticates because she appeared in the pulpit dressed as Little Bo Peep, may be having the last laugh.

Aimee Semple McPherson was the principal pioneer in what has become one of the most characteristic—and most problematical—qualities of pentecostalism, its uncanny ability to utilize the prevailing popular culture for its own message, while at the same time raising questions about that culture. I am convinced that Sister Aimee's own spectacular success in this lover's quarrel with Tin Pan Alley was due in some measure to the fact that as a woman she did not have to conform to the role expectations set down for male ministers. She could innovate and experiment, which she did, with real panache and obvious enjoyment. As a woman and a pentecostal, McPherson's very success probably helped other women in the struggle for equality within the movement. But what about those other, lesser known pentecostal women preachers? How do they justify their calling in biblical terms?

My best clue to an answer to this question came when I visited what everyone in Kanawha County always referred to as "Bill Carter's church." The church stands on a hill at the end of a long winding road through deep valleys and steep gorges about twenty miles south of Charleston, West Virginia. This is coal mining country. It has a radical political history. It gave a larger majority to Eugene Debs's Socialist candidacy for president in 1924 than any other county in the nation. And it is religiously conservative. This is where the famous school boycott broke out in 1974 when parents refused to allow their children to use textbooks that mentioned evolution. The church is called Bill Carter's church not just because he is the preacher, but because he owns the property and building, a common practice among rural, independent pentecostals. This is also a church where, up until a few years before my visit, the worshippers sometimes handled snakes.

At this evening's service Betty Lou, Bill's twenty-four-year-old daughter, is in the pulpit. There are perhaps thirty people in the congregation. Unpressed trousers and shapeless dresses suggest that they are continuing to endure hard times. We have just sung a chorus accompanied by two amplified guitars. Betty Lou has her long brown hair tied with a single white ribbon. She wears a long, off-white dress with simple embroidery around a neckline that plunges a bit deeper than some pentecostals would countenance. In an excited voice that rushes on almost without a pause, she is giving a testimony about the healing she experienced after a serious car crash about a year earlier.

"There I was," she cries, "lyin' on that hospital bed in Charleston, *wracked* with pain. The doctors couldn't do nothin' for me. No matter what medicine they give me, I just felt worse 'n' worse. I couldn't eat, couldn't hardly drink. I thought I was gonna die and—I hate to admit it—sometimes I wished I would. I felt that bad. I really did. I tried to pray, real hard I tried. But somehow the words wouldn't come and I'd just see these giant big red flashes. And sometimes I'd see that there truck come swoopin' over to our side of the road, and I'd hear that awful bang. I just couldn't get it out of my head. And my back and neck and arm hurt so."

She pauses briefly to catch her breath, swallows, then goes on. "But then I saw this bright light at the window. It was so bright I could hardly look at it. It scared me at first. Then I seen in the light, like inside it, with the light all around, a person. I looked. It sure enough was *somebody*. First I thought it was an

angel, an angel . . . of . . . light. But then my eyes got used to it
a little and I looked again. It was *him*. It was Jesus Christ. I knew
it was him 'cause I could see his beard, and he held up his hands
and I could see . . . [here she paused and swallowed] . . . I could
see the cruel nail marks where they nailed him to the cross."

"Well, he come to my bedside," she continues, "and he took
my hand in his hand. He held it for a while and I could feel my
pain just slippin' away. And he spoke to me ever so soft, and just
kept holdin' my hand. Well then, after a while, he stooped over
and he picked me up. Just like a momma or a daddy picks up a
little baby. He just scooped me up and held me close. Then he
turned and flew with me right out of that window, holdin' on to
me real tight. At first I was scared but he told me not to fear. So
I just trusted in him.

"Well, he carried me way up till when I looked down, all the
cars and houses looked like little bitty ones, like dolls' houses.
Then he carried me over the bridge and up the valley, and when
I looked down I could see Crayton's store and the old lumber
mill and everybody's houses, only from way up, so they looked
so tiny. Even them big trucks looked *so* tiny.

"Then Jesus says to me, he says, 'See all these people. Many
of them are lost and lonely, many are living in sin, many are sick
and lots of them don't know where the next meal is comin' from.
Lots of 'em had no work for months, welfare's runnin' out. What
they need most though, what they need is me, my Gospel and
my Holy Spirit to comfort them.'

"Then he says, 'Betty Lou, you listen to me. I want you to
bring my word to them. I want you to tell them about how I died
for their sins and how I sent the Holy Ghost to comfort them. I'm
gonna take you back to that hospital now, and you're gonna be
alright. But I want you to become a bearer of my word.'

"'Well,' I says to him, 'I think you got the wrong party. My
papa's the preacher in my family. I got my hands full with a husband and two kids. I didn't even finish high school. I thank you
for the healin,' I really do, but you got the wrong addressee for
this letter, especially me bein' a woman and all, and what the
Bible says about women preachers and all that.'

"Well, by this time we was headin' back for the hospital. And he says to me, 'Betty Lou, I don't *make* mistakes. I *know* who I am talkin' to. I am healin' you for a *purpose*. Now let's not hear any more complaints.'

"So I says, 'Well, Lord, I guess you're right. You don't make no mistakes. I know that. So if you're really healin' me and this is not just a dream, then I'll do what you say. I'll preach your word, in season and out. I do promise. But I got to make sure.'

"Well, he took me back to the hospital and laid me ever so gently back on that bed. Then he smiled, and then he was gone. Well, next day the doctor came by, and he took one look at me and he said, 'What's gotten into you, Betty Lou? You look 100 percent better." [Here Betty Lou mugged the astonished look on the doctor's face and the congregation laughed.] Well, at first I was embarrassed to tell him what had happened, but then I did. I said it was the Lord himself who healed me. He smiled like he didn't quite believe it. But then he examined me and he told me that he had a hard time believing it but it looked now like I'd be out of there in a few days. Well, three days later I was out. And here I am standin' here, not because some man told me to, not because I just took a mind to, but because Jesus Christ him*self* told me to. And [here the congregation joined in the refrain] he . . . don't . . . make . . . no . . . mistakes."

I have often thought about Betty Lou's testimony. It went a long way in answering my question about how so many women win the right to preach in a church which, at least technically, forbids it. It clearly demonstrated why pentecostals, who take the authority of the Bible very seriously but also believe in direct revelation through visions, have opened a wider space for women than most other Christian denominations have. What the Bible says is one thing, but when God speaks to you directly, that supersedes everything else.

But I continued to think about Betty Lou's sermon-testimony for another reason. It was also a kind of Chartres Cathedral, a perfect embodiment of its genre. It had all the elements one finds in several different testimonies all artfully rolled into one. It included a mystical vision, an almost shamanic flight, a miraculous healing, a glimpse of human need, a divine "call" to preach, resistance to the call, and then an acceptance. It was delivered with warmth, eloquence, passion, and a touch of humor.

Betty Lou's testimony also illustrated a more general element in the appeal of pentecostalism, one I have called the recovery of primal spirituality. In this case we find a classic call-refusal motif. It appears frequently in the Bible. Most people are familiar with the reluctance—at least at first—of Moses to accept God's charge that he lead the Israelites out of their Egyptian captivity, or of the initial unwillingness of Amos to become a prophet. The same theme is given a comic twist in the story of Jonah who tries to run away from God's directive to him to preach to Ninevah; Jonah starts off in the opposite direction, but is swallowed by a great fish who delivers him to Ninevah anyway. This summons-refusal theme is not just a biblical one. It is far more widespread. Joseph Campbell in his *Hero with a Thousand Faces* claims that the pattern of a divine call and an initial refusal to obey appears in the myths of almost every culture. For pentecostal women, of course, it is especially important since they have to demonstrate that they are aware of the religious and cultural strictures against becoming preachers ("You got the wrong addressee . . . what with what the Bible says about women preachers and all"). They have to make it clear that this was a matter over which they had little choice.

Elaine J. Lawless, a student of American folklore, has listened to the testimonies of dozens of pentecostal women preachers and has written about them with a great deal of discernment and sympathy. She sees testimonies as a form of folklore, a kind of art form in which individuals weave and reweave a narrative using not only their own life histories but a set of commonly held anecdotes and plots. In such stories a certain amount of embellishment is expected and some elements, especially the dialogues, follow a familiar pattern. Lawless describes them in the following terms:

> It is . . . a story delivered to make a certain point. . . . It will therefore have a focus. History will be modified, melded, pushed and molded to create a story that is based on truth, but is, in fact,

a created story; there is a pact between the narrator and the listener that disallows scrutiny and allows a measure of fantasy, within mutually agreed bounds.

I am not sure that Betty Lou Carter would agree with this description of her testimony. I think that she truly believed she was telling God's own truth, and the fact is that within a religious context, the possibility of visions and dreams and voices is more allowable than it is in others. But not always. Andrew Greeley is a widely respected sociologist of religion. His continuing research on the mystical experiences of ordinary Americans has shown that a much larger number of people has had them than anyone had supposed. The problem is that in a culture in which both the scientific climate and the teachings of the established religions tend to disallow such experiences, the people who have them are reluctant to talk about them, even to ministers and priests. They understandably feel that they may be referred to a psychotherapist. What the pentecostal meeting provides, among other things, is a setting in which people are encouraged to talk about such out-of-the-ordinary events in their lives without embarrassment.

For women preachers in particular, these testimony stories fulfill a dual function. They not only give them access to a leadership role that is normally reserved for men, but they also provide the occasion to reassure themselves about who they are. Feminist scholars have written a lot about how important "telling my story" is to all women, especially to those who have been deprived of a voice. Hearing oneself tell the story and seeing that it is confirmed by those who hear it gives the narrative a firmer place in one's own identity. Also, since one tells these stories again and again, new elements and additional nuances can always be added. The story is an open-ended one. Both women and men can redefine who they are as life unfolds in a process that Lawless calls "rescripting."

What needs to be added to this folkloristic view of the value of the testimony for pentecostal women—and for men too—is that the reweaving includes not only key incidents from one's own life, and appropriate nuggets from the store of common folk stories. In addition it also incorporates elements from what the literary critic Northrop Frye calls "the great code," the biblical narrative that forms the basic plotline for the whole culture. The result is a complex tapestry of larger and smaller threads, a tapestry that is woven and rewoven for as long as a person lives and needs to assimilate new installments of his or her ongoing life story.

Even after hearing Betty Lou's dramatic testimony at her father's church, my second question still continued to nag me, and I know it has bothered many other people too. Why would these women *want* to be pentecostals, let alone pentecostal preachers? Why would they want to become part of a religious movement which still, at least formally, insists that the man must be "the head of the woman" at home, and also in the church (unless God makes exceptions)? Why are women drawn in such lopsided numbers to pentecostalism? The question especially puzzles those who have observed that the headlong expansion of the pentecostal movement in Latin America can be traced in many instances to women who first join a church and then bring their families, including their husbands, along later.

I had the chance to ask this question very directly to a number of women who had gathered for a prayer and Bible study session in a pentecostal church a few miles outside San Jose, Costa Rica, in a small community devoted largely to the production of coffee. At first they seemed reluctant to answer but then Caterina, an outgoing married woman of about twenty-five with two children, broke the ice.

"When I first came to this church," she said, "I came with my sister-in-law who told me what they teach here could help me with the problems I was having in my family. I didn't believe her, but she insisted, and I was getting pretty desperate, so eventually I came. What I heard, from the other members and from the preacher too, was that the Bible tells wives to obey their husbands, but it also tells *husbands* to love and respect their wives, and to be good fathers. Well, at that time—I don't mind telling you this—my husband was drinking and staying away from home, and I didn't know what to do. I was afraid I might lose him. I don't know if he was fooling around with other women or not, and I was afraid to ask, but sometimes when he went in to San Jose to do a plastering job, he'd be gone for days.

"I started coming more regularly, and I saw men here, the same age as my husband, who were not drinking or fooling around. And they didn't flirt with me either. Something had happened to them. I tried to get Lorenzo to come but he just laughed at me. But eventually I asked God to help me and I felt He was speaking to me, right here in church. He was telling me that everything would turn out okay. I accepted Christ and got baptized. When I told Lorenzo, he didn't laugh, he just looked at me. It seemed to me that he could just *tell* that something had happened to me. I was different. It took me a long time and a lot of prayer. But finally, three months ago, he came along. He just sat there and listened, didn't miss a word. Now he comes with me a lot. He has not joined the church yet, but two weeks ago he helped the men here paint the walls, and I have only smelled tequila on his breath once. I am still praying for him. I know he'll come around. It's wonderful what God can do, like a miracle."

Her words started the ball rolling. Elsa, a somewhat younger woman who is not married, and the only one wearing slacks, said that as soon as she joined the church she bought one of the Bibles they sell and carried it whenever she had to go downtown and walk past the men who had always whistled at her and sometimes tried to touch or pinch her. She laughed. "Last time," she said, "as I walked by, one of the guys looked me over and said to his buddies so I could hear it, 'Man, look at that pair of'—well you know what he said—and one of the other guys said, 'Hey man, don't do that with her. She's one of the alleluias.' That's the nickname they have for us in this town—alleluias—because that's what we say sometimes when we pray, especially when we're happy. In fact, sometimes when I get off the bus and have to walk by those guys, one of them might say, 'eh, alleluia, alleluia!' But I don't mind that. I just pray for them, like they tell us to do here at church, and sometimes I say 'alleluia' right back to them.

Now, Irena, a somewhat older woman, spoke. "I believe the husband *should* be the head of the house," she said, "what's the matter with that? But being the head means he has to take some responsibility. He has to earn some money and bring that money *home*. He has to stop playing the lottery or playing cards and losing it. My own husband died five years ago. And he was not saved, and I cried and cried about that. But he did come to church with me sometimes, and he did stop playing poker, though he still bought a lottery ticket now and then. When I sat next to him in church sometimes I saw him cry, and I think he was remembering our son—our only child—who left home when he was sixteen and lives in San Jose. I think he regretted that he was not a better father. I think he was getting ready to join. I think the Holy Spirit was working on him. But when he got sick, the priest came, and warned him to stay away from our church. I think my husband did not feel he wanted to leave the Catholic Church although he hardly ever went. When he died I was so sad, not just because he died but because he never accepted the Lord. But the pastor here told me not to cry about that. He said Enrique was in God's hands now, was with God, and that God is merciful. Still, I miss him."

Our conversation went on; later when I added what these women had told me to what I heard on other occasions, the pattern was becoming clear. For decades pentecostals were persecuted in many parts of Latin America. So, since they could not gain access to the public arena, they worked mainly through family networks. This happened just as the old family structure was being weakened by new forms of production that made cooperative family work less economically viable and often took the man out of the home for long periods of time. But, the importance still attached to traditional familial connections provided a ready-made network for recruitment. The pentecostal conviction that everyone has the responsibility to spread the word did the rest. Wives brought husbands, children brought parents, in-laws and cousins and aunts testified to each other. For women, the pentecostal message provided the best way they could see to effect a genuine change in their family relations, to get their men to forgo some of the macho posturing the popular culture encourages, and to reorder the priorities on how the limited family income was spent. As Elizabeth Brusco, who has studied pentecostals and other evangelicals in Colombia, puts it, this kind of religion "literally restores the breadwinner *to* the home and restores the primacy of bread *in* the home."

There can be no doubt that, for whatever reason, women have become the principal carriers of the fastest growing religious movement in the world. Eventually this is bound to have enormous cultural, political, and economic implications. There is considerable evidence that once women join pentecostal churches they learn skills they can utilize elsewhere. They read and travel more. In what could be most important of all her discoveries, Brusco found that the women pentecostals she interviewed in Colombia were planning to have fewer children so they could give them a better education, and I have noticed in the many pentecostal bookstores I have visited in both Latin America and the United States that family planning is considered to be an important Christian responsibility. This suggests that the rapid spread of pentecostalism in third world countries where the Catholic Church opposes birth control could make a tremendous difference. It could be a major factor is reversing the deadly momentum of the population explosion.

Dr. Edith Blumhofer, one of the most outstanding historians of women in pentecostalism, does not believe there was ever a golden age in the early days of the movement when women were treated equally. After all, the first pentecostals all came into pentecostalism from other denominations, bringing along their established biases. Maybe the daughters could prophesy, men conceded, since prophets were conduits of God's word and you did not need any brains to be a mouthpiece. But they should not be allowed to preach. Adding to insult, some pentecostal men saw the eloquent testimonies of women as proof of God's power to use even the weakest and most inept creatures to make His word known. The main advantage that Aimee Semple McPherson had was that her pentecostal faith kept her going against all the opposition, and even she eventually had to found her own denomination.

Yet either because of or despite their pentecostal faith, women continued to lead. Barred from the pulpit, they preached in the streets. Refused ordination, they became missionaries and went to places where men were afraid to go. They became healers and teachers, writers and editors. Without them, pentecostalism would probably have died out long ago. Blumhofer likes to recall that in the early days when no women were ordained and the railways gave half-fare privileges to clergy, an announcement appeared in a pentecostal newspaper about a forthcoming pentecostal camp meeting. It urged everyone to come and reminded the ministers they were eligible for half-fare tickets. Then it added: "Sisters, trust the Lord for the full fare!" For nearly a century the sisters have been trusting the Lord for full fare, but there is a strong conviction abroad in the movement today that the era of male dominance is fading.

Toward the end of his splendid biography of Sister Aimee, Daniel Mark Epstein describes some of the intricate sets her talented designer contrived for those elaborate "illustrated sermons" she produced at Angelus Temple. These included a Gold Rush town, a giant radio set with a movable dial, a twenty-foot-tall Easter lily from which Aimee preached in a gown the color of a golden stamen. But my favorite is the "fully operational Trojan horse." I can imagine Sister Aimee, emerging from a door in the side of the horse, sword in hand, to subdue the startled Trojans. And I think of the verse in the Acts of the Apostles that anoints both sons and daughters as prophets as a kind of theological Trojan horse. Having been dragged into the center of the stronghold of male-dominated Christianity, the door has now opened. And even Homer could never have foreseen what the result will be.

CHAPTER 8

"Music Brought Me to Jesus"

Praise God with fanfares on the trumpet,
Praise him on harp and lyre;
Praise him with tambourines and dancing,
Praise him with flute and strings;
Praise him with the clash of cymbals.

Psalm 150:3–5

ONE SUNDAY morning in September 1993 I attended a lively Latino pentecostal church housed in a former synagogue in what had once been the German-Jewish section of Chicago. While the mostly Puerto Rican worshippers were swaying and singing "Dios Está Aquí" ("God Is Here"), I spotted a small sticker. It was attached to the gleaming red and white mother-of-pearl trap drums a young devotee was beating with an astonishing series of slams, rolls, and paradiddles. From my location about a third of the way back I could see that the first word on the placard was "Music" and the last word was "Jesus." But the intervening words were in smaller print, and no matter how hard I squinted I could not quite make them out. My curiosity had been piqued, so after the service I slipped up to the band area to take a closer look. Now I could see the whole message. It said "Music Brought Me To Jesus."

That had not been quite my experience as a boy. In fact it had been almost the opposite. Music had come perilously close to taking me away from Jesus. It is not that I disliked singing hymns and anthems, or the ebullient gospel songs we unleashed when I attended the "little church" with my friend Lois. But on my fourteenth birthday my parents surprised me with the gift of a used C-melody saxophone, the kind you can play along with a piano without needing to transpose. Suddenly my whole musical existence moved into a new key signature.

I am sure my parents thought of the saxophone mainly as an instrument you played in high school and community marching bands, at summer concerts on the green and at Fourth of July parades and football games. And indeed I worked my way up through marches like "High School Cadets" to the "Washington Post" and "El Capitán." But as even the most innocent of parents must have known, there is another whole world of saxophone music, a demi-monde that comes to life after the marching band has packed up its horns and gone home. For me, the saxophone is and always will be principally a night-time thing, a jazz instrument. Giving one to a fourteen-year-old and expecting him to play it only to cheer on the local eleven at halftime is like giving him a thoroughbred and hoping he will only ride it around the backyard. Within a year I replaced the C-melody with a used alto sax, the kind Charlie Parker blew, and I was already playing in a dance band led by an energetic Italian American guitar player who preferred Count Basie and Duke Ellington over John Philip Sousa. Soon not even the more advanced Sousa compositions could hold my interest, and I found myself sitting in the band section at the Saturday afternoon games mentally rehearsing "Take the A Train" or "Satin Doll," my fingers silently picking out the inventive improvisations I would toss out the next time we played at the Bocce Club.

My changing musical tastes also precipitated a small crisis in my religious development. At the Baptist church I attended, the piano and the organ normally carried the full load of instrumental support for the congregational singing, the choirs, and the soloists who sometimes sang at the services. On Easter Sunday it was also thought proper to invite a local trumpet player who did not belong to the church to accompany the hymns, especially "Christ the Lord Is Risen Today." Also, once in awhile at an evening service a plump young woman named Lillian, whose father had managed to assemble an amazing collection of different-sized cow and sheep bells, would race back and forth behind a long table and ring out familiar hymn tunes while her daddy sat in the first pew beaming with pride.

But the saxophone? Even after I had thrown out a series of broad hints about my willingness to accompany the singing, and—when no response came—had resorted to shameless offers, I was met only with polite refusals from the deacons, the minister, and especially the organist. Maybe I could play at the Sunday School picnic or for the youth group's Halloween party, they suggested. It soon became clear to me that although the harp and the timbrel could claim a legitimate place in divine worship (though we never saw either one in our church), the instrument Adolphe Sax invented in 1840 by mating a brass horn with a clarinet, the one whose throaty sobs and sinuous inflections I drank in from my bedside radio after everyone else was asleep, definitely did not. My chosen instrument, like the Gentiles who visited the ancient temple in Jerusalem, was never going to be admitted into the inner court.

I was discouraged. But I did not stop going to church. I was too caught up in a series of adolescent spiritual crises and resolutions for that. And church was too important to my social life. But I did sadly file away the information that there were two sides of my life that I would have to keep in different cabinets, my growing love for jazz and my church life. Gradually I adjusted to the inner schism. Sometimes I would play at dances on a Saturday night until one o'clock in the morning with the Mainliners, not get home until two, and still be in the choir loft on Sunday morning when the organ prelude started. I continued singing "The Stranger of Galilee" and the other anthems our organist selected from a publication called *The Volunteer Choir*, which I found anything but demanding even though I rarely appeared at choir practice.

This schizophrenic musical existence dragged on for years. Then all that changed too. It happened one July evening in the late 1970s when my family and I were spending the summer, as we often did, on Martha's Vineyard, where I gardened, prepared the lectures for my classes at Harvard, and played my saxophone with local musicians whenever I could. One night my friend Walter, a black jazz bassist, asked me if I would like to play with him and a guitarist once a week at a local Greek restaurant where the manager had agreed to give us each a meal in return for the music. I gladly accepted. We had a great time playing tunes such as "Autumn Leaves," "Green Dolphin Street," and "April in Paris." We took turns improvising the choruses. The diners wiped their lips and applauded politely whenever we finished a song, and the moussaka and stuffed grape leaves were marvelous.

After about three weeks, one evening as we were packing to leave, Walter asked me if I would come to his church with him the following Sunday evening, bring my horn, and help him accompany the singing. I was surprised. I had never seen or heard a saxophone in a church, not even in the "little church" I had gone to with Lois years before, where they had settled for a slightly out-of-tune upright piano and tambourines. I hesitated, and asked him if he was sure it would be okay. Wouldn't we have to tone down the major seventh chords, sustained fourths, and gut-bucket endings a bit? Walter zipped up the battered black case he carried his bass in. Absolutely not, he told me. We would play the hymns just the way we played here at the Helios. But instead of playing for our suppers, he added with a smile, "We'll be playing for the Lord." I accepted, and that Sunday evening, bringing along what had now evolved into a tenor saxophone (the kind Stan Getz and John Coltrane played), I arrived at the Fellowship Pentecostal Temple in Oak Bluffs, Massachusetts, and for the first time in my life I played *my* instrument for the Lord.

Knowing what I do now about pentecostal churches, I am sorry it took me so long to discover that I had lived for too many years with an unnecessary disjunction in my life. Most pentecostals gladly welcome any instrument you can blow, pluck, bow, bang, scrape, or rattle in the praise of God. I have seen photos of saxophones being played at pentecostal revivals as early as 1910. Nor—despite television evangelist Jimmy Swaggart's vilifications of rock-'n'-roll—is there any style of music that is deemed irredeemably profane by pentecostals. I have heard congregations sing to the beat of salsa, bossa nova, country western, and a dozen other tempos. In recent years I have heard some of the finest jazz improvisations and chordal innovations to be found anywhere in pentecostal churches, and I have come to believe that there is a special kinship between the religion that was born in America and the music that was born here too, between pentecostalism and jazz.

As we have seen, pentecostalism has many predecessors. It stitches together threads from a wide variety of religious practices—Wesleyan Holiness, African American ecstatic praise, millennial eschatology. But whatever its many antecedents and its present international variants, it is a child of the multiple mutations and intermixings that make up American religious culture. And so is jazz, for the truth is that just as the nineteenth century was turning into the twentieth, not one but two powerful and interrelated American cultural expressions—one musical and one religious—came to birth. Pentecostalism and jazz are undeniably siblings, with all the consanguinity and rivalry such a blood link always brings with it.

Try as they have at times to deny their common parentage, jazz and pentecostalism belong together. Each sprang from the obscure underside of the society. Each first appeared in one of the great polyglot cities of America, jazz in New Orleans and pentecostalism in Los Angeles. Each was despised and ridiculed at first, but both then went on to become major vehicles through which the American spirit—or better, the Universal Spirit with a distinctly American accent—would reach virtually every corner in the world.

Jazz was born in the early years of this century when African rhythms, secondhand American band instruments, and the hymnody of southern revivalism—both black and white—all met each other in the steamy back streets of New Orleans. The highly complex counterrhythms, scarcely known before in European music, came with the slaves who also brought work songs, field hollers, and circle shouts. But it was also in that cosmopolitan gulf-port city that many of the military units from the Spanish-

American War were demobilized after the fighting ended in 1898, and their cornets, drums, and trombones went on sale cheap. Revivalism, with its strong emphasis on ecstatic song was already the principal religious practice of most African Americans and of most southern whites as well. The ingredients that were to coalesce into the new music were all there. Now all that was needed was something to push them together.

The push came with two fateful decisions, one made by the Louisiana state legislature, the other by the city fathers of New Orleans itself. The state legislature, riding the wave of Jim Crow policies that followed Reconstruction, redefined the legal meaning of race by designating all individuals with "negro blood" as "colored." This new policy now shoved a variety of people—former slaves and their offspring, black Creoles, the so-called octoroons, and others who had not previously mixed together very much—into the same social space. The town fathers made their unconscious contribution to the future of music by setting aside one section of New Orleans, Storyville, as a district where prostitution would be legal, thus creating new employment opportunities for musicians in bars, restaurants, and hotels. It was in this heady environment that jazz, a powerful new fusion of previously disparate musics, emitted its birth shriek. It has never been quiet since.

Pentecostalism draws on the energies of many of these same ancestors. Though it had a long gestation period, when black and white religion interacted in an ad hoc manner, what we now refer to as "the pentecostal movement" is largely traceable to the revival that took place under the guidance of William Seymour in an abandoned church on Azusa Street in Los Angeles. It is true that some of the characteristics we now associate almost exclusively with pentecostalism—such as healing, speaking in tongues, and prophesying—were hardly new. Each has a long history dating back to the earliest years of Christianity and before. But it was in Los Angeles—like New Orleans, a cauldron of American urban heterogeneity—that they all came together and the pentecostal movement began its earth-encircling career. It was at Azusa Street that Seymour injected the rapturous intonations of African

American spirituality into the ecstatic Holiness piety he had picked up a few years earlier at the Holiness school run by Charles Fox Parham in Houston, Texas. The mixture was highly flammable.

Just as white musicians sought out the French Quarter dives where the blacks were playing jazz, and learned to play it too, at Azusa Street, during a period when segregation was on the increase, white people flocked into a revival in what was in fact a black church, and they were welcomed. For the whites the revival was a thrilling demonstration of novel and refreshing ways of worship. For the blacks, of course, there was nothing terribly new about most of the elements, though the particular mix Seymour presided over was original. Many African Americans were accustomed to shouting and dancing and to being possessed by the Spirit. The whites, under the influence of John Wesley's Aldersgate experience in which he reported that his heart had been "strangely warmed," were used to expecting something ecstatic at the moment of conversion, but not on a continuing basis. Now, however, these familiar themes of African American spirituality and white Holiness were converging and, as though by a miracle, the walls of segregation were tumbling down.

Neither jazz nor pentecostalism is a purely African invention, though both are now spreading through Africa. But neither jazz nor pentecostalism would have been possible without the influence of the distinctively African American experience of resisting oppression through exuberant worship. One historian of the pentecostal movement has written, "For Black Christians . . . the experience of the Spirit was more than personal holiness, it was also power from God to triumph over injustice and oppression in the social sphere." Both jazz and pentecostalism stand as powerful reminders that who we are as Americans—though we often try to deny it—is a direct result of the unique mixture of black and white which has shaped us.

Some musicologists trace one of the sources of jazz to the African American funeral procession in the south, in which the band escorted the mourners to the cemetery with doleful dirges, but then led them back to the jaunty syncopations of "Didn't He Ramble?" From the start, the new music and the new spirituality, though they worked different sides of town and fired occasional salvos at each other, interacted continuously. Jazz musicians freely borrowed the call and response style of the black preachers, a pattern imported directly by slaves from West Africa. Meanwhile, in church on Sunday night, the piano and cornet players who accompanied the hymns threw in the growls and blue notes they picked up from fellow jazz men who might have learned them in a cabaret in the red-light district. From the earliest years these two characteristically American statements of the same creative Spirit carried on a long and tempestuous rivalry that enriched and enlivened both. Now they have gone forth to be the principal heralds of how our racially mixed society feels about love and sex, sorrow and happiness, life, death, and the great mystery. Even if jazz did not actually originate in the black funeral procession, it is a legend worth preserving, because it enshrines an important symbolic truth: jazz and black American religion sprang from the same womb.

The more I attended pentecostal churches, the more I continued to play jazz as a hobby, and the more I read about the history of the two movements, the more startling the parallels appeared. For example, both jazz and pentecostalism possess an uncanny capacity to combine with indigenous cultural features and still retain a recognizable integrity. Jazz in the Caribbean absorbs the rhythms of Jamaica and Martinique and produces calypso, mamba, and reggae. In Brazil the same syncretic admixture becomes bossa nova. In West Africa, jazz filters through swing and becomes a music known as "High Life." But nowhere does the jazz component lose its identifiable tone. By virtue of something like a musical equivalent of transubstantiation, jazz—whether in Finland or Japan or Mexico—sounds both indigenous and also like jazz. In fact, this sweaty distillate of the smoky taprooms of Bourbon Street has become the first truly universal music in human history.

Pentecostalism has the same uncanny capacity to be at home anywhere. It absorbs spirit possession in the Caribbean, ancestor veneration in Africa, folk healing in Brazil, and shamanism in Korea. It is now spreading in the republics of the former Soviet Union and in China, eastern Europe, and Sicily. But everywhere it remains recognizable as pentecostalism. In Latin America it is growing very rapidly today among indigenous Indian peoples who find that they can now worship in Tzeltal or Queche and retain many of their pre-Columbian healing practices under new auspices. Indeed pentecostalism's phenomenal power to embrace and transform almost anything it meets in the cultures to which it travels is one of the qualities that gives it such remarkable energy and creativity. And the same is true for jazz.

Pentecostalism and jazz also resemble each other in one central characteristic both share: the near abolition of the standard distinction between the composer and the performer, the creator and the interpreter. The key defining quality of jazz is improvisation. Without it, however competent and polished the performance, it is not jazz. The jazz musician, usually working carefully within the chord structure or rhythmic pattern of a given tune, creates an original musical work every time he or she plays. Jazz that is written out or fully scored may be jazz-like, or jazz-derived. But from the viewpoint of a bona fide jazz musician, it is not really jazz.

It is the same with pentecostal worship. The message of the Bible is taught, sung, and celebrated with heartfelt enthusiasm. The basic chords, as it were, are there. But the message is delivered with what might be called "riffs," with a free play of Spirit-led embellishment and enactment. At a black pentecostal church I attended once, I watched in wonder as the pastor not only preached about David and Goliath but acted out the young shepherd's gathering of the stones, the proud chest thumping of the haughty Philistine warrior, the swoosh of the pebble as it careened through the air, the surprised look on Goliath's face, and the crash of his ungainly body as it hit the ground. He even invented some highly plausible dialogue between the Israelites and their foes to lead up to the denouement. The similarity between this style of preaching and the way Charlie Parker dances around the theme of "Embraceable You," or John Coltrane embellishes the melody of "Favorite Things" is hard to miss.

Besides the free-play riffing, the other prominent similarity both jazz and pentecostalism have preserved from their common roots is what scholars of religion call "possession." In fact the anthropologist Clarke Garrett has claimed that spirit possession is the most powerful and most common characteristic to be found in folk religion worldwide. It is being possessed by the Spirit, passing into a form of consciousness some would call "trance," that convinces people that the divine is acting directly and intimately in their midst. For such people, he says, trance and possession are not "extraneous bits of deviance"; they are, rather, "the very stuff of religious experience." But anyone who has watched a jazz trumpeter or clarinetist get caught up by the music senses that something very similar is going on. Again, the roots of both jazz and pentecostalism are to be found in Africa, where music is not an incidental part of worship but provides its substance. For centuries, in slavery and after emancipation, black people had continued to practice the African "ring shout," a religious group exercise that combines a swaying movement with verbal ejaculations. This same practice was brought into Christian worship. When the first black Methodist and Baptist denominations were organized in the nineteenth century, however, some of their early leaders strongly discouraged ring shouting as a holdover from superstition. But it never died out, and when the pentecostal revival came it gave African Americans a chance to reclaim this element of their spiritual heritage.

The structural affinities seem endless. Even speaking in tongues has its equivalent in jazz, or at least some people claim. Walter Hollenweger, the distinguished historian of pentecostalism, has suggested that there is an important parallel between the kind of "scat singing" Louis Armstrong made famous and the glossolalia that occurs in a pentecostal church. Both are forms of verbal expression that transcend the normal limitations of language, though they are used for quite different purposes in the different contexts. Whether or not this is the case, music historians are now quite certain that both jazz and the type of music called "gospel" have roots in the "moaning" of early African American worship. "Moaning" is the folk term for the chants and hums—without words—that so often accompanied the singing of hymns and spirituals.

Like the history of jazz, the history of pentecostalism has been a story both of the breaking down of racial barriers and of erecting them again. No one disputes that the original jazz was created and performed by black Americans in and around New Orleans in the early years of the twentieth century. It was quickly picked up, however, by white musicians who, also by common consent, learned to play it very well. It is a considerable irony that the so-called Original Dixieland Jazz Band which made the exciting new music famous nationwide almost overnight when they played in New York in 1917 was an all-white group and anything but "original." Still, its great success only demonstrates how quickly this African American music suffused an entire culture.

Likewise, no responsible historian of religion now disputes that pentecostalism was conceived when essentially African and African American religious practices began to mingle with the poor white southern Christianity that sprang from a Wesleyan lineage. But it was a long gestation, and a fierce debate still simmers about when and where the birth actually took place. Some trace it to New Year's Eve, 1900, when a white woman named Agnes Ozman is said to have spoken in tongues at Charles Parham's Bethel Bible School in Topeka. Others locate it at the Azusa Street Revival in Los Angeles, led by William Seymour. Those who hold that tongue speaking is *the* defining characteristic of pentecostalism insist on the Topeka advent. But the dispute will probably never be settled since both Topeka and Azusa Street have now achieved a certain mythic quality. Those who take a broader view of what the pentecostal movement is, and who underline the power of the Spirit to break down racial and ethnic walls, claim that the former stable on Azusa Street is the real manger scene. I personally find it hard to accept the case for Topeka, since glossolalia has been documented in virtually every period of religious enthusiasm since Paul both commended it and warned about its excesses in the first century A.D. Emissaries from Azusa Street, on the other hand, fanned out all over America and into several foreign countries sowing the seeds for what became "the pentecostal movement" of the following decades.

It is a sad commentary on the first decades of pentecostal movement that—due largely to the discomfort of whites—it did not retain its revolutionary interracial quality. Before too long, just as there were white bands and colored bands, there were white and colored pentecostal churches. Still, it must be said that even today, despite the rebuilding of racial barriers, pentecostalism, in America and elsewhere, is one of the least segregated forms of Christianity; just as jazz, which also endured a long period of color separation, may now be the least segregated form of music.

On the debit side of the ledger, both jazz and pentecostalism have had to contend with an endless succession of fakers, shill artists, overpublicized buffoons, self-promoters, and cynical exploiters. Both have suffered their share of fallen idols. Among the pentecostal preachers, the lapse from glory has often been tinctured with stories of sex and greed. Charles Parham and Aimee Semple McPherson have been accused of stumbling into the first snare (though in both cases the allegations have been challenged), while Jimmy Bakker and a host of others have fallen afoul of both. Among the jazz artists, drugs and liquor have exacted a terrible toll. Both Charlie Parker and John Coltrane fell prey, in different ways, to these perils. It is important to remember, however, that when a religion or a musical style cuts as deeply into human emotion as these two do, ordinary human frailty is stretched and tested to an unusual degree. At least some of the people who toppled under the strain, though not all, were victims of what the public came to expect of them and of what they came to expect of themselves. This does not justify gross self-serving or self-destructive behavior. But, on the other hand, it is mistaken to think that, preacher for preacher or musician for musician, either jazz or pentecostalism has produced more than an average quotient of bad apples.

The analogies between jazz and pentecostalism continue into more recent years. Both have endured countless efforts—mostly unsuccessful—to tame them down, domesticate them, and use their driving energies for extrinsic purposes. George Gershwin, it was once said, tried to "make an honest woman out of jazz," but I think the statement is wrong. Gershwin loved jazz, and he recognized as much as anyone how honest she already was. But nearly from the outset jazz has been copied, packaged, and replicated, its scorching and erratic elements softened, its temper toned down. The music we usually call "swing" is really domesticated jazz. On the other hand, jazz has also been coarsened and trivialized, as is the case with some (but not all) rock-'n'-roll. It seems hardly surprising to learn that the televangelist Jimmy Swaggart, who carried a certain garish version of pentecostalism to dizzying new heights, is the blood cousin of the rock performer Jerry Lee Lewis. But despite all this, jazz has somehow usually been able to survive its latest profanation and continue to sing its own, constantly re-created, song.

Likewise pentecostalism has gone through the same attempts to tame it. Its history is a saga of efforts, also largely unsuccessful, to smooth it over so as to make it more acceptable to "mainstream" American religion. When Charles Parham arrived in Los Angeles to witness the fruit of William Seymour's work he was shocked by what he saw and later described its "disgusting similarity to southern darkey camp meetings." He tried as hard as he could—without success—to get the thing under control. But one of the key features of pentecostalism is the chronic uncontrollability that some see as its greatest strength and others as its fatal flaw. The Spirit "bloweth where it listeth," and no effort to contain the pentecostal impulse within ecclesiastical or doctrinal boundaries has ever succeeded for very long.

The battle between spontaneity and order does not always fall out along racial lines. It has raged on in pentecostalism for nearly a century now, with splits and divisions the rule rather than the exception, and the struggle sometimes takes the form of a contest between lay people and preachers, with the preachers trying, often in vain, to harness the essentially unharnessable surge of the Spirit. One need not say much about the "rock" as opposed to the "swing" versions of pentecostalism since the highest-decibel evangelists are the ones who tend to get on television most, and they make up in hoarseness and volume for what they lack in originality. But, like jazz, pentecostalism seems to hold within itself an unfailing self-renewing quality. Try as they will to spoil it, it seems to survive with style.

Sometimes the more domesticated expressions of pentecostalism last for a while. Sometimes they do not. A couple decades ago motifs of worship borrowed from the pentecostal churches across the tracks began to crop up in mainline, middle-class churches. Episcopalians and Roman Catholics here and there began speaking (discreetly) in tongues, and Lutherans and Presbyterians began placing their hands on people's heads and praying for healing. This "charismatic movement" was dubbed by scholars of religion, ever handy with a useful label, "neo-pentecostalism." The movement still continues, especially in middle-class parishes of the Roman Catholic Church, but its growth now seems to have slowed, except perhaps in Germany and France where it is the main form pentecostalism now takes.

From the beginning of the charismatic movement, however, "real" pentecostals were suspicious. They were leery of this sleek new, tidied-up version of their boisterous faith in part because, since the charismatic movement stayed carefully within the confines of the existing churches, it could always be trimmed and tailored by nail-biting bishops and apprehensive clergymen into something that threatened no one. If Jimmy Swaggart is the Mick Jagger of pentecostalism, the charismatic movement is its Guy Lombardo.

When I first became interested in pentecostalism, I was urged to attend some of these "charismatic" services, and I did. But to me they seemed tepid and derivative. The praying in the Spirit appeared stagey and contrived. I decided that if I had to choose between the Mick Jagger and Guy Lombardo versions of pentecostalism, I would probably choose Jagger. But I was glad I did not have to make that choice, since the authentic—call it the "jazz" version—of pentecostalism was—and is—alive and thriving, while the charismatic movement remains a kind of toned-down and primly packaged pentecostalism, especially appealing to people who might be embarrassed or put off by the real thing—a pentecostalism, so to speak, without blue notes, drum breaks, or gut-bucket choruses.

Recently I have moderated my earlier distaste for the charismatic movement, however. I have reconciled myself to the fact that there will always be people who prefer musical and religious expressions that annoy or bore me, and that I should be more tolerant. Maybe I had even unconsciously absorbed some of the aversion "real" pentecostals feel toward neo-pentecostals. In any case, the present surging growth of pentecostalism worldwide has nothing "neo" about it. True, sometimes its most vigorous outbursts appear within congregations bearing the names of other denominations, especially in such churches as the Baptist where an independent local polity and the lack of any hierarchy capable of enforcing liturgical or doctrinal standards enable it to flourish. But when that takes place, as it frequently does, especially in the third world, no matter what the sign on the church door may say, what is happening inside is pentecostalism, not something derivative.

My own convoluted history with the church and the tenor saxophone seemed to come full circle in the spring of 1993 when I discovered a congregation in San Francisco that has chosen the late jazz saxophonist John Coltrane as its patron saint. A storefront located on Divisidero Street two blocks off Haight Street, it is called St. John's African Orthodox Church and claims its apostolic succession through Ignatius Peter III, the Patriarch of Antioch. The mixed black and white congregation, under the leadership of Bishop Franzo King, exhibits a fascinating mixture of exuberant pentecostal and traditional Eastern Orthodox elements. On Rogation Sunday, the fifth Sunday after Easter in 1993, introits, collects, and the Apostles' Creed alternated with gospel songs, selections from Coltrane, and a tune called "Natural Mystery" by the late reggae artist Bob Marley. The weekly bulletin of the congregation lists such standard items as the time of the choir rehearsal, that week's birthdays, a free hot meals program, and a swimming party for the youth group. Just to the left of the altar hangs an iconic-style representation of Coltrane, painted in the traditional Byzantine manner by one of the church's ministers named Mark C. E. Dukes. It depicts the church's patron in a green velvet jacket and formal shirt. In his left hand he grips a glistening gold tenor saxophone with flames leaping from the bell. His right hand holds a scroll with the words "Let us sing all songs to God." His head is surrounded by a golden halo.

The newsletter of St. John's reports that in December 1992 a delegation of its members visited the Stanford Memorial Chapel and "celebrated the ancient African liturgy to the music of John Coltrane." At the service, which the account says drew 1,000 people, Bishop King told the worshippers why Coltrane is so important. "We don't hold a monopoly on John Coltrane," he said "because John is a saint among Buddhists; he is a saint among Moslems. He is a saint among Jews. And I think there are even a few atheists who are leaning on that anointed sound." He explained why the grating, dissonant passages in the music were also vital. They remind us, said, that "faith is not accomplished without coming to the crucifixion of ourselves." Quoting the text from Job 13:15, "Yea though he slay me, yet will I trust him," he alluded to a persistent pentecostal theme: "We must find the courage to be slain." He ended with a reminder, also vintage pentecostal stuff but completely congruent with Eastern Orthodox belief, that a truly evolved faith is one that is quickened by the baptism of the Holy Ghost.

At first the theology and liturgy of St. John's may strain the equanimity, or the credulity, of even the most ecumenically oriented Christian. But to me it makes sense. Although most Protestants do not continue to canonize saints, and remain content with those mentioned in the Bible, Roman Catholic and Orthodox Christians do continue the canonization process into the present. Pope John Paul II has made more saints than his five predecessors put together. The recognition that exceptional holiness and spirituality continue to manifest themselves in our own time is also a central pentecostal conviction. But John Coltrane?

That also makes a kind of sense. There is hardly anyone who symbolizes the consanguinity of jazz and spirituality better than Coltrane, the acknowledged grand master of the tenor saxophone, who died in 1967. Born and raised in North Carolina, in the venue of black church music, Coltrane began playing with dance bands in the late 1940s and eventually joined the famous Miles Davis Quintet in 1955. A painful bout with heroin addiction eventually led him to a spiritual rebirth. This launched him on a new phase of artistry as he tried to use his music to create an equivalent of what William James once called the "oceanic feeling" that underlies all religious experience. Leaving behind the familiar phrasings, Coltrane began to produce swirls of sound and visceral shrieks that puzzled and angered music critics. But he persisted, turning to Africa for more complex rhythms and to Indian sitar styles for a brooding bass drone.

Coltrane became consumed with his quest. Like a man on a desperate pilgrimage he pushed his instrument beyond its known limits. As the jazz critic Edward Strickland writes, "Coltrane was attempting to raise jazz from the saloons to the heavens. No jazzman had attempted so overtly to offer his work as a form of religious expression. . . . In his use of jazz as prayer and meditation Coltrane was beyond all doubt the principal spiritual force in music."

Coltrane's undisputed masterpiece is an album issued in 1965 called "A Love Supreme." Like a worship service it begins with an invocatory piece called "Acknowledgment" and ends with a clamor of praise in "Psalm." A year later another album entitled "Meditation" appeared. It opens with a yearningly throaty statement called "Father, Son and Holy Ghost," followed by a series of wails and groans that Strickland calls "glossalalic shrieks." The critic's choice of metaphor is accurate. When Coltrane breathed into his instrument his entire life seemed to pass through the reed and mouthpiece into the resounding metal. His music combined raw feeling with technical brilliance in a sophisticated echo of the sounds that once arose from the black churches of North Carolina and were still in his bloodstream. But, as with the genius of unfettered pentecostal praise, his arpeggios fused themselves with musical modes from other climates into a unified paean. "My goal," Coltrane himself once said in an interview, "is to live the truly religious life and to express it in my music. . . . My music is the spiritual expression of what I am."

The church historian Jaroslav Pelikan's book *Bach Among the Theologians* skillfully places Johann Sebastian Bach within the religious currents of his time and credits him for bringing the message of the Reformation to ordinary churchgoers. (Bach owned the entire collected works of Martin Luther.) Pelikan reminds us that Bach always began his compositions by writing "Jesu Juva [Jesus, help]" and closed them by writing "Soli Deo Gloria [to God alone be the glory]." He also quotes biographers who believe that Bach was a mystic and an ecstatic. If the Lutheran Church still beatified people, can there be any doubt that there were would be at least one Church of St. Johann Sebastian in every town in Minnesota? Admittedly, one should be cautious about such comparisons. Unlike Bach, many people still find Coltrane's music harsh, cacophonous, and at times almost unbearable. But like the plaintive chaos and outcry of pentecostal worship, it also pierces the skin of convention and can touch the hearer at a vital core. No one embodies better than Coltrane that strange kinship between pentecostal incantation and the spiritual lineage of jazz. No wonder they finally named a church after him.

Some years ago the distinguished American composer and critic Virgil Thompson described jazz as "the most astounding spontaneous musical event to take place anywhere since the Reformation." The judgment is significant not only because of the authority of the man who made it but because of his use of an explicitly religious event—Luther's religious breakthrough—in his comparison. Some scholars describe pentecostalism in the same terms—as "the most important event in religious history since the Reformation." Others believe it marks the rebirth of a more catholic, mystical, even medieval spirituality. In any case, it is well to recall that the religious reform that Luther and Calvin set in motion moved across Europe to the tune of a new kind of music. It was the Bach chorales, congregational hymns, and, later, shape-note singing and gospel songs that carried the message to the masses. In our time as well, as the sticker on that drum in Chicago proclaimed, music is still bringing people to Jesus.

In 1919, many years before Thompson made his statement about jazz, the famous Swiss conductor Ernest Ansermet surprised his classical associates by writing an essay on the black jazz clarinetist Sidney Bechet. He concluded with the statement that perhaps the kind of music Bechet was creating "is the highway along which the whole world will move tomorrow." No such prediction about pentecostalism is on record so early from any representative of what might be called "classical" religion. But in one sense both jazz and pentecostalism, the neglected and even for a time abused children of the American experience, have become highways along which the whole world is moving.

PART
III

CHAPTER 9

"We Shall Do Greater Things": Pentecostalism in Latin America

In very truth I tell you, whoever
Has faith in me will do what I am doing;
Indeed he will do greater things still
Because I am going to my Father.
John 14:12–13

*T*HE PENTECOSTAL congregation called Amor de Deus meets in the huge courtyard between two adjoining apartment houses in a part of Rio de Janeiro where peeling lower middle-class tenements meld almost imperceptibly into a dilapidated slum. On this clear, cool Sunday night in June, some 600 people are crowded into the area, most seated on folding chairs and long wooden benches, but many standing. Guitarists strum vigorously. The congregation is linked to the Assembleia de Deus, a Brazilian pentecostal denomination with ties to the Assemblies of God, a worldwide organization with its headquarters in Springfield, Missouri. Pentecostalism began its spectacular career in Brazil shortly after the turn of the century when two Swedish laymen, Gunnar Vingren and Daniel Berg who were living in Belem, Brazil, were excommunicated from its tiny Baptist church for speaking in tongues. Like religious expellees before and since, however, they did not give up. Instead they left Belem and headed for Rio where they founded Brazil's first pentecostal congregation. That church grew and later affiliated with the newly organized Assembleia de Deus. This denomination spread with breathtaking rapidity to every state and region in the country, and now claims somewhere between 11 and 15 million Brazilian members. It is still growing and is only one, albeit one of the largest, of several hundred pentecostal groupings in Brazil.

There is more than a little irony in the fact that this congregation has ties to the Assemblies of God. Many black pentecostals claim that the denomination was founded in Hot Springs, Arkansas, in April 1914 by white North Americans to avoid the nonwhite leadership that was so prominent in the early pentecostal movement. Some historians reject this contention, but in any case, on this balmy evening, 3,000 miles from Hot Springs, almost all the worshippers at Amor de Deus are brown and black. They belt out joyous choruses, clap their hands, and raise their arms toward the stars, dimmed but not defeated by Rio's mantle of smog. The lyrics proclaim that God is here, that rivers of blessings are flowing, that Jesus loves us. Sometimes the mood changes and the people sing a muted, almost mournful melody about the sorrow and heartbreak of life, but underneath a *cantus firmus* about the love and nurturance of God continues to pulsate.

Three different singing ensembles—a youth choir, young adults' chorus, and a women's choir—all perform. The pastor is a lively young man in his thirties wearing an impeccable brown suit with tiny blue stripes and a white shirt, but sporting a fuchsia and orange tie that might be judged too splashy by North American clerical standards. Speaking into a microphone that picks up every intonation, he leads a prayer, his voice rising and falling with emotion but with the mellifluous Portuguese always fluent and distinct. Two worshippers, one a middle-aged woman, the other in her thirties, stand and briefly "speak in tongues." As frequently happens in pentecostal churches, another worshipper, this one a man wearing a plain black suit, white shirt, and dark blue tie, "interprets." Exercising another of what pentecostals believe is a gift of the Spirit, he renders what the tongue-speakers have said in biblical phrases that sound very much like verses from Isaiah or Jeremiah. So far it has been the kind of service one might expect in a pentecostal congregation almost anywhere. But now something quite extraordinary happens.

The pastor calls to the pulpit a tall, handsome black woman who is neatly but inexpensively dressed in a ginger and white dress and light-tan open shoes. It's Benedita da Silva, a member of this congregation. She marches confidently to the platform, tests the microphone, looks out across the sea of expectant faces, smiles, and then begins to give her "testimony." In pentecostal parlance, a testimony is a short, first-person narrative about the course of the individual's own life, the trials and difficulties they have struggled with, the disappointing paths they once followed, the way the Good News came to them, and how the Spirit-wrought salvation has changed them. Both the testifier and the listeners sometimes punctuate it with grateful "alleluias" and this is what happens tonight.

Benedita's testimony was not unusual. At least not at first. She was raised, she says, in an impoverished *favela* (shantytown) by semiliterate parents who were often sick and out of work. Her grandmother had been a slave (slavery was finally abolished in Brazil only in 1888), and her own mother did washing for the rich people who, in Rio, continue to live in close proximity to the poor. Benedita, as a young girl, often delivered the heavy baskets of freshly ironed shirts and embroidered linen to the wealthy families, always to the back door. As a black child, even in allegedly color-blind Brazil, she felt the sting of racial insult when people sometimes called her a "preta" (the Portuguese equivalent of "nigger").

The religion of Benedita's dingy neighborhood, she says, was a mixture of popular Catholicism and "Umbanda," a Brazilian version of African folk beliefs. But, she tells the congregation, these customs and practices did not help her to know who she was and what God wanted her to be. She became discouraged. In her early twenties things got so desperate she felt she wanted to die. But it was just then, when she was twenty-six, that God spoke to her, the Holy Spirit entered her life, and she felt the joy of salvation.

"Alleluia!"

I was impressed with Benedita's eloquence and pace, and by her sure-footed sense of timing. This was a testimony which, even though she had probably given it many times before, still rang true. Except for her unusually winning manner and commanding personal presence, however, there was nothing uncommon about it.

But then, Benedita began to weave into her narrative some observations about the cruel way Brazilian society treats poor people. She mentioned corrupt politicians and big businesses. She talked about how she had been working as a street vendor when God had led her to want to do something about all this misery; how she had then taken a course to become a nurse's aide, then became a volunteer community organizer. Still dissatisfied, she had become active in the newly formed Partido dos Trabalhadores, "Workers Party," the left democratic coalition that first appeared in Brazil in the late 1970s as the major opponent to the military regime. In 1989, a couple years after I first met Benedita, the party's presidential candidate, Luis Inacio da Silva, known to almost everyone as "Lula"—and no relation to Benedita—came within a few votes of winning the first really free presidential election in the history of the country. In 1994, as I finished writing this book, Lula was running for president again, and the early polls gave him a strong lead over all of his opponents. I knew something about this party when I heard Benedita mention it. Many of the progressive Catholic priests, lay activists, liberation theologians, writers, and labor union leaders I had met in Brazil were members of it. But a black pentecostal? When Benedita talked about her work in the party, commonly known in Brazil as the PT, I leaned forward. This was not going to be your ordinary testimony.

Benedita did not miss a beat. She seemed now to be reminding the congregation of something they already knew, but they appeared to like it. Several years back, God had seen fit to allow her to be elected to the city council of Rio where she sought to serve Him with all her heart and soul. ("Alleluia!") And, as it happened, the elections for the federal congress were coming up soon and she had consented, after praying about it for days, to allow herself to be a candidate. Perhaps, indeed, God wanted her to continue to use the gift He had so mercifully bestowed on her in a higher and more influential office. The congregation murmured in assent, indicating that this might be exactly what the Spirit had in mind for the towering sister with the broad smile. Benedita wrapped it up, after exactly eight minutes of testimony, with a ringing thanksgiving to the God who in Jesus Christ had made this all possible. The congregation alleluiaed and applauded as she strode majestically back to her seat in the congregation.

I was puzzled. What about all those articles I had read that told of the "otherworldliness" of pentecostals? What about the accusations that pentecostalism itself is the product of a calculated right-wing North American effort to woo Latin Americans away from Catholic liberation theology and radical social movements? This woman could out-preach every liberationist priest I had ever met, and she was a member of the left opposition party.

I learned later that Benedita had indeed been elected to congress in 1986, the first black woman ever to serve. She went on to make an unsuccessful run for mayor of Rio de Janeiro in 1992. Today this young-looking fifty-one-year-old grandmother (she was married at sixteen) is a person of considerable influence in the PT and a strong advocate of children's rights. But that night at Amor de Deus, most of this lay in the future, and as I returned to the home of the friends with whom I was staying in Rio, and thought about what I had heard, a sinking feeling came over me. I realized that nearly all my preconceptions about pentecostalism and politics, race and women, would now have to be junked, and that this was going to require considerable effort. Benedita was a six-foot, three-inch detonator who exploded books full of theories and generalizations in minutes. I decided I wanted to meet her, so I called the pastor, and he said he would be glad to arrange it.

Benedita, faithful to her commitment to continue to live among the poor people she represents, resides with her family in a simple painted wooden house on a steep hillside just at the edge of a *favela* not far from the gleaming luxury hotels and condominiums of Copacabana. When I arrived with the pastor and a couple of other friends the next afternoon she was wearing a dark red dress and open shoes with blue and red straps. A serious-looking leather briefcase rested near the chair where she eventually sat down, and the blue cloth coat draped over it suggested that she had other business to attend to that day. She served us each a small cup of thick black coffee and poured one for herself.

When Benedita found out that I teach religion she launched into a vivid discussion of the only trip she had ever made abroad, the visit of a PT delegation to Israel the year before. The tour was paid for in part by the Israeli Labor party which is trying to build better relations with comparable parties in Latin America. What Benedita wanted to tell me about, however, was not the geopolitics of the trip but how inspired she was by Galilee, Bethlehem, and the Mount of Olives, places she had read about in the Bible but never thought she would see.

She soon left her wide-eyed account of the pilgrimage, however, and began talking about the social and racial crisis of Brazil in the tones of a mature and tempered political leader. She talked about the murders, which had started even then, of the street children of Rio. From this she moved easily into a discussion of pentecostalism, in which she said she felt at home because it reached out to the poorest people, those who had no time to learn theology and might not even be able to afford a Bible. "The pentecostals tell people they *need* to change and that they *can* change," she said, a startling idea in a culture where people often believe you just have to play the cards fate has dealt you, and street wisdom ascribes all misfortune to the implacable will of God.

As for the Bible, she went on, patting the fat, morocco-bound one that lay on the table beside her, it was not only a religious book for her. It was the source of her political "project," she said, using a word the liberation theologians also like. It not only told of a Jesus who was a true revolutionary, who fought against wickedness in high places, but who also promised "that we would do greater things than He did." This seemed to be one of her favorite texts and she repeated it again. "Imagine," she said, "we will do *greater* things than He did."

The phone rang and Benedita chatted briefly. When she hung up she turned to a subject I had not asked about, but apparently others had—the pentecostals' attitude toward women. "Lots of people think we don't like it that we are supposed to dress modestly," she said, "but actually most of the women I know like it a lot. We feel safer, less like a target for whistles and sexual advances, more dignified." This led her to remark that struggle, hardship, and opposition are spiritually important in life, because it is during such times that you learn who you are and how much you need to rely on God.

After a half an hour of conversation, interrupted by two more brief phone calls, the door opened and the driver of the city council car that whisks Bendita around to her many engagements looked in and pointed to his watch. He was a short, fair-complexioned man wearing blue slacks, a tieless white shirt, and wrap-around sunglasses. Benedita took a last swallow of her coffee and walked toward the door still answering my last question: how did she now feel about her younger years in the Catholic Church? Her answer came as a surprise. It was not lost time at all, she said. She paused at the door so I would not miss the point. In fact, she said, she was grateful for the political education she had received from the progressive Catholics she had met. But it was finally the doctrines (she did not specify which ones, and the driver was looking at his watch again) that had caused her to become a pentecostal. With that she was out the door.

Benedita's story is not unique. In 1992 a religious census carried on by a research center affiliated with the World Council of Churches revealed that in the previous three years approximately 700 new pentecostal churches had opened in Rio. Two hundred forty new spiritist temples had also started, mostly of the Umbanda variety that Benedita had once taken part in. But, despite population increases, only one new Roman Catholic parish had been founded. The pentecostal growth is most evident among the poorer communities. In the thirteen municipalities of Rio, there are three times as many pentecostals in the peripheral *favelas* than in the more well-to-do and sophisticated southern zone, and pentecostals are also three times more numerous among people with less than eight years of school and among those with the lowest wages. Once merely quick, pentecostal growth has now reached the proportions of a tidal wave. Besides, there are not many "nominal" or "nonobservant" pentecostals. Scholars now estimate that on any given Sunday morning there are probably more pentecostals at church in Brazil than there are Catholics at mass.

A similar picture is emerging all over Latin America. In his book *Is Latin America Turning Protestant?* David Stoll pulls together statistics from a number of sources to show that non-Catholic Christianity is growing in many of the continent's countries at five or six times the rate of the general population. If the statistics in Brazil are any indication, 90 percent of this non-Catholic increase is pentecostal. Stoll predicts that if current rates of growth continue, five or six Latin American countries will have non-Catholic—mostly pentecostal—majorities by 2010. In several other nations the non-Catholic percentage of the population will have reached 30 to 40 percent.

I had first become aware of the rumbles foreshadowing this landslide in the Latin American religious topography almost two decades earlier, during a visit I made to Chile in 1970. I had flown to Santiago at the invitation of a well-known Jesuit priest and sociologist named Renato Poblete to attend a seminar at the Centro Bellarmino, a Catholic think tank closely related to the Christian Democratic party of Chile. The center is named after the highly respected theologian named Robert Bellarmine (1542–1621), a Jesuit who was canonized by Pope Pius XI in 1930. Bellarmine was a social theologian who used the analogy of the body and the soul to argue for the interdependence of the church and the state. He is sometimes credited by Catholic scholars as being one of the sources of modern Christian democratic movements. Bellarmine's shade must have been bending attentively over the center that bore his name at the time of my visit: I had arrived during the hectic political campaign that was to turn the ruling Christian Democrats, headed by Eduardo Frei, out of power and vault Salvador Allende into the presidential office. Allende's brief tenure would be followed shortly thereafter by a grisly military coup and the long reign of General Pinochet.

I had accepted the invitation to come to Chile mainly to find out more about Latin American Catholic theology and to observe the election campaign. I soon discovered to my surprise, however, that the Catholic scholars I met—even in the midst of a fierce electoral battle—seemed even more interested in the growing Chilean pentecostal movement and anxious to get my help in understanding it. (Not too many Protestant theologians found their way to Chile in those days.) I told them I would like to meet some of the local pentecostal leaders, and the very next day Father Poblete drove me out to a shabby suburb where the local mayor, a member of the Christian Democratic party, was to meet with a delegation of pentecostal pastors. With obvious enthusiasm Poblete told me this was something quite new, that until recently pentecostals had avoided contact with political figures, viewing them as representatives of a sphere they considered hopelessly enmeshed in the "fallen world."

At that time there were already hundreds of pentecostal churches in Santiago, most of them very small, although one boasted a towering edifice on a prominent downtown street. There are many more now, and some of their buildings are enormous. We met this time, however, at one of the smaller ones, a white frame structure on a rutted unpaved street with clouds of gritty dust and no shade trees. The pastors, all carefully dressed in neatly pressed dark suits and subdued ties, were already there when we arrived. They were polite but guarded. The Christian Democratic mayor explained how advantageous it would be to their people to continue him and his party in office. He mentioned a number of improvements that (under *his* auspices) had recently been introduced, among them the paving of a road two blocks away. He did not, I noted, warn them against Allende's Popular Unity Front by using the anticommunist rhetoric that was being widely employed during that campaign. Maybe he thought it was not necessary.

The pastors listened, asked a few questions, then shook hands with everyone and left. They made no promises. Still my hosts thought it significant not only that they were clearly concerned about the election (obviously they did not expect the Last Days all that soon) and that, since pentecostal preaching in Latin America often carried a sharply anti-Catholic animus, they would agree to meet with people who were rightly identified in the public mind with the Roman Catholic Church.

As I continued to talk with politically engaged Catholic priests during my stay in Chile I could understand why they were concerned about the expansion of pentecostalism in their country. It was still the heady period just after the Second Vatican Council, which had brought all the Catholic bishops to Rome for a series of sessions held from 1962–1965 in order to reform and update the Church. These priests were enthusiastic supporters of the Council and they saw themselves as part of a new generation of socially committed Catholics who were interpreting the Church's social teachings in a way they thought would help the masses of the poor in Latin America. They envisioned their "project" as one that was threatened from the right by conservative Catholics and from the left by Allende and his Popular Unity coalition. They represented a "third way." But now, just as they were in a position to consolidate their gains, pentecostalism was spreading like wildfire among the very people they most wanted to help. What was going on?

I returned from Chile before the voting but later learned that Father Poblete's surveys had indicated three things about the pentecostals and the election. First, they had indeed voted in considerable numbers. Their allegedly otherworldly orientation had not prevented them from exercising their franchise. Second, the pentecostal leaders had generally opposed Allende's Popular Unity Front, and had supported the Christian Democrats. Poblete's interviews suggested that the leaders had done so both because they felt more secure with the status quo and also because they were suspicious of Allende as a socialist who was said to harbor atheistic elements in his party. But the third finding was that the ordinary members of pentecostal churches—most of them poor people—had, despite the admonitions of their leaders, voted for Allende. Whatever authority those meticulously dressed pastors had *within* their congregations—and every study has shown it to be enormous—it apparently did not extend to what their members did in the voting booth.

One of the first scholars to try to understand the sudden expansion of what had previously been considered a small, marginal movement in Latin America was Emilio Willems. His important book *Followers of the New Faith* was published in 1967. It concentrates on the growth of Protestantism—in which he included pentecostalism—in Chile and Brazil. A close observer of the wrenching social dislocations that were then—and still are—tearing the fabric of Latin America, Willems believed that these changes produced a sense of *anomie*—moral meaninglessness—that was becoming simply unbearable. Pentecostal congregations, he contended, counteracted this *anomie* by supplying their members with a new sense of coherence and a strict set of rules to live by. Also, by enlisting every convert as a missionary, expected to go out and win others to the new faith, the pentecostals broke the monopoly the Catholic priests had held for so long as purveyors of salvation. Imagine the sense of empowerment that must have come to ordinary people living in a highly religious culture who normally felt weak and devoid of any authority when they suddenly became—with the help of the "gifts of the Spirit"—active agents in bringing spiritual deliverance to others. Ecstasy, as students of comparative religion all recognize, is about power, and as Harold Bloom wrote in 1992 about pentecostals in his thoughtful book *The American Religion,* "If you share in the force of the Holy Ghost, with your tongue on fire and miraculous healing breaking out on every side of you, then you may well scorn every lesser manifestation of power."

There was something else as well. The pentecostal faith strictly forbids drunkenness, carousing, and infidelity. Consequently pentecostals have gained a reputation for sobriety, punctuality, and honesty. They are sought after as employees even by people who find their religion peculiar. Thus not only do pentecostals replace the *anomie* with a new community, one with very explicit codes of behavior and moral rules, they and the other Protestants in Latin America, Willems held, were—without really knowing it—

producing something the continent had always lacked, a middle class. They were therefore contributing, albeit perhaps inadvertently, to the process of modernization.

Willems's theories did not go unchallenged for very long. The debate his book caused continues to rage around a wide range of interpretive schemes. Most sociologists, like Willems, believe that pentecostal churches help people "adapt" to a changing world. But they differ about just how this adaptation takes place. Some believe that other Christian traditions—especially popular Catholicism in Latin America—actually *prepare* people for the pentecostal experience. Others emphasize the radical, sometimes even personally risky, break that a new convert must make. Some see pentecostalism as a modernizing process, providing a transitional holding pattern for people who are uprooted from traditional cultures but not yet prepared for the radical individualism of modern urban life. Others hold that pentecostalism is a "social strike" against modernity, a desperate attempt to reclaim at least some elements of a quickly fading past. Still others see it as an ingenious combination of old and new, premodern and postmodern. But they all agree that Latin American pentecostalism is growing at an amazing rate and that careful factual descriptions from different settings are still hard to come by. Therefore the terms of the debate shift as the focus moves from pentecostalism in Latin America to the Caribbean, or from rural congregations to urban areas, or from white churches to black. So far there is a lot of controversy but not much clarity.

While pentecostalism everywhere seems to baffle social scientists, the Latin American branch of the movement has particular features that defy schematic interpretation. Why, for example, when worship is so spontaneous and highly emotional, do the ministers and other leaders usually appear to be so securely in control of the services? If adherents truly believe—as they often say—that we are living in the Last Days, then why do they save money, buy homes, and send their children to school with more regularity than other people who share their general social status? If they hold to the biblical teaching about the man being the "head of the woman"—as they insist they do—then why do so many women not only join pentecostal congregations but bring their husbands and relatives along? If they are so attracted to the "other world," why have they become increasingly more active and effective, even politically, in this one? If God distributes spiritual gifts to lay people, young and old, educated and illiterate, in such an even-handed way—as they claim is the case—then why does the leadership of their congregations often appear so authoritarian? If in some places, especially Latin America, their movement has become an alternative to liberation theology, and even a protest against it—as many analysts claim—then why have pentecostalists begun to develop very similar social theologies and even an explicit "pentecostal liberation theology"? How can people who dance, shout, gesticulate, and seem to go into trances during worship be such models of sobriety, seriousness, and steadiness on the job? How can they, in times of illness, rely both on prayer and the laying on of hands, *and* on antibiotics, chemotherapy, and CAT scans?

To the outsider pentecostalism seems to be drenched in paradoxes and contradictions. But this may be the outsider's predicament, not the pentecostals. As the frontiers of explanation change, merge and separate, there is one interpretive fissure that has continued since the first outbreak of pentecostal fireworks in the upper room in Jerusalem: insiders and outsiders have a quite different take on what is going on.

This is understandable. The people who consider themselves to be pentecostals are uncomfortable with explanations of their movement that seem to explain it away. They simply do not see themselves as victims of *anomie*, refugees from modernity, or deprived searchers for some form of psychological compensation. To add to the confusion, many pentecostals know how confusing their faith appears to outsiders and they seem to take some quiet pleasure in deepening that puzzlement. This does not make the task of understanding their movement any easier.

The scholarly disagreement is indeed serious. On the day after our meeting with the pentecostal pastors in Santiago I met the scholar who was one of the first to take sharp issue with Willems. Christian Lalive d'Epinay had just published *Haven of the Masses,* a study of Chilean pentecostals, and he happened to be back in Chile for a visit. At that time he was a young man enthusiastic about his research, full of opinions and eager to talk about pentecostals. Differing sharply from Willems (he actually turned his thumb down when I asked about him), he told me that the single greatest reason for pentecostal growth was the vast migration of rural folks to the cities. He insisted that their congregations represented not the *collapse* of the folk Catholicism they had practiced in the village but its *transplantation* into the urban environment. He emphasized the continuity, not the break, between the rural village and the city church. Although it surprised me at the time, he was arguing in effect that Latin American pentecostals are not really "Protestants" at all. They represent the newest variant in popular Catholic folk religion. Pentecostals were not "modernizers" either, Lalive said, they were vainly trying to reconstitute a lost past. Don't be misled by the neckties, he warned. These pastors were powerful, not because they were imbuing their people with a modern life-style, but because they had taken the place of the old *patron.* And in neither case was there any question of democracy. Rather, in both situations a severe authoritarian style reigned. These congregations were not, he believed, contexts in which modern attitudes could be learned; rather the old folk beliefs in miracles and supernatural intervention were simply being perpetuated under new auspices. Those pastors in the polished shoes and clean shirts, he said, were only doing what any wily *terrateniente* (landowner) would do. They were keeping on the right side of the powers that be. Far from vanguards of modernization, their congregations were sanctuaries for the frightened masses, shelters designed to protect them from the assaults of modernity. As such, Lalive felt, they would ultimately not succeed; and the rapid growth of pentecostalism in Chile, and elsewhere in Latin America, would eventually slow down and stop.

I remember feeling that Lalive's ideas seemed quite plausible when I first met him in 1970. But the twenty-five years that have passed since *Haven of the Masses* first came out have poked a number of large holes in his thesis. Instead of slowing down, the pentecostals are growing faster than ever. And now they are running for congress and for mayor. Rather than mere "havens," their churches have become powers to be reckoned with by political leaders.

The question of why pentecostalism is expanding so rapidly on a continent that has been thought of as Catholic for so many centuries continues to puzzle Latin American scholars. Sixteen years after I met Lalive in Chile it came up again, but now with a new forcefulness. It happened the day after I attended the service at the Amor de Deus congregation and heard Benedita da Silva give her testimony. At a cozy restaurant in Rio de Janeiro, I was savoring a long lunch of *bacalhau,* the local codfish dish, with a dozen church people and scholars from different fields who had been invited by an old friend who lives in Rio. All of them shared a common interest in the interplay of religion and society in Brazil, and since there is hardly anything Brazilians like to do more than eat, drink, and talk about religion, I knew it would be a great symposium. There were sociologists, theologians, a political scientist, a Brazilian Methodist pastor, a Catholic priest, an activist nun, and a cultural anthropologist. Over the rice and vegetables that accompanied the fish, they all chatted amiably about a number of questions, but it soon became evident that the question which animated them most was exactly the one that was on my mind: why are pentecostals growing so fast in Brazil and in other Latin American countries?

It was at this luncheon that I first heard some of the startling statistics that have become more widely known in the last few years. There were now more pentecostal pastors in Brazil, the historian said, then Roman Catholic priests, and, unlike the priests, they were almost all native Brazilians. The growth was so swift, the sociologist said, that some sections of Brazilian cities already had pentecostal majorities. If things continued to go this way, commented the Catholic priest with three decades of experience in Latin America, within thirty or forty years the Roman Catholic Church would be reduced to serving a largely ornamental function ("like the Church of England," he added ruefully) while the real religious life of the vast majority of the people would be lived in pentecostal congregations. The downturn Lalive had predicted was still nowhere in sight.

I listened as much to the *tone* of the conversation as to its content. They did not seem to be angry or worried, not even the practicing Catholics or the "mainline" Protestants present. They were, quite simply, awed. The once steady and plodding growth of the pentecostal movement in South America had now become exponential. It was a religious change of the first order, the theologian said, comparable in scope only to the so-called "spiritual conquest" of Latin America by the Spanish and Portuguese in the late fifteenth and early sixteenth centuries. So far there seemed to be little disagreement among my table companions. They all agreed on the empirical side of the equation.

When I asked *why* the pentecostals were growing so fast, however, consensus dissolved. Everyone, it seemed, had an explanation, but their ideas contradicted and collided. One suggested that since the pentecostals were so often poor, displaced, and powerless people it was obvious that their religion functioned as a psychological compensation, a spiritual reimbursement for what they were missing on earth. Another explained pentecostal growth in terms of urbanization or class conflict. Two people at the table attributed the expansion to the deep pockets of North America and the machinations of the CIA. One said that for centuries the Catholic Church had ignored the plight of the disadvantaged and now, despite all the liberation theologians' brave talk about a "preferential option for the poor," Mother Church was paying the price for all that neglect, and it served her right. "The Catholic bishops may want to encourage a preferential option for the poor," declaimed the historian, "but the poor seem to have a preference for the pentecostals." The nun, wearing the contemporary "habit" of a modestly cut dress, a denim jacket, and a small wooden cross around her neck, nodded in vigorous agreement. She had been working for three decades in Brazil, as a school teacher and an organizer of community health services. She said she remembered how, when the Baptists and Presbyterians first appeared in Latin America, the authorities of her church warned about the invasion of the *sectas*. But then, as the mellowing influence of the Second Vatican Council set in, Catholics and Protestants become more fraternal.

Now, however, she said she had begun to receive panicky mail-ings from organization sponsored jointly by both Catholics and Protestants that warn about the *sectas,* and this time they mean the pentecostals. But she paid no attention to the admonitions, she said. It was high time that her church—and the staid old-line Protestants—got a run for the money. Besides, the pente-costals were doing a lot of good things. Why, look at Benedita da Silva.

The argument raged on and their voices grew more strident. Everyone seemed to be talking at once. I was not surprised that my table companions could not agree. Ever since the very begin-ning the pentecostal phenomenon has been the subject of con-flicting interpretations. To view it, with Saint Peter, as evidence of the activity of the Spirit, is something few scholars are willing to do. If anything, the dispute is now infinitely more complex since—as our lunchtime hub-bub in Rio had amply demonstrated—there is little agreement even among those who bracket whatever role the Spirit plays and look for psychological or sociocultural expla-nations of pentecostalism's growth.

One of the most articulate voices at the luncheon was a Brazilian sociologist of religion named Francisco Cartaxo Rolim. A small, chubby, balding man, Rolim is the victim of something close to a scholarly obsession with the subject of pentecostalism (he has written three books and a half dozen articles on the sub-ject). But he disagrees sharply with both Willems and Lalive, and he is also suspicious of any *anomie* theory of pentecostal growth. Rolim believes one must start, at least in most Latin American countries, with the assumption that there is genuine conflict between classes, and that religion—of whatever type—will inevitably fulfill one of two roles. It will either mask the conflict and thereby contribute to alienation and oppression, or it will become a vehicle of protest. He believes that pentecostalism is an expression of rebellion, not of alienation.

But Rolim does not stop there. In an obvious thrust at his scholarly opponents he adds that these same two possibilities—alienation or protest—also apply to *theories* of religion as well, and the *anomie* theories his scholarly opponents pander contribute

177

to alienation by obscuring the real situation. They imply that the cause of the pentecostal explosion is a passing jagged blip on a normally smooth line, a temporary disjuncture in an otherwise stable situation. Wrong, says Rolim. The cause is not transient but structural and deep-seated. He also insists that pentecostalism does not merely alleviate the alienation from society many people feel. Rather, it transposes it into another key. Their faith does not "adjust" pentecostals to a society of class conflict. It gives them a way to "just say no." It is social protest expressed in religious form.

Rolim has done most of his research in the vast industrial and slum suburb of Rio de Janeiro called Nova Iguacu, not far from where we ate lunch. He found that most of the people from Nova Iguacu who joined pentecostal churches had not been religiously illiterate before but had been more or less active participants in some form of popular or folk Catholicism. Rolim sees folk Catholicism—with its unauthorized shrines, amulets, *milagros* (miracles), and fiestas—as itself a popular protest against hierarchically controlled religion. From this perspective, pentecostalism merely takes another step. It provides unmediated access to God and healing that comes from prayer and does not even require holy water, scapulas, or tiring pilgrimages to holy places. Instead of a pantheon of saints to be invoked for various kinds of help, pentecostals now have the Bible. (I had noticed that Latin American pentecostals love to carry around the biggest, thickest Bible they can find, with gold piping and colorful ribbons, and I remembered the huge one I had seen on Benedita's living room table.) Rolim also interprets "speaking in tongues" as a kind of protest that verbally unskilled people can use to be heard, and to gain some of the attention that normally focuses on "speakers." In effect, says Rolim, folk Catholicism is a kind of staging ground, a personal and cultural preparation for pentecostalism, and pentecostalism is *not* Protestantism. It is what another writer calls "Catholicism without priests," a radical religious and symbolic movement that could eventually bring a thorough-going, even revolutionary change to the South American continent.

Rolim seemed to know what he was talking about. But as I listened to his carefully formulated description of the how and why of pentecostal growth, and later as I read his books and articles, a question kept occurring to me. It is one that lies close to the heart of any study of the interaction of religion and society. What exactly is "symbolic protest"? Should it be called "protest" at all? Most Marxists, for example, have contended that precisely by "transposing" rebellion from the "real" to the "symbolic" realm, religions divert energy from the actual causes of misery and thus help perpetuate it. One can engage in symbolic protest forever, they argue, and never change the "real situation."

Rolim disagrees with this Marxist rejection of the value of symbolic protest. Symbols, he claims, are not just confectioner's decorations sprinkled on the cake. They have a genuine and potent social power. To protest against the hierarchical monopoly on the creation and use of religious and symbolic power, to take at least some of that power into one's own hands as the pentecostals do, is a form of *real*, not illusory, protest. Rolim is a persistent critic of what he believes are atrociously unjust social conditions in Brazil (including hundreds of thousands of homeless children on the streets of Rio itself), and he sees the pentecostal movement in a positive light. He believes that it holds the potential for long-term and social change in Brazil and elsewhere in Latin America.

I found Rolim's theories intriguing: they certainly made some sense in Brazil. But what about elsewhere? I thought about the recent success of pentecostals in China, Russia, and Ukraine. If pentecostalism is a sort of "seizure of religious power," one that takes control of what he calls the "means of symbolic production" of the dominant religion, and if it removes this authority from the hands of its traditional wielders, then how does one explain its growth in these formerly Communist countries? Christians were until quite recently themselves an oppressed minority. Why would anyone wish to seize the symbolic power in such a hounded institution and risk exposure and persecution?

And what about the rest of the world? If popular folk Catholicism supplies most of the underlying archetypes and thus "prepares" people for pentecostalism, as Rolim says it does, how is one to make sense of its rapid growth in places like Africa where the converts come mainly from indigenous spiritual traditions? Or Korea, where a fusion of diluted Confucianism, Buddhism, and folk shamanism forms the main religious tradition? If class conflict is such a potent factor in pentecostal growth, then why are there people from different classes in many congregations, and why has the growth occurred not so much among the poorest of the poor, but among people who are somewhere between the upper fringe of the impoverished and the lowest rung of the middle class? Rolim's theories, based almost entirely on his research in Brazil, and in Nova Iguacu in particular, certainly help to explain the pentecostal boom there. But they are of less help in other parts of Latin America, let alone in Indonesia or Zimbabwe.

As I listened to the high-spirited luncheon discussion in Rio, I occasionally smiled to myself, thinking about how much many of my pentecostal friends would have enjoyed hearing it and how much merriment they would have derived from the incapacity of these brilliant scholars to understand what makes them tick. But they would also have found in it a certain confirmation. Pentecostals insist, often quite stridently, that it is the *same* Spirit that has touched them all with its searing and life-giving power, and they often seem to take pleasure (at least in the eyes of outsiders) in their ability to disagree so freely with each other. The fact that outsiders find them contradictory and paradoxical does not bother them a bit.

I had another thought as I listened to the scholars. I remembered Benedita's testimony, and many other testimonies I had heard, some in congregations almost within shouting distance of where we were eating. After all, I thought, maybe the best location from which to understand pentecostalism is neither that of the outside analyst sipping coffee nor that of the Spirit-baptized insider, but somewhere in the middle. And at that time, that was exactly where I felt I was. I realized that to most scholarly theorists and to many pentecostals, the middle would seem to be not the best but the worst place to be. But I continue to believe that this stance—being a "sympathetic outsider" and a "critical partici-pant"—may eventually cast the clearest light on the subject. After all, who is inside and who is outside is not all that obvious: pen-tecostals share a significant portion of their reality with everyone else. Must the participant-observer who finds herself participating more deeply thereby cease to be an observer? Does the worship-per who begins to reflect on his worship become less of a wor-shipper? I think that the answer to both questions is no, and that pentecostalism, the faith built on the belief that "the Spirit bloweth where it listeth," may by its very nature require a whole new approach to the study of religion, one that will ultimately deepen and clarify the study of other religions as well.

These are the kinds of thoughts that were going through my head as we ended our memorable luncheon in Rio de Janeiro. As the last of the *cafe zinho* was being drained, on impulse—and maybe emboldened by two bottles of the local beer I had enjoyed earlier—I asked my table companions if any of them had them-selves ever "spoken in tongues" or "prayed in the Spirit" as the pentecostals say. There was an awkward silence. The priest glanced at his watch. The historian brushed crumbs from the tablecloth. The rest looked doubtfully at each other. None, it seemed, ever had. Nor had I, I admitted. They seemed relieved. But then I asked whether anyone had ever *wanted* to. Here again, the response was negative, and most seemed surprised when I revealed that I had at times wanted to. I told them that I was not at all sure what the wordless "praying in the Spirit" phenomenon means, but that I had witnessed it enough times, and seen the joy and serenity it brings, to have felt—against my more restrained instincts perhaps—that I would like that too. I admitted, warming to my subject now that I had gotten started, that I had not always felt this way. In fact sometimes I had even been put off, or a bit disquieted, when such "praying in the Spirit" was going on. Still, there were times—a few—when disquietude or curiosity changed to a kind of envy.

For me, saying all this to my lunch companions was a small moment of truth—not for them, but for me. It taught me some-thing about pentecostalism. It produced the kind of insight that sometimes comes when you finally *say* something that has been lingering in the back of your mind. The fact is that I will probably never "speak in tongues." I am too self-conscious, too inhibited, maybe too old. And as I write these words I am not even sure I would really want to. But my recognizing publicly, if only to a small circle of friends and acquaintances, that there *have* been times when I *have* wanted to, still seems very important to me. It was a bit like the testimonies the pentecostals give: once you have said it, it becomes part of your personal history. This insight taught me something about the enormous power that is generated by *desiring* something very much. And it occurred to me that pentecostals must be understood as people who have become what they are because they *wanted* something badly enough to allow themselves to be changed in a fundamental way, and they were willing to embrace the elemental terror that sort of change requires. However vaguely or incoherently, they yearned for something—healing, fellowship, salvation, empowerment, dignity, meaning, serenity, ecstasy—they saw in other people, and decided to claim it for themselves; then, having done so, they became the glad bearers of its message. I am not sure my scholarly compatriots understood this point. But, in any case, our three-hour lunch provided all of us with a lot to think and talk about. As they left in groups of two and three, I could see the discussions continuing through the rear windows of their taxis.

In the spring of 1991 I returned to Latin America, and to the same debate, this time at a conference of the Latin American Association for the Study of Popular Religions held at the Institute of Anthropology in Mexico City. One of the scholars present was a brilliant Swiss historian named Jean-Pierre Bastian who has spent most of his adult life in Mexico. Bastian was the bearer of bad news. He warned that pentecostalism in the present Latin American context may be "Catholicism without priests," but it lacks the internal democracy of the previous Protestant movements. He pointed out that it is developing an ominous authoritarian character and that its leaders, instead of helping their people nurture democratic attitudes and skills, are becoming wheeler-dealers who trade blocs of votes for spoils and patronage. They have become the *caciques* and *caudillos* of religious movements that they pass on to their sons according to the age-old nepotistic custom. He did not believe that pentecostalism was going to contribute much to the advancement of democracy in Latin America.

I was sorry to hear what Bastian reported. But unfortunately some of the other news I picked up during that trip confirmed his negative impression. A Brazilian participant told me that the fastest growing pentecostal church in her country, known as *Brasil para Christo*, seems to have become an absolute despotism. And in Guadalajara, the leader of the church called *La Iglesia de la Luz del Mundo*, originally founded by a poor migrant worker in 1926, had taken the name Aaron and made quasi-messianic claims. When he died in 1984, his son succeeded him under the name Samuel. In Peru, the chief of a pentecostal group called Los Israelites has proclaimed himself a messiah by taking the following titles: "Grand Biblical Compiler, Grand and Unique Missionary General, Spiritual Guide, Prophet of God, Master of Masters and Holy Spirit and Christ of the West." This trend toward highhanded overlordship also infects smaller pentecostal bodies where the pastor frequently not only holds title to all the church property but rules like an oriental potentate. Given this regrettable pattern, Bastian fears that the hopes many people once held out that pentecostalism would become a seed-bed of democracy in Latin America may prove to be a sad disappointment.

Not all the news I heard about pentecostalism at the Mexico City conference was bad. Two younger anthropologists reported that the indigenous tribes they were studying seemed to be able to retain their native practices and healing rites better after they became pentecostals than before. Another reported that, despite Bastian's warnings, pentecostals in Costa Rica and Nicaragua, where they are closer to the Baptists and Moravians, were evolving genuine democratic practices in their congregations.

As I reflected on the disparate theories and ideas I had heard at the Mexico City meeting, I began to see at least two reasons for the massive contradictions that characterize these opinions. One is that each theory represents only a partial view of the whole. The other is simply that *the pentecostal movement itself is a highly paradoxical one.* It is diverse, volatile, and mercurial. It will not sit still long enough for someone to paint its portrait, or stop changing long enough for anyone to chart its trajectory. One of the sociologists at the meeting had summed it up quite well. "What we are dealing with here," he said, "are, without a doubt, paradoxical visions of a paradoxical religion." In fact, it may be this polychrome character that makes pentecostalism so attractive to so many people. Its appeal is multifaceted, and the feature that draws one new believer in may not be what attracts the next one. Indeed, even after they join, because of the multivalency of its teaching and practices, different believers may make something very different of their common pentecostal faith.

I am still trying to keep up with the flood of interpretive articles on pentecostal growth in Latin America. But all of their theories seem to pale beside the one Benedita da Silva offers whenever she is asked. After her unsuccessful campaign for the mayoralty of Rio de Janeiro, a journalist interviewed Benedita about how she had taken the defeat, and what she planned to do now. As I read her response, I remembered the evening I heard her testimony amid the guitars and the animated hymns under the stars and the Southern Cross. And I remembered our conversation at her little home on the rocky hillside overlooking the tar-paper shacks and the glass hotels of Copacabana. Was she discouraged?

"Look," Benedita answered her interviewer, "we believe that Jesus performed miracles, that He rose from the dead, that He distributed the loaves, that He said, 'I depart but will not leave you orphans. You will have the power to do greater things.'" Then I could almost see her pause before she added the final words. "My God," she said, "if we keep the word of God, we will do greater things than he did!"

CHAPTER 10

Sibyls and Madonnas: Reclaiming Archaic Spirituality in Europe

I say you are mad with love, my Jesus, and I
will always say it. You are altogether lovely
and merry, you refresh and console, you nourish
and unite, you are torment and relief, effort and
rest, death and life in one.

Maria Maddalena De'Pazzi (1566–1607)

*I*N THE SPRING OF 1993 the Center for European Studies at Harvard hosted a conference on "The Failure of Modernization Theory: Is There a Religious Renaissance in Europe?" The question posed to the fifty-odd scholars who attended was a straightforward one: given the resurgence of religion in most places in the world, is something similar afoot in Europe, or is Europe an exception?

I listened carefully to the various presentations. There was not a full consensus, but the majority seemed to hold that Europe was indeed an exception. Church attendance was still declining. Even in the former Soviet satellites of eastern Europe, the religious revival that some had thought would take place after the Berlin Wall came down seemed not to have occurred. The newly liberated populations of what were formerly East Germany and Czechoslovakia seemed more interested in buying VCRs and vacationing on the Greek islands. Even in Poland, in many ways the most religious country in Europe, an accelerated disaffiliation from the church appeared to be under way.

A few weeks after the conference I went to Manchester, England, to deliver some lectures. It became evident to me during my visit that at least for the Church of England and the other mainline Protestant denominations in Britain, the findings of the conference seemed to be accurate. Attendance was indeed down, way down. Buildings were decaying, and nearly every church I walked into was sponsoring a fund drive to preserve the stained glass and keep the steeples from falling. Interest in religion seemed to be at a low ebb. There was no renaissance in sight.

But then one day I told my host, a professor of philosophical theology, that I would like to visit some of the pentecostal churches in Manchester. At first he looked at me quizzically and appeared not to have understood. Then he told me he had his doubts about whether such a visit could be arranged since all *those* churches were in the section of town called Moss-side which was considered dangerous. It was where the Caribbean immigrants had settled, and there had actually been a murder there only last year.

But I gently persisted, and with the help of a friendly graduate student I managed to visit two congregations, one of the New Testament Church of God and the other of the Church of God of Prophecy, the two largest pentecostal denominations in Britain. The two buildings had both previously belonged to other denominations. Now they were being used by very lively Caribbean pentecostal congregations. At one church I attended a revival where in addition to the usual trap drums, electric guitars, and keyboard, we also heard a sweet gospel song sung to the tune of "Danny Boy" by a black woman who had obviously been listening to both Aretha Franklin and Billie Holiday records. While the instruments played, a small black boy of about five in a white shirt and red necktie stood next to his mother in the pew in front of me and shook the tambourine he had brought with him to church.

When I returned to London after giving my lectures at Manchester I spent some time looking into the religious situation of the United Kingdom. What I discovered did not surprise me, but it raised some doubts in my mind about the findings of the conference at Harvard. Professor Eileen Barker, a sociologist at the London School of Economics who specializes in studying religious movements, told me that by her count there were approximately 600 "new" religious groups in the United Kingdom. She added that they were by far the fastest growing ones in the country. Among these she included the "immigrant religions" such as Hinduism and Islam, hardly "new," but relatively new to the U.K. religious scene, at least in the numbers they now represent. She also included what she called "cults" and "new age" groups in her estimate, but said they did not account for much of the growth. The groups that are really increasing, she said, are the pentecostals.

The statistics she showed me were very revealing, but again not surprising. They told what had become a familiar story. In the years between 1985 and 1990, the research shows, Baptists, Methodists, Presbyterians, Anglicans, and Roman Catholics in the United Kingdom have all *lost* members, with the Catholics and the Anglicans taking the biggest losses, down about 10 percent each. During the same five-year period, "independent Christian churches," which includes mainly pentecostals and charismatic "house churches," *gained* nearly 30 percent. I began to think that maybe Europe was not such an exception after all.

On the Sunday before my return to the United States I tried to find a pentecostal church in East London that one of the ministers of the church I had visited in Manchester told me about. But I mistakenly took the wrong bus, and by the time I arrived at the Holy Spirit Apostolic Church in the Stepney section, the worshippers were filing out. I introduced myself to a young Caribbean man who seemed to be a leader and he told me not to feel bad about missing the service since some of them were on their way to Hyde Park's famous Speakers' Corner where they planned to hold a street meeting: I was welcome to come along.

Six of us—all Caribbeans except myself—traveled to the Hyde Park stop on the top of a double-decker bus, singing rousing hymns to the amusement of the few other passengers who had ventured out on a day that threatened rain. At Hyde Park, the young preacher—his name turned out to be Tom Harrison, formerly of Jamaica—set up a ladder, climbed to the second step, and opened a large leather-bound book which I of course thought was the Bible. It was not. What he held in his hand was an English translation of the Koran, with the verses that mention Jesus underlined in red pencil. He was there not just to preach, but to preach to the Muslims. I could see right away that this might get very interesting indeed, and not wanting to be drawn into any fisticuffs, I stepped back a couple of yards to try to blend into the audience. While Tom got ready I walked around the area to check on what the other orators at Speakers' Corner were saying.

Tom was not the only preacher plying his trade that day. Just down the way from us stood an immaculately dressed Korean gentlemen preaching, albeit in a somewhat subdued voice, a rather formulaic fundamentalist message. Across from him another West Indian, whose accent sounded very much like Tom's, seemed to be giving a lecture on personal character building. On a much higher ladder, a man with a picture of Saddam Hussein and an Iraqi flag behind him was giving a fiery denunciation of the United States and the Gulf War. Not five yards away, on a somewhat smaller ladder, a young man in a *yarmulke* was extolling the virtues of Israel while his companion stood next to him holding the blue and white Israeli flag and looking warily at the curious crowd that had gathered around them. There was also an advocate of world government, speaking in measured tones to a very small cluster of listeners, and a short, grizzled old gentlemen who, without any ladder at all, was standing on the ground and attacking the British Labour party for abandoning true socialism. His only audience consisted of two American tourists who appeared to be looking around uneasily for a way to escape without hurting his feelings.

After my tour of the oratorical offerings, I bought an ice cream on a stick and started back toward Tom, now holding forth with full arm gestures; he had a book in each hand. One was the Koran. The other was the Bible. Even before I could get back to his outdoor pulpit I could see that he had attracted the largest crowd, and as I pushed to get closer I could see why. The four other church members who had come with us were all standing near the ladder. But in front of Tom, some fifteen Muslims had gathered to heckle, throw questions, interrupt, and argue with him in the old Hyde Park tradition. It was obvious to me that they had been here before and that they were enjoying the exchange. And so was Tom.

"What do you mean, Jesus didn't really die?" Tom asked, in response to a frequent criticism that Muslims make. Since they believe that Jesus was a prophet of God, they often insist that he could not possibly have died on the cross, but must have escaped, and that the New Testament documents are doctored. But Tom was not buying this delivrance-from-the-cross plot. "Just give me one witness, one eyewitness for your version," he pled, "one *little* witness is all I ask for. Look. Here we have *four* eyewitnesses, Matthew, Mark, Luke, and John, and they all say he died."

Then Tom took up a very delicate subject. "Look," he said, pointing to a passage he had underlined heavily, "your Koran says that a man can beat his wife, but the Bible says we should love our wives. What kind of a holy book is that?"

Again I took a couple of steps back to fade into the crowd of spectators. I didn't want to be caught in the crossfire, but at the same time, I wished that some of my scholarly Christian colleagues who engage in well-mannered dialogues with Muslims could have been there. This was interfaith dialogue in the raw.

But the Muslims did not seem disquieted. They laughed and shook their heads, and seemed to be having a good time. Then one of them told Tom that the translation of the Koran he was using was not a valid one. Tom led him on like a cat with a mouse. "Not a valid translation, eh? Oh, so you say the *translation* is not valid. Well, who do you think *did* this translation? Then he triumphantly opened the first page to show that the translation had indeed been published by a Muslim organization.

"The Koran is only valid when it's in Arabic," shouted one of the Muslims. "It cannot be translated."

"What?" said Tom in feigned surprise, "you don't believe in *translations?* But we're in *England* now, my friend. We're both speaking *English.* My God speaks to me in English. Alleluia!"

As I listened to the exchange and watched the arm waving that both Tom and the Muslims were engaged in, I had the impression they were playing a game that was both sportive and in earnest. I also noticed that they both carefully respected the rules of the exchange. Once one of the Muslims reached out as though to take the Koran out of Tom's hands, but his coreligionists stopped him, and warned him with whispers and stern looks that this was out-of-bounds behavior. After a while, Tom's voice began to give out. The other pentecostals then handed out leaflets inviting people to their church, and to my amazment, some of the Muslims accepted them. As Tom folded his ladder, I had a suspicion that all this would happen again next week. I wanted to stay and chat with Tom some more, but I was already late so I thanked him and said goodbye.

"God bless you," he said cheerily, his voice having recovered its full timbre. "Be sure to come to the church the next time you're here. Cheerio."

When I got back home to Cambridge, Massachusetts, I decided I was not ready to accept the conclusions of the Harvard conference. If religion was a dead letter in Europe, no one had heard about the death in either Moss-side or in Hyde Park. Thirty years earlier, when I had visited London as a divinity student almost all the debates at Speakers' Corner were about politics. Socialists debated with Tories and members of the IRA tried to recruit members. Today, religion is even *more* in the public eye than it was then, when the only religious speakers I heard were one American Mormon and an aging member of the British Catholic Evidence Society. So I decided I would reopen my inquiry, and try to find out whether pentecostals and other similar movements were growing at anything like the same rate elsewhere in Europe. What I discovered raised some serious doubts in my mind about whether the global religious renaissance had bypassed Europe as completely as the participants at the Harvard conference had thought.

For example, on November 1, 1992, the Church of God, an American pentecostal denomination with headquarters in Cleveland, Tennessee, held its first public meeting in Moscow.

The scene in the large rented hall, as described in the church's publication *Save Our World*, was a remarkable one by any standard. Huge crowds were waiting an hour in the cold before the service was scheduled to begin. Some 1,500 people jammed the auditorium designed to hold 800. Another 2,000 people crowded the lobby. After only a week's efforts—utilizing television announcements, newspaper notices, printed invitations, and wall posters—the church had signed up more than 4,000 new members. It is now preparing 100 Russian pastors to fan out into the former Soviet Union.

Pentecostalism is not new to the former republics. It arrived in Russia in 1911 and has been present there ever since. During the period of communist rule pentecostals often joined with Baptists and other evangelical Christians in holding semiclandestine meetings for prayer and Bible study in the kitchens of the believers' homes. Others worhipped more or less publicly in the handful of Baptist churches that were permitted to remain open by the government. Sometimes tensions arose between the Baptists and the pentecostals in Russia. As might be expected, the Baptists were uncomfortable with tongue speaking and with the more emotionally demonstrative expressions of pentecostal worship, but the more severe the government repression became, the more willingly they cooperated with pentecostal groups.

Now pentecostals, along with Catholics, Baptists, and others, are free to worship and even to try to win other people to their movement. The Russian Orthodox Church is, of course, free as well. But the years that the Orthodox Church enjoyed a virtual legal monopoly, as well as the years of persecution under communism, have made it less prepared to compete for members in this newly open situation. Also, the fact that many Russians distrust the Orthodox Church for what they believe was its hierarchy's willingess to compromise too easily with the Communists makes its situation even more difficult. Recently leaders of the Orthodox Church tried to get the government to pass legislation that would have limited the freedom of other churches, especially those coming in from outside. Boris Yeltsin refused to support the proposed law. In any case, it would not have affected pentecostals as much as many other groups, since they have been present in Russia for eighty years.

When I hear about the current growth of pentecostalism in Russia, I sometimes wonder how this "free market in faith" may change religions such as the Orthodox Church, which have not had to face such competition for hundreds of years. Will the Orthodox Churches in the east or the Catholic Church in Poland and elsewhere turn now to more vigorous forms of evangelism and marketing? How will the resulting impact of these techniques and forms of self-presentation modify these religions themselves? This is only the beginning. With mass media now available, televangelists are already at work in eastern Europe, and their political and cultural agenda will surely follow. The question may soon arise, what has Dostoyevsky to do with Pat Robertson?

The former Soviet Union is not the only place on the European continent where pentecostalism is spreading. There is a small but vigorous charismatic movement in the Catholic churches of France, involving mainly middle-class technical professionals. There is a similar trend, also small but lively, in the German churches, where the movement is having some difficulty because it has been criticized by both the state church and the small, theologically more conservative "free churches" such as the Baptists and the Methodists. But what surprised me most was to learn that pentecostalism is also expanding in Italy, the home of the Vatican, the international headquarters of the Roman Catholic Church. Since I was planning a visit to Italy the following summer, I tried to find out as much as I could about the movement there, so I would be in a position to understand it better after I arrived.

It was not easy to find information about pentecostalism in Italy. But then I discovered that for a number a years an anthropologist named Salvatore Cucchiari had been publishing field studies of women in pentecostal churches in Sicily. I was astounded. I had not known that there even *were* pentecostals in Sicily, a land I had usually associated with fossilized catholicism, olive groves, and the Mafia. But the best estimates now place them at about 350,000 and growing rapidly. I was also a bit disquieted that anthropologists, who are known for studying peoples on the verge of disappearing, were now scrutinizing pentecostals. Since I was planning to visit Italy that summer, I looked up some of Cucchiari's articles, hoping that he might turn out to be a kindred spirit instead of a collector of chipped pottery or shrunken heads.

· As soon as I began to read Cucchiari's articles I was relieved and drawn in. Although he is not a pentecostal himself, Cucchiari obviously respects and even admires the people he studies. Furthermore, what he said about pentecostals in Sicily, which I have never visited, turned out to be true for the churches I attended on the Italian mainland. Then, as I started to look at pentecostals in Italy with the help of a sympathetic anthropologist, I began to wonder whether the predominance of women in this movement could eventually make some impact on the gender relations of the larger culture. Now it struck me that Italy, and especially Sicily, could be the test case. Here was the ultimate challenge to pentecostalism's capacity to contest a patriarchal culture at its most entrenched. Both in legend and in fact, Sicily is surely one of the last redoubts of the most traditional brand of male domination, at least in the western Christian world. If pentecostal women could crack the barnacled iron-clad male dreadnaught of Sicily they could probably do it anywhere.

Admittedly, few people think of pentecostalism as being in the forefront of feminism. Fewer consider Sicily the most promising site for a fruitful field study of the prospects for women's liberation. But even Sicily is changing. Recently a few courageous shopkeepers banded together and refused to pay "protection" money to Cosa Nostra dons, such as Salvatore "Toto" Riini who police say strangles his victims and dissolves their corpses in vats of acid. In June 1993, the *New York Times* reported that Toto had finally been taken into custody and indicted for murder. The Sicilians are fighting back. But then the island was already changing in the 1860s, as Giuseppe Tomasi de Lampedusa's novel *The Leopard* reveals. In the 1962 film version by Luchino Visconti, the prince—the proud, cunning, but strangely likable lead character, brilliantly played by Burt Lancaster—suddenly realizes during a formal ball at his estate that his world is dying. At first he is devastated, but later he devises a brilliant coping strategy. "One must change," he muses in an often-quoted line, "so that things can stay the same."

In a sense, he was right. Many things have changed on his old island, but many things remain the same. Today's Sicily would, in most respects, be unrecognizable to the prince. Modernization has marched across the land from Messina to Marsala. Television antennae perched on roofs in villages where ancient Roman citizens once lived now pull "Dallas" reruns and game shows out of the ether. Fiats and mopeds clog the streets of Palermo, Ragusa, and the smaller cities. Young people demonstrate in the streets against the Mafia. But there is one thing in Sicily that has changed very little, as even Lampedusa's melancholy prince would recognize. Men still dominate women, or try to. And a rigidly enforced code that stakes every man's "honor" on his ability to control the public and sexual behavior of "his" women still stands. It would probably comfort the prince to know that even during a social hurricane, certain things remain in place. In modern Sicily, men are still expected to make sure that women abide by the severest standards of demure and modest public deportment and submit unquestioningly to male authority.

This does not mean, of course, that mama cannot be a benevolent despot at home, as long as she defers to her husband in public. Within the household, the world can be, and usually is, "mother-centered." But the Sicilian cosmos is divided into domestic and public, feminine and masculine spheres. And it has always been the men who have set the boundaries and enforced them. This code is firmly embedded in the Sicilian worldview and, together with Sicily's sad reputation for dealing mercilessly with subverters of traditional values, it might suggest to the prince that he can rest easy. Even if patriarchy is teetering in some places, Sicily could be its stone tower and inner keep.

The fact is that the change is already under way. According to Lucia Chiavola Birnbaum, whose grandparents came from Sicily, and who has written two books on the subject, Italy has one of the most energetic women's movements in the world, and its strength comes in part from its power to tap into ancient religious practices. Birnbaum distinguishes between the "official"

Catholicism of Italy and the tenacious folk beliefs which the Church has frequently tried to eradicate but which stubbornly persist. In many places, she reports, it is Mary Magdalene, not Jesus, who is the central figure in the unofficial celebrations, which thrive despite the disapproval of the local priests. I think that Italian pentecostalism has to be understood as the most recent outcropping—under a new aegis and with a contemporary twist— of this age-old religion of the back streets and the side alleys. But to understand how it works for women in Sicily, and the kind of potential it carries for a more sweeping change, one has to be prepared for an element of irony.

Pentecostalism came to Italy when a migrant worker named Giacomo Lombardi, who had been converted in the United States in 1908, returned to spread the new faith among his neighbors and family members. It expanded quickly, and in 1929 there were already 149 pentecostal congregations in the country. Membership has swelled since then despite the opposition both of the Catholic Church and, during the Mussolini period, of the state as well. Today pentecostals constitute the largest non-Catholic religious grouping in Italy. Most of them are drawn from the lower and middle classes. These are the very people Lampedusa's prince once feared would someday topple his beloved aristocracy. They may indeed topple it, but not in the way he anticipated.

When I got to Italy in the summer of 1993 and began to visit churches, it was clearly evident that, like their fellow believers in many other places, Italian pentecostals place most of their *formal* leadership in the hands of male preachers. They also promulgate a Pauline ethic of male authority: women are to obey their husbands, and "husbands are the head of their wives as Christ is head of the church." As we have already noticed in West Virginia, Latin America, and elsewhere, this seems at first like stony soil for aspiring women. It has even occurred to many observers that in Italy some men are drawn to pentecostalism because it seems to shore up the patriarchal cosmos they feel is threatened by such social changes as the increasing numbers of women in the work force.

But first impressions can be deceiving, and in this case they surely are. If many men, and even some women, initially join the pentecostal movement in the hope of salvaging "traditional" family values, what happens is that they end up undermining them. In Italian pentecostal churches women play major roles in worship and even hold a near monopoly on some of the leadership positions. Also, if you listen carefully, you can hear that the way pentecostals talk and pray and testify refers to a God who is very different from the Great Patriarch of traditional Christianity.

Italian pentecostal churches open a door for women. Unlike most other Christian churches, they place at least as much emphasis on the "Spirit" as they do on the "Word," often even more. This means that the spiritual authority in the congregation is vested not just in the Bible, which can be quoted to undergird male control, but also in the free gifts of the Spirit which are showered on all without reference to rank or gender. It is this tension between Word and Spirit, a classic one in Christianity but more explicit in pentecostalism, that women seize upon to create a new space for leadership, empowerment, and—possibly one day—the reconfiguration of a centuries-old cultural pattern. And there can be little doubt that, at least within the pentecostal congregations of Italy, a radical metamorphosis in how men and women understand themselves and their relations to each other is occurring.

The pentecostals I met in Italy, like the ones in Sicily, obviously believe that the best way to handle the religious norms and conventions that pervade the atmosphere is to "just say no." In a society where for centuries a close alliance of church and state has set the tone, they vigorously reject the dominant religious symbols and practices. They will have nothing to do with Catholic baptisms, marriages, or last rites. They do not accept the authority of priests, and their refusal to dance or get drunk at religious holidays, saints' days, or Madonna festivals causes some people to think of them as spoilsports. But anyone who has visited pentecostal churches and met the people who attend them can tell you that they seem anything but gloomy. Their weeks are filled with convivial church suppers, musically upbeat prayer meetings, and jubilant testimony services. They have nothing against dancing in the Spirit and making glad noises with amplified keyboards and electric guitars, sometimes to the chagrin of the same neighbors who claim the pentecostals never have a good time.

But there is something more going on. Within the fast growing pentecostal counterculture, and in the personal lives of pentecostal women and men, a change is taking place which even Lampedusa's prince could hardly have foreseen. Women are coming into their own. Two out of every three pentecostals in Sicily are women. This may not sound surprising at first. Italy has for centuries been a country where the black-clad womenfolk were customarily packed off to church by the men. But this is a different case, indeed nearly the opposite, for many of these women have become pentecostals in defiance of the express prohibition of their fathers and husbands. In other words, by the sheer act of converting to this often despised and ridiculed faith, they have taken a risky and venturesome step against Sicilian patriarchal culture. They have disobeyed the men whose honor depends on controlling them, and in a manner which—because of its openly public character—was bound to bring shame and censure on those men. Such women often have had to endure enormous hostility from the men, and from other women who, though they may secretly admire the courage of these daring sisters, feel they must keep up the appearance of subservience. This "unauthorized" movement of women into the pentecostal churches in Sicily has given rise to much public criticism, and their opponents sometimes impugn pentecostal congregations with a colorful insult: they call them "dens of witches and whores."

Both parts of this crude epithet are significant. But both are initially puzzling. Pentecostals are widely known, in Sicily and elsewhere, as people who disdain all varieties of black or white magic, including witchcraft. Then why does it occur to anyone to call pentecostal women "witches"? The answer becomes clear when one looks deeper into the history of popular religiosity and superstition in Sicily. Well into the nineteenth century the local witch was still a recognized figure on the Sicilian landscape. She sometimes led the peasant women in rituals that linked breast milk with the fertility of the earth, in the face of the stern disapproval of Catholic authorities. Witches are simply women who control symbolic power that neither men nor established religious authorities can wrench from them. On the lips of fearful men and apprehensive church officials the term "witch" is certainly one of disapprobation. But, given the local history, it is understandable that their opponents should apply it to pentecostal women, the unauthorized wielders of female religious power.

The use of the term "whore," especially in the light of the pentecostals' strong and well-known condemnation of sexual promiscuity, seems even more baffling at first. In Italy, as in many places in the world, pentecostal women dress more plainly and wear less makeup than other women. They often do so gladly, not grudgingly, because it reduces the amount of sexual violence and catcalling they have to put up with. They do not frequent the bars and clubs where men on the lookout go to pick up prostitutes. If anything, pentecostals are generally viewed as being *more* puritanical than other women, not more promiscuous. So why do their antagonists refer to their meetings as "dens of whores"?

Again, upon further reflection the intent of this derisive language is obvious. "Whore" is simply the Sicilian male argot for a woman whose public behavior is not controlled by her husband, brothers, or father. A "whore" is a free agent, applied to any woman who in some respects lives her own life. Maybe this helps explain why Mary Magdalene continues to be such a popular figure among many Italian women and why she has the place of honor in some of the unauthorized festivals. In any case, when "whore" is paired with "witch" the combination is potent. It suggests that many of its opponents fear Italian pentecostalism as a sinister and threatening feminist movement.

In trying to understand how pentecostals impact the culture around them, on the issue of gender or anything else, it is important to remember to watch what they *do*. Their theology is in their practice. Here again it is important to recall that although women are technically forbidden to preach, if God calls them—as he did Betty Lou Carter and many thousands more—they do preach. Also, they do "prophesy," since prophecy and testimony, as well as healing and praying in the Spirit are understood to be "gifts" that are distributed without reference to status, education, or gender. "Ministries," however, are something else. They are formal, official positions within the church organization. But as I have noticed in many pentecostal churches the difference is not as great as it sounds. The distinction between the "ministries" of preaching and teaching, on the one hand, and the "gifts" of prophecy and testimony on the other, is often hard to make out.

Cucchiari has noticed the same thing. He writes, for example, that one of the most forceful and eloquent exhortations he has ever heard in a pentecostal church was delivered, Bible in hand, by a woman at a congregation in Palermo. "The woman's inspired appeal," he writes, "went on for a full 15–20 minutes and evoked an emotional response from the congregation." But when he asked some of the people in the church if this had not been a fine sermon indeed, they quickly denied that what she had done was preaching. The woman, they said, had given her personal "testimony."

This is far from uncommon. Indeed in some pentecostal churches in Italy *only* women prophesy, and as anyone who has visited such churches anywhere in the world knows, the prophesying and the testimonies often far surpass the sermons in power and brilliance. It should also be remembered that for pentecostals, healing is also a gift, and in most places—Italy included—most of the healers are women. In short, within pentecostal congregations, women are learning to exercise important expressions of symbolic and personal power which they are generally denied elsewhere. If this sometimes worries the men in the congregations, they can take some comfort from the assurance—however thin—that the women are not really ministers but are merely exercising gifts.

But there is more fig leaf than fact in this rationalization. The reality is that in Italian pentecostal churches women are extending their authority well outside the kitchen and the living room into a public area which has heretofore been the men's exclusive domain. The once housebound sisters and daughters are getting a taste of power, and they are learning how to use it. It is hard to imagine that, once having learned these new skills and gained this new confidence, they will not also exercise them in other parts of the society. No matter how much Lampedusa's crafty prince bends, it seems unlikely that the change he so dreaded can be headed off much longer.

But the new confidence and novel skills women learn in Italian pentecostal congregations are not the main key to the change in gender status. That key appears in two other places, in the actual *experience* pentecostals have when they worship, and in the *religious worldview* that their worship exemplifies. Central to pentecostal worship is the experience of being possessed by the Spirit, receiving the Spirit's gifts, and breaking out of the constraints and limitations of everyday life. Worshippers ignore grammar and syntax. They shout and weep. They laugh and dance. In warm weather they perspire. To the uninformed observer, or to someone who listens to rumors about "what happens in those churches," this animated hand-clapping and rhythmic swaying might appear to be sexually lax.

Pentecostals are very sensitive to such gossip and are extraordinarily careful to prevent sexual hanky-panky under cover of prayer. But at a more profound level, pentecostal worship is, in fact "aberrant": it challenges the normal rules about how women should act in public, which is one of the things Sicilian men are honor-bound to guarantee. When women dance and testify at a gathering where anyone who wants to can come in, they violate the long-standing boundary between the private and the public sphere, a barrier that feminist scholars claim has always worked to disadvantage women. At a still deeper level, the seeming chaos that characterizes pentecostal worship services at times, what students of religion call "liminality," can easily be seen as posing a threat to the entire social order. Of course, sociologists claim that such periods of fluidity and formlessness can actually stabilize a society by providing an escape valve for accumulated tensions. But the curious spectator peeking in the open door of a Sicilian pentecostal church on a hot Sunday evening would have no knowledge of this esoteric theory. Besides, ecstasy is not always just an escape valve; so the scandalized onlookers who see pentecostalism as a threat to traditional sex roles ("witches and whores") and to the long-standing value system that undergirds those roles might just be on to something.

There is another and possibly even more fundamental threat that pentecostalism poses to the traditional male domination of Italy, and other parts of Europe, and indeed the world. It inheres in the pentecostal theology itself. There are, of course, theologians who take exception to the phrase "pentecostal theology" as a kind of oxymoron. But I disagree. By its "theology," I mean the symbolic cosmos of the pentecostal movement, which is articulated not through formal treatises but in the songs and prayers, the sermons and testimonies. This is where the most fundamental revolution is going on because what is being altered is nothing short of what might be called "the gender of God."

The process is a subtle one. There is no goddess worship. Pentecostals do not say prayers to the Virgin Mary. But, nonetheless, the qualities that pentecostals attribute to God, the Holy Spirit, and Jesus Christ combine to produce a radical repainting of the traditional Sicilian portrait of the deity. The result is nothing short of a different God, because those qualities include distinctively feminine ones. The distant, jealous, and judgmental God of some traditional Catholic theology gives way to a Jesus who longs to embrace sinners, to enter into their hearts in what Cucchiari aptly calls a "soteriological romance." God courts human beings and is broken-hearted when men and women resist his gentle advances. For pentecostals God is more lover than judge, "more concerned with human affection than with commanding obedience," and is sympathetic with "the murky emotions of the heart."

This change in how God is envisioned is crucial because, as feminist theologians frequently point out, the dominant male role in society is often anchored in images of the male deity. As Mary Daley once put it, "If God is father, then father is God." Obviously, any change in this archetypal symbol will eventually have an enormous impact on how male and female roles are understood in the society at large. Some sociologists contend that it works the other way around and that a "softer" picture of God reflects changes in male roles already going on. The truth is that the two processes probably influence each other. In any case, "God-the-lover," as eloquently advocated by such American feminist theologians as Sally McFague, may already be courting the hearts of unlettered men and women in Sicily and elsewhere, albeit unnoticed by theologians—whether men or women—because academic theologians have so far demonstrated little interest in the worldwide religious transformation that pentecostalism represents, even though it is going on under our noses.

Not only do pentecostals invoke God as wooer, they also often refer to God and even to Jesus Christ in songs and sermons with explicitly female imagery. To take only one example, Cucchiari records this brief extract from a pentecostal sermon delivered by a male preacher in Palermo:

> How marvelous that look of Christ's must have been. He was looking at the man, not with hostility, not with severity, but with a look full of grace. A look . . . like that of a mother at her child, a defenseless small child. She will never look at it with a severe or cruel look. She will look upon it with all her love.

This is a truly remarkable bit of sermonic theologizing, and for a number of reasons. First, it is not only God but Jesus Christ who is here depicted with feminine qualities. In the long run this could have a much more profound impact on gender roles and sexual stereotypes in Sicily—and elsewhere—than any recovery of goddess worship such as is advocated by some feminist theologians. The problem with goddess worship is that although it may strengthen the spiritual powers of some women and perhaps even of some men, it leaves the image of the remote and aloof patriarchal God undisturbed. Remember that when Betty Lou Carter testified about her healing and calling in West Virginia, Jesus had picked her up from her hospital bed "just like a mama or a daddy picks up a little baby." To endow Jesus and the Christian God with female qualities is at once far more radical and paradoxically more easily assimilable to the existing religious symbol system. Furthermore, this change is being introduced, in Sicily and elsewhere, not by academically trained women and not in elite groups, but by people at the bottom of the social ladder, frequently uneducated, who convey these fresh images through rite and ecstasy, an infinitely more powerful idiom.

The second noteworthy feature of this sermon extract (and many more examples could be given) is its deft use of the phrase "full of grace" to refer to Jesus. Every single person within earshot of these words, men and women alike, would have recognized instantly where the words "full of grace" come from. They are borrowed from the most common of all Catholic prayers, the "Hail Mary." Here, with remarkable boldness, the preacher is drawing a central symbol of the most widely venerated female saint (in fact, a near deity in popular piety), the Madonna, into the description of Jesus and thus of God. Most pentecostals already think of the Holy Spirit as a feminine figure, the consoler and the comforter. In gendered languages, like Italian, "Spirit" is almost always feminine. Here, in addition, the preacher also frontally challenges the traditional specialization of sex roles according to which God and Jesus are the judges and Mary is the soft-hearted intercessor.

This change in the "division of labor" within the heavenly family could also have a decided impact on the earthly one. The traditional divine model has always symbolically reinforced the structure of the average Italian family where the patient, warm-hearted, and long-suffering mother intercedes with the less accessible fathers and brothers—always aware that their "honor" is at stake—to soften their anger and mitigate their punishment. Now, however, if the Holy Spirit is female, and if God and Jesus exemplify both male and female qualities, not only is the divine family redefined, the earthly one is as well. The traditional anchor is gone, and a new model of family relations, one in which both parents share both male and female qualities, begins to take place.

By the time I was scheduled to leave Italy I was convinced that the religious resurgence was also gathering steam in Europe. I was also certain that—as everywhere else—it involved the recovery of a kind of primal spirituality. Knowing that pentecostals have a knack for mining and refining older religious practices, I suspected that the startling inversions of the "gender of God" I had witnessed in their churches had not been created ex nihilo. It must lie somewhere in the subsoil of European religious culture, but where?

Soon I was asking everyone I met in Italy this question, and since it was Italy, I got lots of different answers, all cheerfully delivered with complete assurance. But perhaps the one I heard most frequently came first from a professor of history at the University of Siena I had met at an ecumenical conference in Rome. An affable man in his forties, with absolutely no hair on his head and wearing glasses with the thickest lenses I had ever seen, he told me he was convinced that the pentecostals were in fact digging into something very old and very Italian. It was, he said, a lively undercurrent of religiosity which in recent centuries had been repressed and excluded by the official Catholic Church— the tradition of erotic mysticism. Without even the tiniest hint of embarrassment about boosting his hometown he told me that the best representative of this tradition was none other than Saint Catherine of Siena, who had lived from 1347 to 1380, so I had better come to that city to find out more about her, perhaps in the research center there devoted to the study of her life and its significance. So two days later, my previous plans scrapped, I found myself sitting on the veranda of the Santa Caterina hotel on the Via Piccomolini in Siena.

The city of Siena reposes like an intricate nest made of ocher and off-white leaves on the lovely hills of Tuscany, due south of Florence near the Chianti Hills which give their name to the most famous of all Italian wines. A fine Gothic cathedral, its facades faced with white, green, and red marble, stands on the highest point in the town, and a soaring Romanesque campanile continues even today to hold its centuries-long dialogue with the brick and travertine Palazzo Publico on the Piazza del Campo a few blocks away.

I had not come to Siena, however, to enjoy the architecture. I had a very specific question in mind. I wanted to look for clues to the nature of this primal spirituality, this buried religious wellspring that was now resurfacing and threatening to change something as basic to a culture as its way of envisioning God.

Consequently, on the table in front of me, propped between a cup of cappucino and a buttered croissant, stood a recently acquired copy of *La Vita de Santa Caterina da Siena*, the biography of the saint by her confessor Raimondo da Capua which my shiny-domed new friend had lent me.

After two hours of perusal I came upon the following passage, which I quote in a standard English translation. It comes in a paragraph in which Father Raimondo, who seems alternately shocked and overpowered by his saintly client, breathlessly describes one of his encounters with her. The moment I read it I knew I had found the traces of the primal spirituality I was looking for. Father Raimondo writes that one day when Catherine was lying in her bed, "burdened with many pains," she had called him, in secret, to come to her bedside. She wanted to talk with him about "certain things which the Lord had revealed to her." He entered her chamber and stood by her bed.

> She began, though feverish, to speak in her usual way of God and to tell of the things that had been revealed to her that day. But when I heard such great and unheard of things, I said in my heart . . . "Do you suppose that all the things she says are true?"

It is not hard to understand the confessor's hesitancy. Catherine spoke with unusual authority at a time when men held a near monopoly on religious power in the church. She had little reticence even about telling the pope what to do. But in a hierarchical church, Father Raimondo must have known that both he and his celebrated adept were skating perilously close to the edge of heresy. Catherine was reporting on revelations that had come *directly to her*. They had not been mediated by a priest. The flames of the *auto-da-fé* had crackled in recent years for people who made such claims. On June 1, 1310, for example, only a few decades earlier, a respected teacher named Marguerite Porete, the author of *A Mirror for Simple Souls*, had been burned as a heretic at the Place de Greve in Paris partly because she claimed to receive direct revelations from God. So Catherine's adviser was understandably nervous.

What happened next between Catherine and Father Raimondo is highly significant because it shows that when today's pentecostals, in Italy and elsewhere, transform the gender of God and of Jesus in their preaching and prayers they are delving into something much older and deeper. While he stood there in doubt, Father Raimondo records, he looked more closely at Catherine and "her face was changed in an instant into the face of a bearded man who, gazing at me with staring eyes, gave me a great fright." Who was this bearded man the confessor saw in the face of Catherine?

> The face was rather long, of middle age and had a beard that was not long, the color of wheat, and in appearance it displayed such majesty that it thereby revealed itself as the Savior.

Now nearly speechless with terror, Father Raimondo records that he raised his hands in consternation and cried out, "Who is this who is gazing at me?"

Catherine answered, "He who is." And with this, the face of Christ disappeared, and the confessor once again saw only that of Catherine.

It is hard not to conclude that in retrieving something like this fourteenth century mystical transformation of Jesus, the Italian pentecostal movement is exhibiting the same uncanny ability to reclaim powerful features of folk religious and mystical motifs it demonstrates elsewhere: healing practices in Colombia, the veneration of ancestors in Zimbabwe, shamanic visions in Korea. Here in Italy, and in many other places, they have uncovered a long repressed and forbidden expression of Christian piety. And once again, they have packaged it in a new and more accessible way, so that the current generation can sense its power.

In other writings of and about Saint Catherine, and other Italian women saints, an erotic component lurks just below the surface. The same Father Raimondo tells us, for example, that Catherine once reported to him that Jesus, the eternal bridegroom, had slipped into her chamber one dark night, opened the left side of her breast, and removed her heart. The vexed confessor says that when he heard this he at first tried to use humor to calm his charge down, reminding Catherine that she could not possibly live without a heart. But this was only the beginning. Some days later, he reports that she told him:

> When she arose upon waking from sleep . . . a light of heaven suddenly shone around her, and in that light the Lord appeared to her, bearing in his consecrated hands a reddish and shining human heart. . . . [Then] the Lord approached her, opened her left side once more, placed inside it the heart which he bore in his hands, and said, "See, beloved daughter, just as I took your heart from you the other day, so I am now giving you my heart, with which you will live from now on."

Historians of religion are familiar with these words of Saint Catherine, but one rarely finds them in popular devotional treatises. Still, if her words sound like a somewhat muted expression of erotic mysticism, those of her Italian sister of two centuries later, Maria Maddalena De'Pazzi were more explicit. She once wrote to her fellow nuns:

> my Jesus is nothing else but love, he is mad with love. I say you are mad with love, my Jesus, and I will always say it. You are altogether lovely and merry, you refresh and console, you nourish and unite, you are torment and relief, effort and rest, death and life.

I find it impossible to read this prayer and exhortation without thinking of the erotic imagery in the Hindu tradition, the passionate love of Krishna, the debonair prankster, for Rhada, the lovesick goatherd. But Sister Maria Maddalena's erotic mysticism goes even further. In the Hindu tradition, a favorite devotional practice is the clothing of the images of the gods. Maria went the other way. She became convinced that her plaster image of the child Jesus needed to be stripped, in part to divest him from worldly ornaments, but also to reveal him in his "naked humanity." In her own writings she went considerably beyond the biblical Song of Songs or even Hindu devotional language in her descriptions. Reporting on one vision she writes:

I saw that Jesus united with his bride in the closest union, laid his head upon the feet of his bride, his eyes on hers, his mouth, his hands, his feet, all his limbs on hers, so that the bride became one with him.

At times Maria Maddelena's mysticism took a near pantheistic turn, generating a vision that comes close to some Buddhist expressions. Thus, not only does God unite completely with the soul, God also "sees himself in all creatures, even those that have no sensation." Perhaps the late Catholic theologian Thomas Merton was right when he said that if the people who engaged in interfaith dialogue would pay more attention to the mystics in their traditions instead of to the theologians, a lot more common ground might be found.

I cannot resist the temptation to ask whether Sister Maria Maddalena, if she could rise from her resting place and return to modern Italy, might not find herself much more at home among the pentecostals than in the average convent. Admittedly, she might have to modulate her erotic imagery, but not very much. She could probably join easily in the fervor of a pentecostal service without causing much notice. According to one biographer, Maria's ardor was so intense, it "made her heart melt" and sometimes "bereft her of her senses." Normally a pale and sickly person, a condition caused in part by her persistent fasting, she nonetheless regained her full strength "when she was surprised by these flames of love." During these periods of intense gaity she would "move about in a wondrous manner" and could be seen "running swiftly from place to place . . . as if raving with love." As she ran she often prayed with a loud voice the single word, "Love, love, love." Finally, when she was exhausted by these exertions she would breathe heavily and pray, "O my Lord, no more love, no more love," and fall in happy exhaustion to the ground. I somehow doubt that pentecostals would be offended by this behavior, though I cannot imagine that it would be permitted in Catholic churches, even ones bearing the name of Mary Magdalene, to say nothing of the local Presbyterian or Baptist congregation.

As for Maria's references to Jesus the lover and Catherine's vivid language about exchanging her own heart with the heart of Jesus, most pentecostals would not find this at all unusual. How many times, I wonder, have I heard pentecostals (and even Baptists and Methodists for that matter) sing and testify about "giving my heart to Jesus," or "opening my heart to the Spirit," or "taking Jesus into my heart"? Not only are pentecostalism and the Christian mysticism of which it is a contemporary expression religions "of the heart" as opposed to religions of the intellect, they are also religions that make frequent use of the imagery of the heart.

We have already noted how, although attendance in the Catholic and Protestant churches in Europe has reached new lows in recent years, millions of Europeans are crowding into the old and new but unauthorized pilgrimage sites. Many of these sites are associated with apparitions of the Virgin, the Mother of God. Is it possible that these masses of restless moderns, dissatisfied with male-dominated, institutional piety, are on the track of something like the primal, more feminine spirituality of their own continent, the spirituality that, as Henry Adams once said, "built Chartres cathedral"? And is it possible that the pentecostal women of Italy are on the same track?

The day before I was scheduled to leave Siena, with questions like these still nibbling at me, I stopped into the cathedral to say goodbye. But three days of swimming in the "sea of joy . . . of delights, flowing, streaming down from the godhead," which is the way Marguerite Porete described the ecstasy of the mystical life (in words very close to those of psychologist-philosopher William James), had done something to me. As I stepped through the huge doors under the rose window into the cool interior and paused to let my eyes adjust I saw the old *duomo* in a different light. Suddenly its pavements, capellas, and sacristy seemed to be crawling with inspired and angry women. Somehow during my earlier visits I had stumbled along looking upward toward the stained glass and the ceiling with its gold stars on a blue background. Now, for some reason I glanced down underfoot.

There they were—all ten sibyls, the classical female prophetesses from pagan times, staring up from the mosaics on the paving tiles. One of the most prominent is the Cumaean Sibyl who is described by Virgil in the *Aeneid*. The poet reports that when she offered the head of the ruling family of Rome her prophetic writings, the famous Sibylline Books, he refused to pay the price she asked. Enraged beyond words, she lit a fire and began to burn the priceless volumes one by one as the ruler looked on in horror. Finally he gave in and paid her full price for the remaining three. For many years these precious tomes were kept in the Capitol by the Romans who consulted them in times of crisis. They were eventually destroyed when the Capitol was burned in 83 B.C. Now here were the sibyls, 2,000 years later, ensconced in the church of a Roman Catholic bishop, gazing up at the suntanned legs and plastic flip-flops of tourists from Hamburg and Stockholm, largely ignored but still decidedly present.

Then I saw Judith. Why had I not noticed her before in the mosaic just behind Nicolo Pisano's famous white marble pulpit? Her story has a harder edge than the Cumaean Sibyl's. In the account found in the apocryphal Old Testament book that bears her name, Judith lived at the time when an Assyrian commander named Holofernes was besieging the Jewish city of Bethulia. All seemed lost. But then Judith, a brave and beautiful widow, slipped into the Assyrian camp and seduced Holofernes. In the midst of their lovemaking she killed him and returned to the city carrying his head, severed by his own sword. The mosaic spares none of the pertinent details of this ill-fated assignation.

Of course the cathedral also has statues of Saint Catherine and Mary Magdalene, reliefs of the life of the Virgin, and a fresco of the canonization of Catherine, all properly decorous. But somehow, as I emerged into the bright sunlight of the Piazza de Duomo I could not get Judith or the Cumaean Sibyl out of my mind. Here was primal spirituality with a vengeance. For millennia, men have been cowed and disconcerted by the power and sexuality of women: let them into the tent and they will chop off your head. They have also been unwilling to accept the wisdom that women offer. Only as the smoke curls up and pages crinkle do they realize they may be losing insights they cannot live without. So women like Judith are banished to apocryphal books of the Bible and the sibyls are consigned to the pavement. Nowadays their detractors call them witches and whores.

But they will not go away. Despite centuries of effort, in neither Judaism nor Christianity has the male leadership ever succeeded in extirpating or excluding the influence of suspect women. Even King Saul once crept out by night to a place called Endor to consult a witch he had banned from the realm. And Jesus once told some pharisees, to their considerable surprise, that the prostitutes would undoubtedly precede them into the Kingdom of God. Maybe in our time, at last, in a movement that allows the Spirit to emerge from the submerged underside, these long silenced and disparaged voices are beginning to have their say. In any case, as my flight took off from Rome, and I gazed at the dim outline of the dome of St. Peter's on the horizon, I was certain that the resurgence of primal spirituality had not bypassed Europe after all.

CHAPTER 11

Shamans and Entrepreneurs: Primal Spirituality on the Asian Rim

*I know a Christian man who fourteen
years ago (whether in the body or out
of the body I do not know—God knows)
was . . . caught up into paradise, and heard
words so secret that human lips cannot
repeat them.*

Paul, 2 Corinthians 12:2–4

LATE ON THE AFTERNOON of February 8, 1991 the house
lights in the Royal Theatre of Canberra, Australia, dimmed
dramatically, and a petite Korean woman named Hyun Kyung
Chung entered from the rear of the hall. She was accompanied
by nineteen Korean dancers with bells, candles, drums, gongs,
and clap sticks. As a vast crowd of nearly 4,000 people craned to
watch, the retinue advanced toward the stage led by two
Australian Aboriginal dancers dressed only in loincloths and body
paint. Both were playing a traditional wind instrument known as
the didgeridoo. When they had all reached the stage, Chung and
her companions stepped through a synchronized pattern which
combined Aboriginal movement with traditional Korean folk
dance.

If this had been a traveling Asian folklore troupe the scene might not have been noteworthy. But the audience was not the usual matinee crowd. It consisted of Anglican priests, Lutheran bishops, Baptist and Methodist lay leaders, Presbyterian ministers, journalists, and theologians from 100 different countries who had gathered in Canberra for the Seventh General Assembly of the World Council of Churches. And the dancer was not an international entertainment celebrity, but a professor of Christian Studies at the Ewha Women's University in Seoul, Korea. Dr. Chung had been invited to give one of the two keynote addresses at this, the opening session of the gathering. The topic she had been asked to address was the overall theme of the assembly: "Come Holy Spirit, Renew Thy Whole Creation." The other keynote, scheduled just before Dr. Chung's, was entrusted to a venerable Eastern Orthodox theologian, His Beatitude Parthenios III, Patriarch of Alexandria and All Africa. In inviting both a Korean women and an Orthodox patriarch to address the assembly's theme at the same session, the planners were no doubt making an important symbolic gesture. They were publicly signaling the importance of women, third world churches, and Christians from the long-repressed Orthodox realm in the ecumenical movement. They were also acknowledging that both the Eastern Orthodox tradition and the lively new nonwestern churches focus more attention on the Holy Spirit than most western churches, either Catholic or Protestant, do.

What the leaders did not anticipate was that Dr. Chung's keynote would come to overshadow almost everything else that took place at the assembly and would stir up a dispute within the council's membership that eventually came perilously close to splitting it apart. Both the address itself and the controversy it sparked constitute a kind of epiphany. Taken together, they reveal much, both about the rapid spread of the Spirit-oriented forms of Christianity in Asia, and about the unsettling feeling this expansion stirs up in many people, including Christians.

The World Council was founded just after World War II as a largely pan-Protestant network, but by the time of the Canberra meeting the council included the major Eastern Orthodox churches based in Russia, Romania, and Greece. It also included many of the so-called new churches of Africa and Asia. Since only two of the many hundreds of pentecostal denominations in the world belong to the World Council of Churches, this movement was dramatically underrepresented. But, even though pentecostals had not selected the theme of the meeting, it was one that was obviously influenced by their burgeoning presence in the world. "Come Holy Spirit, Renew Thy Whole Creation" is a topic dear to their hearts.

In fact, as the weary delegates climbed off their planes after the long flight there was every indication that some acknowledgment of the reemergence of suppressed and neglected spiritualities, and some recognition of the growing strength of the pentecostal wave would have to be part of the assembly's agenda. A self-conscious openness to indigenous practices has become a hallmark of the new generation of Asian Christians who had come to Canberra. But just *how much* these issues would dominate the meeting was probably not foreseen by the leaders of the World Council when they invited the slight, soft-spoken Korean woman to deliver the second keynote. The World Council has never been quite the same since.

Hyun Kyung Chung is one of an emerging group of theologians from the fast-growth area of Christianity who like to refer to themselves as the "second generation." They are the young scholars and intellectuals from areas such as Asia, Africa, and Latin America which were once looked upon as "mission fields" but now contain the majority of the world's Christian population. The term "second generation" cannot be taken literally, of course, since various forms of Christianity have been present in some of these areas for centuries. But these theologians have gone beyond either slavishly embracing or mechanically rejecting the versions of the faith the missionaries brought to them. Instead they are crafting theologies and liturgies that draw on their own indigenous cultures. A prominent European Roman Catholic thinker once remarked that Catholicism would never be securely grounded in Africa "until the Mass is drummed and danced." An equivalent observation could be made about Christianity in other parts of the nonwestern world. Dr. Chung and her colleagues in the "second

generation" are—quite literally—the drummers and dancers of this
new theology, as the thousands of delegates gathered in Canberra
were soon to find out.

The established rubric for keynote speeches in such assemblies as the Canberra meeting is clear . . . a straightforward address
usually read from a prepared text. The contribution of the
Orthodox theologian was read by another representative since
the patriarch was unable to attend. Though Parthenios is himself
a lively and engaging person, the fact that his scholarly address
had to be delivered by someone else gave it a more than usually
stodgy and arid character. His Beatitude argued that the kind of
unity Christians seek already exists in the Holy Trinity, but needs
to be made visible, and this was the task of the Seventh General
Assembly. People applauded politely. But when the house lights
went down and Dr. Chung with her troupe filed to the podium
something new in the annals of World Council of Churches presentations took place.

True to her "second generation" vision, Chung not only spoke
about the importance of the Spirit in a faith which, while claiming to honor the Trinity, has lavished nearly all its attention on
God and Jesus Christ, she also provided a living demonstration of
what she was talking about. When the dance procession had
reached the stage, Chung stepped to the microphone and invited
all those present in the audience to take off their shoes. She
explained that this followed the custom of many Asian and
Aboriginal peoples and was meant to honor the holy ground on
which they were meeting. She also reminded them that God had
asked Moses to remove his shoes at the burning bush. The gesture, she said, would help everyone to assume an attitude of
humility before the Spirit of God.

As she began her talk, Chung invoked "the spirits of the
women, children and men killed by oppression." She specifically
mentioned the victims of the Gulf War which had just broken out
when the meeting started. She also invoked the spirits of the rain-
forest, the earth, the air, the water, all the sea creatures and—
finally—"the spirit of the Liberator, Jesus Christ." Next she set fire
to long strips of rice paper on which she had written the names

of the spirits she had summoned. Then, with considerable panache and dignity she held the flaming papers high in her hands until they disappeared in smoke.

When she addressed the audience directly Chung explained that in Korean folk tradition, *han* spirits are the wandering souls of those who are filled with anger, bitterness, and resentment because they were killed or died unjustly or for many other reasons. It is because of these *han* spirits, she said, that "we can feel, touch and taste the concrete, bodily historical presence of the Holy Spirit in our midst." Turning to the theme-prayer of the assembly, "Come Holy Spirit, Renew Thy Whole Creation," she insisted that it should not be used as an excuse for passivity, merely waiting for the Spirit. Rather it required active solidarity with all forms of life. "I no longer believe in an omnipotent God," she declared. "I rely on the compassionate God who weeps with us in the midst of the cruel destruction of life." She ended her address by describing her personal image of the Holy Spirit. The Spirit, she said, is like a bodhisatva, an enlightened being, a goddess of compassion and wisdom. Indeed the Holy Spirit "might also be a feminine image of the Christ . . . who goes before and brings others with her." She closed with a ringing appeal which, though delivered in a very different tone from that of Parthenios, actually echoed the same sentiment: "Let us tear down the walls of division which separate us." When the verbal part of her address ended, she concluded the session with a dance meant to dramatize the recent coming to awareness of Korean women and to contrast with the overly verbal idiom of many western liturgies.

The presentation was greeted, as one delegate later observed, with both "thunderous applause and thunderous silence." Some hailed it as a long-needed step toward the recognition of an authentically Asian Christianity. They called it electrifying, powerful, evocative, haunting. Others termed it pantheistic and outrageous and dismissed it as syncretism of the worst order, the abject surrender of Christianity to a pagan environment. Some thought Dr. Chung's performance was merely an example of youthful excess, understandable if not wholly excusable. After all she was only a woman. Several of the Eastern Orthodox delegates, who had for a long time nursed other complaints about the World Council, threatened to withdraw their churches from the organization completely. Their millennia-old devotion to the Holy Spirit plainly did not encompass the invoking of the spirits of the land.

For the next days the thousands of delegates and visitors sang and prayed and discussed the other papers and reports. But what continued to buzz at the coffee breaks and dinner conversations were the questions Dr. Chung's keynote had raised about the future direction not only of the World Council of Churches but of Christianity itself. In fact what had happened at Canberra was the dramatic eruption of the primal spirituality that we have charted in several other areas. Only this time the geyser of underground energy spouted before the very eyes of the stolid old World Council of Churches itself.

Spirit and fire, cleansing rituals, shamanic invocations, Aboriginal blessings, all under the auspices of the oft-neglected third person of the Christian Trinity: what Hyun Kyung Chung did might have seemed unfamiliar, even menacing, to many of the delegates at the World Council of Churches. But those familiar with the varieties of pentecostalism would recognize this cluster of elements immediately. That is why Dr. Chung's keynote performance and the anxious response it generated can rightly be referred to as an epiphany. Her performance and the reaction to it point beyond Christianity itself. They reveal something both about the other fast growing religious movements in this decidedly post-death-of-God era and also about the unease their appearance evokes. Finally, the fact that this event happened under the direction of a Korean, whose homeland is itself a paradigm of many of the economic, cultural, and religious changes that are occurring in the nonwestern world today, is highly significant.

Hyun Kyung Chung is not a member of a pentecostal church. But that makes the controversy surrounding her keynote address even more significant because it demonstrates that the energies pentecostalism draws upon transcend its own borders. My worldwide exploration of the expansion of pentecostal types of Christianity has convinced me that for any religion to grow in today's world, it must possess two capabilities: it must be able to include and transform at least certain elements of preexisting religions which still retain a strong grip on the cultural subconscious. It must also equip people to live in rapidly changing societies where personal responsibility and inventiveness, skills associated with a democratic polity and an entrepreneurial economy, are indispensable.

Both of these key ingredients are present in Korean pentecostalism, which helps explain its dramatic success. Despite its own protestations to the contrary, pentecostalism in Korea seems able to incorporate many of the characteristics of shamanism and also to prepare people remarkably well for modern political and economic survival. South Korea is a kind of litmus test. Its religious culture—Buddhism and Confucianism overlaying folk shamanism—is similar to many other Asian countries. Its emerging democratic polity and guided market economy are also similar. Consequently, if we can understand the pentecostal phenomenon in Korea, we may get some important hints about its prospects in China and the rest of Asia, and possibly its global prospects as well. Let us ask first about the issue which—depending on one's point of view—can be labeled either negatively as the "syncretism" question, or positively as the power of the Spirit to transform preexistent faiths.

There may be no better way to grasp the astonishing scope and baffling complexity of Korean pentecostalism than by paying a visit to the Yoido Full Gospel (Pentecostal) Church in Seoul, South Korea. This church, whose pastor, the Reverend David Yonggi Cho has become something of a religious celebrity in Korea, is only a few decades old but has already become the largest single Christian congregation on earth. Such megachurches are not unusual in Korea. On the list of the "top ten" largest churches in the world, three are in Seoul and one is in Inchon.

The Yoido Full Gospel Church is also located in what is a prototypical area for such pell-mell expansion: a pullulating megacity in a rapidly changing third world country. Clearly, in order to appeal to so many people, this church and the wider movement it represents must have satisfied, at least in some measure, the two basic conditions I have just mentioned. First, it must help people hold on to at least some elements of the traditional culture and religion that seem to be falling to pieces before their eyes. In South Korea, as in the rest of Asia, this is a particularly challenging condition for pentecostalism since the culture's historic religious traditions are not Christian. And second, Korean pentecostalism must also help people cope with both the rampant urbanization and the wrenching demands of new economic and political realities, which have completely transformed the once-isolated peninsula known as the Hermit Kingdom. Korea has left its sequestered past far behind and has become one of the most energetic of the newly industrializing east Asian countries. But the pace of change in Korea has taken a toll. Its prodigious economic derring-do and its constant political uncertainties perch uneasily on an underlying cultural edifice that is heaving and straining as people try to embrace modernity while still clinging to whatever bits of tradition they can salvage. Religion is the arena within which much of this wrestling match between old values and new life-style is fought. And pentecostal Christianity is both the principal vehicle and the main battleground of this confrontation.

Protestant Christianity in Korea is only about 100 years old. At the end of World War II, Christians still accounted for only about 8 percent of the populace. But by 1994 the churches had recruited over one-third of the population of South Korea. If current trends continue it will become the majority faith by the year 2000. In Korea Christianity is anything *but* otherworldly. After the Korean War ended in 1951, South Korean churches inspired a courageous opposition to the authoritarian regimes of Syngman Rhee and Chung Hee Park, during which many Christian pastors and students were beaten and jailed. Korean Christians invented their own form of "liberation theology" called "minjung theology," using the Korean term for the ordinary, nonelite people among whom Christianity first spread. More recently, Christianity in South Korea has helped ignite an Asian Rim version of the Protestant ethic, a zest for hard work that has fueled the country's dazzling entrepreneurial take-off and made it one of the most formidable of the so-called seven dragons.

It is true that statistically at least South Korea is quickly becoming a Christian nation. But, as in many third world countries, the traditional western denominational labels mean very little (what does it mean, for example, to be a South Korean Dutch Reformed?). Besides, it is the pentecostals, not the Catholics or the Presbyterians, who are bringing in the most converts. Therefore, to understand the phenomenal growth of Christianity in Korea (and elsewhere on the Asian Rim) we must put to the pentecostal movement the two questions we asked earlier. Does it amalgamate previous, pre-Christian religious practices, which in Korea are a mixture of shamanism, Buddhism, and Confucianism? And how does it assist in providing the essential *Geist* that lubricates the country's rough-and-tumble market economy.

The best way to answer the first question may be to look at the example of the Yoido Full Gospel (Pentecostal) Church. As we have noted, the Yoido congregation is a megachurch. Its 800,000 membership makes it the largest congregation in the world. With an initial membership of 5 in 1958, its rapid growth is a parable of pentecostal expansion both in Asia and in similar areas elsewhere. In some ways its story reminds me of one of those time-lapse films that chart the blooming of a rose from bud to petals, except that this sudden spurt of increase took place in real time. It compresses into a few decades the whole pentecostal story.

There are many ways to try to explain the eruption of Christianity and pentecostalism in South Korea. Many of these explanations credit the painful aftermath of the Korean War and the rapid economic and social changes that have taken place since then, including the extraordinary concentration of more and more people in the cities of South Korea, especially Seoul itself. But there are other factors as well. The sprouting of giant cities is a common factor in the spread of pentecostalism elsewhere in the world, but there are several factors peculiar to Korea, or at least east Asia. Some characteristics of Korean pentecostalism in particular are deeply embarrassing and upsetting to western pentecostals.

Few pentecostals anywhere in the world would be uncomfortable with the fact that a principal reason for the Yoido church's growth is its reputation as a center for spiritual healing. Healing, after all, is an integral part of the pentecostal message everywhere. But what disquiets them is that one of the key reasons for Korean pentecostalism's extraordinary growth is its unerring ability to absorb huge chunks of indigenous Korean shamanism and demon possession into its worship. This capacity for absorption, as we have seen, is not unusual for pentecostalism. In fact it is surely one of the primary reasons for its spread. What troubles pentecostals elsewhere about the Korean case is that the *degree* of importation is so extensive that some wonder out loud what has absorbed what. Is this a particularly successful, non-Catholic example of "drumming the mass," of the so-called indigenization of Christianity in an Asian culture? Or is it merely the continuation of the most salient forms of previous Korean folk religion wearing a Christian mask? The debate goes on, and the Yoido Full Gospel Church is an especially vivid case in point.

In 1963, within five years of its founding, the church had 2,000 members. Each became a dedicated messenger and recruiter, bringing others into the ever enlarging fold. By 1971 there were 15,000 members; by 1981 there were 200,000. The congregation now lists over 800,000, most of whom take part in small face-to-face prayer and study groups in addition to the plenary gatherings in the church's massive temple. The Yoido Full Gospel Church is still growing and its enthusiastic members insist they will top a million by the year 2000. They probably will. This church's story is singular but not unique. While it was growing, pentecostalism was expanding all over South Korea. A reliable recent estimate says there are now more than 5,000 Christian church buildings in Seoul alone. That number, as Koreans wryly remark, even exceeds the count of coffee shops and drugstores. Not all of those churches bear the pentecostal label, of course, but pentecostal congregations, and others with similar modes of worship, are multiplying faster than all the others put together.

As one steps out of the street and into the Yoido Full Gospel Church, even the most practiced observer of pentecostal worship elsewhere is in for a shock. Take what is called "Hallelujah-robics" for example. It is a form of dancing to hymns played to an ear-piercing rock beat by an ensemble of electric organ, drums, accordion, and other instruments. The dancing is led by enthusiastic teams from the church's youth division. When the music stops temporarily the congregation takes up what sounds like the religious equivalent of the cheers used at an Ohio State football game. At full volume they shout "Aboji Hananim" (Our Father, who art in Heaven) and then with hands raised many begin praying in words and phrases of no known language. Then more singing begins, with the songs arranged to the tune of pop melodies. The worshippers rock back and forth and wave their arms. Sometimes the band increases the tempo of the song, the way the Israeli tune "Havah Nagila" is often rendered, and the people move faster and faster until, no longer able to keep it up, they stop in happy exhaustion.

While the shouting and singing goes on, the ministers walk through the congregation sometimes striking the palms of their hands against someone's head or back. The gesture is strongly reminiscent of the practice in some Zen Buddhist monasteries where one of the monks walks up and down among the seated meditators and, to stave off dozing, strikes this or that one on the shoulder with a bamboo rod. Finally, when the singing, shouting, and dancing are over the minister begins leading a prayer which sounds more like an incantation than an invocation. He repeats over and over again, sometimes a hundred times or more, such phrases as "Hallelujah!" or "O Lord!" or "the Spirit fills!" while the congregation joins him. During these incantatory prayers, many of the women and a few of the men begin to weep and cry and flail their arms. Meanwhile, the ministers keep assuring everyone that, whatever their illnesses or infirmities might be, they will certainly be healed.

When the minister returns to the podium people file by to receive both the "laying on of hands" from the ministers and possibly another clap on some part of the back or shoulders. Often a minister will address the "demons of ill health" directly with commands like "Get out!" or the Korean equivalent of "Scat, shoo!" As the service ends, the people who believe they have been healed shout out short prayers of gratitude and stream out of the church, leaving behind those who are still caught up in the fervor and continue to sway and pray until evening comes, the lights are extinguished, and the building is closed. Now everyone leaves. But those who have clearly not been healed do not appear discouraged. They will be back another day.

To a visitor schooled in comparative religion, the worship at the Yoido Full Gospel Church bears a striking resemblance to what is ordinarily known as "shamanism," but when one points this out to Korean pentecostal ministers they firmly deny that there is any similarity. They open well-thumbed Bibles to the passage in 2 Corinthians in which Paul describes his ecstatic experience of being "caught up into the third heaven," and of hearing "words so secret that human lips can not repeat them." If the Apostle himself could have such visions in a trancelike state, they argue, why shouldn't we? They also point out that the New Testament is full of demon possession and exorcisms. They recall the Garasene demoniac and the description of Mary Magdalene as one from whom Jesus expelled seven demons.

It is hard to refute these biblical arguments. But something sounds out of focus, and as their explanations continue, the Koreans do not always reassure their western brethren that they are operating within the usual parameters of pentecostal practice. The sources of these illnesses, some pastors explain, are dead relatives and ancestors who never accepted Christ and are therefore angry and troubled. They return to afflict the living, so they have to be sent packing. Hence the commands to "get out, shoo!"

The underlying issue is not unfamiliar to students of the history of religion. The living are frequently anxious about the condition of the dead. The Catholic Church, over many centuries, evolved the doctrine of Purgatory to respond to precisely this anxiety. Praying for the souls in Purgatory enables those who are still in this world to assuage their own worries and to do something they believe will help those who have already passed on to the next. But making the departed ones the agents of disease represents a twist on this theology that is virtually unknown among Christian in the west. It sounds much more like the familiar pattern of demon possession, still found in many places in the world, but here the demons turn out to be one's departed kinfolk.

A day spent at the Yoido Full Gospel Church, or at any of several thousand Korean pentecostal churches, provides a vivid demonstration of a religion that can swallow and metabolize seemingly indigestible elements in the local folk religion. Ecstatic trances, demon possession, exorcism: all seem to find their place in the worship of "Hananim," the name Korean Christians call God, which is, however, also the same name borne for centuries by the high God of the pre-Christian folk rituals. The delicate question of which divinity is absorbing which is not always clear. Is Hananim displacing the God of the Bible? Or is Hananim just the name Korean pentecostals apply to that God? What is clear is that Korean pentecostalism has become a powerful vehicle within which hundreds of thousands of people who might be embarrassed to engage in the "old-fashioned" or possibly "superstitious" practice of shamanic exorcism can now do it within the generous ambience of a certifiably up-to-date religion, one that came from the most up-to-date of all countries, the United States of America. But after this is said one must still ask the question that was on the minds of many of those at the World Council of Churches Assembly: is shamanism compatible with Christianity? Can there be such a thing as "pentecostal shamanism"?

The word "shaman," which has become so dear to anthropologists and other students of religion over the years, is taken directly from a Tungus word used by the indigenous people of Siberia. But it refers to a religious reality that is so basic and so universal its equivalent has been found almost everywhere. Put quite simply, a "shaman" is one whose power comes directly from the supernatural world rather than through the medium of a traditional ritual or body of esoteric knowledge. For this reason, the shaman is often seen as the polar opposite of the priest, and there is some validity in this distinction. Further, the shaman ordinarily performs his or her ceremony not on stated occasions or in accord with a sacred calendar but when the need, say an illness or a drought, arises and must be dealt with. Most shamans accomplish their task while in a special, trancelike state which they are often able to induce themselves with music, chanting, drumming, or incantation. The important thing about shamans is that they exist in order to bring spiritual power to bear on human pain. For this reason, whatever denominational or agnostic nametag one may wear, there is a probably a shaman lurking inside every human being.

In my opinion, what one finds in the Yoido Full Gospel Church of Seoul involves a massive importation of shamanic practice into a Christian ritual. Many pentecostals deny this. They claim that despite superficial similarities with shamanism, something very different is going on. One Korean pastor pointed out to me that in Paul's description of his experience of hearing words so secret "no human lips could repeat them," the Apostle says that he did not know whether he was "in the body or apart from it." What did they need shamanism for, he asked me, if it was all in the New Testament? He had a point. In fact, recent biblical scholarship has suggested that Paul may have been much more of a mystic, more steeped in the Jewish "hekhalot" literature with its descriptions of celestial journeys, than more conservative interpreters of the apostle like to admit.

I am attracted to this recent understanding of Paul, who appears now to have been something of a shaman himself. It also strengthens my conviction that the primal spirituality now surfacing in Korea (and elsewhere) under pentecostal inspiration also underlies the original biblical faith as well. But many pentecostals, especially American ones, take a different tack. They are reluctant to admit that pentecostalism could ever include pre-Christian or non-Christian religious practices. Consequently, when they acknowledge the shamanic importation in Korean pentecostalism, they suggest that its presence casts real doubt on how Christian the Yoido church really is. This is a debate that the pentecostals will eventually have to settle for themselves.

What is even more important, in my opinion, is that shamanism is the popular, folk religion of vast tracts of the Asian continent; and if pentecostalism can combine with it as it has in Korea, the prospect for pentecostalism throughout Asia is breathtaking. As Tongshik Ryu of Yonsei University in Seoul has observed,

"Shamanism is a common element in the religious beliefs of other Asian peoples, a point of unity amidst the rich diversity of our various cultures." If this is correct, and I believe it is, then in principle there is no reason why pentecostalism could not eventually become a major force in all of southeast Asia, in China, and in Mongolia and Siberia. There are already reports of pentecostal revivals going on in parts of China, despite the opposition of the government. Admittedly, in many of these countries other so-called higher religions such as Buddhism and Confucianism, even Islam, have established themselves on turf once dominated completely by shamanism. But shamanism never really dies. It is just too deeply lodged in the inner recesses of the human psyche, and it frequently survives by wrapping itself in the ceremonies of other traditions. The result is that certain rituals that appear on the surface to be Buddhist or Shinto are essentially shamanistic in content.

Whether there is anything really wrong with what might be called "Christian shamanism" is a question that goes to the heart of the debate that followed Professor Chung's keynote address. The Greek Cypriote scholar Kyriacos C. Markides has argued eloquently in his book *Fire in the Heart*, subtitled "Healers, Sages and Mystics," that what we think of as shamanism is an inherent part of the Christian mystical tradition. From a different angle, Roger N. Walsh, M.D., who teaches psychiatry and philosophy at the University of California at Irvine, suggests that modern western medicine and psychiatry have a great deal to learn from shamanism. "The more we explore shamanism," he says, "the more it points to unrecognized aspects of and potentials of the human body, mind and spirit. For untold thousands of years the spirit of shamanism has helped, healed and taught humankind, and it may have still more to offer us." With both students of Christian mysticism and psychiatrists taking a renewed interest in shamanism, it might well be that Korean pentecostalism is drawing on something much larger than either its defenders or its critics quite grasp.

Setting aside for the moment whether the people who participate in shamanic healing services are "really" healed, there are obviously certain elements of shamanism that cohere rather well with Christianity. Shamanism is based on the premise that neither human beings nor nature itself hold the ultimate power in the universe. The ultimate power is a divine one. Further, it holds that the divine power can be brought to bear positively on earthly sorrow and pain, and that human beings need not be inert recipients of fate but can take measures that will improve their situation. Shamanism is not, like some of the so-called higher religions, fatalistic. It does not encourage resignation. It is, in this respect, more commensurate with certain strains of Christianity than with at least some of the dominant religious traditions of Asia.

From the perspective of some of the current liberation theologies there are positive elements in shamanism. First, it is obviously the preferred religion of the poor and the outcast, the less privileged people of the society. These are the "multitudes" Jesus appealed to. He seemed to know that the people on the bottom are often alienated not only from the economic and political institutions of their times but from the religious ones as well. This is particularly true in east Asia where the religions we study in textbooks such as Buddhism and Confucianism were often the spiritual property of the elite classes, while the masses clung to shamanic practices, though they might deck them out for safety's sake in some of the trappings of the elite faith.

My own observations lead me to believe that the question of whether there can be a Christian shamanism is still open. How it is answered may determine the future of Christianity in East Asia. Pentecostalism in Korea, and elsewhere, while tapping into a very ancient spiritual cosmology finds itself, paradoxically, on the leading edge of both Christian theological reflection and western medical research. In so doing it is evidently fulfilling the first condition for the success of a new religious movement: it is helping people recover vital elements in their culture that are threatened by modernization. But now we must turn to the second condition and ask, does pentecostalism prepare people for the economic and social dislocations of their homeland, especially for a postindustrial, information society?

It was the great German sociologist Max Weber who, in the first decades of this century, systematically probed the question of the relationship between religion and economic life. He saw connections where no one else ever had. His famous thesis about the integral connection between the Protestant ethic and the spirit (*Geist*) of capitalism, though assailed by critics for nearly a century, still offers the most plausible explanation of why modern capitalism first arose in those areas where some variety of the Reformation faith, especially in its Puritan form, held sway. Weber came to believe that the Calvinist doctrine of predestination, which stated that human beings could do absolutely nothing to gain their salvation, released an enormous amount of energy for disciplined activity in this world. The priest could not help. The sacraments were to no avail. Christ had died only for those whom God had previously elected for salvation before the foundation of the world. As for people who still harbored doubts about their eternal destiny, the only thing left for them to do, according to Calvin, was to drive away doubts about their own salvation by faithful and ceaseless work in an honorable worldly calling. Theologians have called this "mundane asceticism," and according to Weber's shrewd observation, the habit of hard work continued long after the supporting theology had faded. In a haunting passage that has now become famous, Weber wrote,

> The Puritan wanted to work in a calling; we are forced to do so. When asceticism was carried out of monastic cells into everyday life, and began to dominate worldly morality, it did its part in building the tremendous cosmos of the modern economic order.

But that was not the end of the story. Capitalism, the unintended stepchild of the Protestant ethic, soon outstripped its birth circumstances and, drawing on—so to speak—the spiritual capital of a previous religious generation, it in effect disowned its parents. Weber did not seem happy with this upshot. He feared that the end result of the obsession for rational management that capitalism required would be an airless "iron cage" that would suffocate the human spirit. People now seemed to work with no larger purpose in mind. Wistfully, Weber wrote what is probably his most widely quoted sentence. The faith itself had faded, he lamented, but "the idea of duty in one's calling prowls about in our lives like the ghost of dead religious beliefs."

South Korea poses an intriguing test case for Weber's thesis. It is hard to imagine a country where people work more assiduously, where diligence has been elevated to a national virtue. It is also true that the spectacular spurt in South Korea's economic growth occurred at exactly the same time Christianity began to spread so quickly. The question of whether there is any connection between the two naturally comes to mind, and there is a strong temptation to see some link between them.

The problem of course is that the *kind* of Christianity that flourishes so remarkably in Korea is of a radically different variety from the kind Weber studied. In fact the two strains—puritanism and pentecostalism—seem in some way to be nearly polar opposites. The puritan sits quietly in church on a rude bench, hands folded, listening to long disquisitions from an elevated pulpit delivered by a minister who is expected to have studied Greek and Hebrew. The only time he shifts position is to stand and croak out a sober psalm or to shift his weight on the hard pew when his extremities fall asleep. The pentecostal prances, jumps, sings at the top of his lungs, waves his arms and interrupts the procedures with shouts and ecstatic prayers. While the puritan may be accumulating a backlog of energy that needs to be redirected into worldly activity, the pentecostal may leave the church exhausted.

At the doctrinal level there are also important differences. For Weber's puritan, any effort to implore or in any way influence God's eternal and implacable decree smacked of irreverence if not of blasphemy. God was the sole and unique author of salvation. Not only could human beings not contribute one iota to their redemption, even the thought of trying counted as an affront to God's power and wisdom. The ancestry of pentecostalism—on the other hand—traces back to mystical, Wesleyan, and Holiness roots. These are all faiths in which some genuine effort to reach out to God on the part of the believer is expected. It is true that God alone saves, but earnest seeking, fasting, arduous prayer, holy living all prepare the soul for grace. It is God who reaches down, but human beings are expected to reach up. In short, pentecostals expend not only a lot of physical and emotional energy, but also a considerable quantity of spiritual capital in their religious life itself. There would not appear to be very much of a balance left for worldly disbursement. So is there really any connection between the soaring numbers of Korean pentecostalism and the Korean economic miracle?

When I put this question to Korean ministers, businessmen, economists, and theologians, most at first seemed hard put to grasp what my inquiry meant. Some thought I might be making things too complicated. Most of the economists thought there was no connection between religion and the economy. Koreans just worked hard and saved their money and were very smart. It was as simple as that. When I asked ministers, most seemed to think that if there was any connection it was a very straightforward one: if people turn to God, God blesses them. Korean prosperity was not the result of some obscure junction between a particular theology and a productive set of work habits. It was just the Almighty's way of demonstrating that He was reasonably pleased with how hard South Korean Christians were striving to win every last person from the East China Sea to the 38th parallel into the fold. Some also attributed it to the Korean Christian practice of tithing, giving one tenth of one's income to the church. "Tithe, and the Lord will bless you," they reminded me cheerily.

I was not completely satisfied with these responses. It seemed to me hardly credible that the two such profound transformations in the life of a very old nation, in its economic and religious life, were not related in some way other than the probably quite salutory benefits of contributing a tenth of the "first fruits of the harvest," the weekly paycheck, to the Lord. After considerable frustration I discovered that the clue lay right before my eyes, in the same place that had provided such a spectacular example of the fusion of Christianity and folk shamanism. It lay in the Yoido Full Gospel Church and the hundreds of Korean pentecostal churches and denominations it so graphically exemplifies. This time, however, the clue was to be found not in the worship but in the absolutely dazzling organizational genius these churches demonstrate.

When you ask Korean pentecostals why their faith has spread with such extraordinary rapidity in the old Hermit Kingdom, they of course attribute the growth to the Holy Spirit. But after the Paracelete has been given due credit for the increase, they start to talk about organization. And, if anything, their level of enthusiasm appeared to me to accelerate when they did. One of the biggest growth spurts in Korean pentecostalism happened in the early 1980s as a result of a nationwide evangelistic campaign called "Here's Life, Korea." The crusade bore all the marks of a massive sales campaign, but its complexity and comprehensiveness would make the national sales executives for color TV sets or compact discs break the commandment against covetousness. The basic unit of the campaign was the local church, but committees for prayer, public relations, visitation, and support were also formed along professional and occupational lines. Committees of college students, school teachers, office workers, lawyers, factory workers, high school students, and so forth were pulled together. They were expected to engage in all-night prayer vigils, Bible study, regional training conferences, and—of course—daily testifying to their neighbors, colleagues, and coworkers about the joy of the Christian life and the gifts of the Spirit. Every single church member was asked to carry a card with the name of a person on it whom they would pray for daily, petitioning God that the person, always someone in their own workplace or neighborhood, would accept Christ during the campaign. This prayer strategy had, of course, an implicit goal: if it succeeded, there would be twice as many pentecostals in Korea at the end of the undertaking as there were before it started.

The flow chart was impressive. Everyone was counting on the Holy Spirit to crown the campaign's efforts with success, but nothing was left to chance. In Seoul alone there were 203 coordinating committees, each one representing 10 churches. Leaders tapped 178 of their most fiery and popular speakers to make the rounds of training conferences, coordinating committees, and district clusters to inspire the troops to further ardor. A twenty-five-minute audiovisual slide presentation with glossy production values and spirited music was used by 230 intermediate training units to equip first hundreds, then thousands of eager lay people to get the message out. Before it was over the carefully kept records show that no fewer than 988,600 lay people received such training. And remember, these were the salesmen, not the customers. They represented the kind of highly motivated and carefully instructed sales force Nike or General Motors would die for.

The climax of "Here's Life, Korea," took place in August 1980. During each of four days, twelve major seminars and fifty church conferences were held in Seoul. Every night fully 2 million people rallied on Yoido Plaza in front of the Full Gospel church for testimonies, songs, and inspirational messages. Then a million and a half stayed there outside all night to pray for a spiritual awakening in Korea and for "national reconciliation," which meant, of course, the reunification of the two halves of the divided country.

The results of "Here's Life, Korea" were not disappointing. Available statistics show that in 1979 there were 2,050 Christian churches in Seoul. By August of 1981, the Korean government's Ministry of Culture and Information estimated that there were 4,700. Most of these are pentecostal congregations. According to a census reported by Modern Society Research Institute, nearly 80 percent of all Korean Christians say that they have experienced "the baptism of the Holy Spirit." At the end of the campaign just over a million people pledged either to spend a year—at their own expense—as lay missionaries at home or abroad, or to undertake the financial support of such a missionary. Most, of course, fulfilled their promise in Korea itself, where the growth of pentecostal Christianity has continued unabated. But it is obvious that one relatively small peninsula cannot contain this missionary zeal indefinitely. It will inevitably spill out, and the mind reels at the prospect of thousands of vigorous young Koreans finding their way to China, Indonesia, India, and the west as messengers of the Spirit. If a comparable, but even more ambitious campaign, perhaps with a name like "Here's Life, Asia" is not already in the planning stages (and I have not heard that it is), then something much like it is sure to appear sooner or later.

When one remembers that this stunningly ambitious evangelistic enterprise was taking place just at the moment of Korea's rocketlike economic take-off, it is impossible to believe there was not some connection. And of course there was. During "Here's

Life, Korea," and in the campaigns that have followed it, and indeed in what has become the routine modus operandi of many Korean churches, hundreds of thousands of people whose parental culture, if not their own, had been rural and traditional, learned the bottom-line skills of a modern market economy. They learned to communicate a simple message with passion and enthusiasm. They learned to organize promotional efforts, to make check-off lists, and to utilize telephones, slide projectors, and tapes. They learned to iron out personality clashes in task-oriented groupings, coordinate their own efforts horizontally with parallel units and vertically with larger coordinating collectivities. They learned to set goals and to reach them. They learned to come to meetings on time, keep them going at a brisk pace, and then go out and accomplish whatever was decided. But they also learned what has become for me one of the most unattractive features of too much of pentecostalism: thinking quantitatively, even about the salvation of souls. Reports on the great crusade list in numbing arithmetical detail just how many people on a given night received Christ as Savior, prayed for the gifts of the Spirit, or signed the missionary pledge.

The people who underwent the training process for "Here's Life, Korea" and all its many successors graduated from a concentrated crash course in what millions of others who fill the lower and middle echelons of modern corporations learn at business schools and sales institutes. It would be silly to imagine that the attitudes and competencies these dedicated people learned in this process did not carry over from Sunday to Monday, from their results-oriented and pragmatic spiritual life to their also results-oriented and pragmatic work life. If it was their austere theology that pushed the puritans out into the world of work, it is not their theology that does this for the pentecostals. It is their uncanny determination to testify, to make the Good News known, to reach every nook and cranny of the earth with the glad tidings of blessing, wholeness, and healing.

Peter Drucker is probably the most prominent philosopher of business management in the world today. One of Drucker's favorite subjects is what profit-oriented corporations can learn from nonprofit ones, and vice versa. He insists that despite their different goals, they have much to gain from understanding each other, especially in the world culture now emerging in the late twentieth century—what Drucker calls "the knowledge society." The point that Drucker returns to time and time again in such books as *Managing the Non-Profit Organization: Principles and Practices* (1990) and *Managing the Future: The 1990's and Beyond* (1992), is that the key to productivity in the knowledge society is the flow of information. Information is the elixir, the staff of life. The key question has become how information is organized, who has access to it, and why. For Drucker, the most effective manager today must be an educator, constantly empowering—not commanding—those with whom he or she works.

Drucker has not written about the relationship between pentecostal Christianity and the economy in South Korea, but I believe his approach can help clarify the affinity. Drucker believes that as we enter the twenty-first century only those nations that have learned how to live in the new global knowledge society will survive economically. Even the command of raw materials and financial capital will now take second place to the question of how a society produces a population that is not simply "educated" but has learned how to continue to educate itself year after year. And for Drucker, the best way for anyone to continue to learn is to teach. "Knowledge people," he says, "learn the most when they teach." But he has a special kind of teaching and learning in mind. He pokes fun, for example, at the colleges and universities of America which, he claims, fail utterly at teaching students the kind of elementary skills they will need to become effective members of an organization. As a professor I know what he means. Grading students for their individual exams and individual term papers may reward a certain kind of midnight oil burning. But it does little to prepare students to accept responsibility not just for their own work but for the accomplishment of the group as a whole. Except in gym and music, and in some laboratory courses, we rarely reward teamwork. We turn out shining stars or burned-out comets who are dramatically *uns*uited for the kind of world Drucker envisions.

Drucker's ideas helped me to understand what had at first so baffled me about Korea. Whatever else "Here's Life, Korea" and the highly effective church growth campaigns that followed it did, they taught people by making them teachers of others. They put hundreds of thousands of individuals into teams in which their own sense of accomplishment depended on how well the team succeeded. Drucker also believes that, ironically, the most successful profit-making enterprises are those that do not focus primarily on making a profit but on something he refers to as the corporate "mission." You have to believe that what you are making or selling will be of genuine benefit to your customers. Otherwise, forget it. Pentecostals, in Korea and elsewhere, know a lot about mission. They are convinced, not just because someone has told them but because they have discovered it for themselves, that what they have to offer the world is important and urgent. But a sense of mission, once ignited, cannot be restricted to the religious sphere. It splashes over into everything the person does. I think this helps explain the Korean "economic miracle." It is impossible to come home from an all-night vigil of your evangelistic prayer and promotion group, in which you have learned—perhaps the hard way—to put the goals of the team ahead of your own, without having it affect the way you approach your secular job.

My guess is that to understand the link between religion and economics in Korea, and perhaps eventually in all of Asia, Peter Drucker is more pertinent than Max Weber. The puritans redirected their excess spiritual energy into their worldly callings because there was no point to pouring it into their religious life. Their eternal destinies had been determined since before the foundation of the world. The pentecostals, on the other hand, pour their spiritually generated zeal into their work because they just can't turn it off. Their whole life is a mission because one of the primary responsibilities of any believer is to convey the message to others. The pentecostal learns because he teaches. Meanwhile, because she belongs to a church that is totally geared to mission and expansion, and that enlists every single member in the effort, she picks up proficiencies that jibe very well indeed with the needs of the knowledge society.

But might they jibe entirely too well? Pentecostalism has succeeded in so many places not just by being up to date, but by
providing an alternative life vision, a way of living that is "in but
not of" the postmodern consumer world. Is Korean pentecostalism blending in so well it will lose its power to present a different picture of what life is about? As I watched the sleek training
films, examined the boxes and lines on the campaign organization charts, and perused wearying statistics, I could not help
remembering that the first pentecostals absolutely disdained organization, public relations, and sales promotion. At Azusa Street
they would not even put a billboard outside, at least during the
first months. Eventually pentecostals—some of them—did organize denominations, establish mission boards, found colleges, and
administer vast, sprawling missionary enterprises. Eventually even
the most Spirit-filled religion has to organize itself in some measure, and most ultimately do.

But are the Koreans overdoing it? I eventually began to suspect that their devotion to organizing things comes perilously
close to an obsession. Does this desperate need to nail down
lines of authority and responsibility arise in part from their impressive willingness to flirt with the chaos of the Spirit world, to court
the "madness" of shamanic flight? Is this, after all, a kind of compensation, a way of staying firmly in control of something because
their worship veers into such giddy gyrations? Maybe there is a
compensatory mechanism working here after all.

Whether or not this hunch is correct, the fact is that Korean
pentecostalism could end up losing any power to bring an ethi-
cal critique to bear on Korean society. It could disappear into the
whirring computers and multicolored flow charts of the economic
miracle. It could become so enamored with quantity—gaining
more and more members—that it loses any capacity to make
qualitative judgments. This would be a sad turn of events because
the Korean economic miracle needs a prophetic critique, not just
blessing and approval, from the churches. The success of the
nation's businesses has exacted a dreadful price from the people,
both spiritually and materially. In order to limit wage increases
so that the country could compete on the international market,

during the 1970s the South Korean government introduced draconian controls over labor unions and cut spending on social services. Rumblings of discontent were heard from workers, students, and intellectuals. Then, arbitrary arrests, police beatings, summary trials, imprisonments, and other human rights violations multiplied.

In the face of this repression, leaders of some of the Christian churches took part in organizing protests and demonstrations. Ministers and priests and lay leaders were arrested and imprisoned. As noted earlier, during these troubled times a special kind of Korean liberation theology emerged, "minjung" theology, meaning the theology of "ordinary people," those not a part of ruling elites. Koreans insist that the word does *not* mean "proletariat" or even merely "the poor." It is a more fluid and elusive term. It means whoever is on the bottom in any power relationship, whoever is getting the short end of the stick. They point out that Jesus was one of the "minjung" in his day; that he also lived in a small nation crushed under the heels of successive conquering empires; that he also grieved for the divisions in his land between north and south, city and country, rich and poor, but that he took the side of the minjung against the unrighteous rulers. All over Korea, but especially in urban slums and factory suburbs, minjung churches sprang up during the 1980s, often led by young ministers who had worked in industrial missions and had read something about Latin American liberation theology.

One of the key elements in minjung theology is the recognition of the *han* spirit, or spirits, that Dr. Hyun Kyung Chung talked about at the Canberra Assembly of the World Council of Churches. Sometimes when I have asked Koreans to help me understand this *han* they simply smile and tell me it is untranslatable. But they also say it is the indispensable key to understanding not only minjung theology but the Korean soul itself. They talk about it a lot. On Korean television and in the coffee houses of Seoul and Pusan young Korean folksingers croon about *han*. Their use of the word recalls German philosophers' use of the term "Angst." Finally, a young Korean minister who had studied and worked for a number of years in the United States told me that the closest he could come to rendering the term with one that was familiar to me was with the word "blues" as it is expressed in American black music. His comparison reminded me of a book on spirituals and the blues, by the black American theologian James Cone, who writes:

"If the blues are viewed in proper perspective, it is clear that their mood is very similar to the ethos of the spirituals. Indeed, I contend that the blues and the spirituals flow from the same bedrock of experience."

This may help explain why Professor Cone, when he visited Korea a number of years ago, says that he felt at home immediately, even though he could not speak the language. There is something similar about the injury and dislocation that Koreans and black Americans have lived through, and it is reflected both in their music and in their spirituality. This may also help explain why pentecostalism, with its roots in black American culture, has been so successful in Korea, and it could point to an eventual coalescing of minjung and pentecostal spirituality there.

The adherents of minjung theology are intense, but there are not many of them. Still, it has had a wide influence in Korea, even in churches such as those of the pentecostals who do not embrace its message fully. It is important to note, for example, that during the "Here's Life, Korea" campaign, church members were taught to pray not just for new converts but for "social salvation," the justice of the Kingdom of God and national reconciliation. Although the Christianity introduced into Korea in the nineteenth century by conservative missionaries was an individualistic version, the Koreans themselves have always understood it as a social faith. Unlike Buddhism and Confucianism, which came to Korea largely as religious movements among the elites and never really trickled down to the populace, which remained shamanistic, Christianity has had a different history. The missionaries who brought it to Korea ignored the ruling circles and took its message to the poor and to rural areas. They translated the Bible not into the langauge of the court but into Hangul, the idiom of the common people. Consequently Christianity in Korea quickly

became associated with the national resistance to Japanese impe-
rialism and, in part because it has blended with shamanism, at
least among pentecostalists, it has retained a strong hold on the
masses. These factors suggest that minjung theology could eventually have a considerable influence on Korean pentecostalism.

But what impact is the pell-mell expansion of Korean pentecostalism having on this residual sense of Christianity as a faith
with a social conscience? When pentecostal preachers tell their
people that if they tithe the Lord will return their gifts sevenfold,
does it help them resist the snares of a rapidly accelerating consumer economy where getting what *I* want is quickly replacing
social solidarity as the First Commandment? After many conversations I am convinced that, hidden below its increasingly slick
veneer, Korean Christianity as a whole still retains a feeling for
the health of the whole society and especially of the less well
off. That sense of compassion could vault to the surface very
quickly if the economic miracle began to curdle. But it needs to
be nurtured. Are the pentecostals nurturing it? Or are they shov-
ing it aside in their compulsive zeal to add numbers?

The historian and theologian Boo-Woong Yoo, a native of
Seoul, has written the only history of Korean pentecostalism available in English. Yoo believes that in recent years he can detect a
convergence between pentecostalism and minjung theology. He
calls it "the meeting between socio-political minjung and pentecostal minjung." If he is right, and if pentecostalism preserves the
inner strength of Korean Christianity, or even develops its own
equivalent of the Social Gospel or of Latin American liberation
theology, then the result could be potent indeed. Whether this
will happen will depend on many factors, among them whether
the "second generation" theologians such as Hyun Kyung Chung
can develop a style of Christianity in Korea that combines the
primal energy of shamanism with the vigor of the pentecostal
evangelism and the passion for justice of minjung theology.

They may just do it. In 1992, Dr. Chung gave a guest lecture
in my class while she was a research associate at Harvard. Dressed
in a stylish gray dress with a sophisticated Asian cut, trimmed with
small gold metal bells, she spoke quietly, almost deferentially, but

seemed anything but humbled by the fracas at Canberra. She said that much of the talk about paganism and syncretism was a smoke-screen laid down to cloud questions about who speaks and who listens. She told us in a soft but firm voice that the reproaches critics had heaped on her had made her even more determined to trust her own judgment and to say what needed to be said. When I asked her after class if she could conceive of any limits at all in the degree to which, for example, Christianity could be combined with shamanism, she simply smiled and shook her head. "You cannot put new wine in old wineskins," she said.

It seemed to me, however, that on this particular question, that famous quotation from Jesus needed to be inverted. What Dr. Chung and her Korean colleagues are doing is not putting new wine into old skins, but putting very old wine—the vintage intoxicant of primal spirituality—into the new wineskins they are trying to design. But I decided not to offer my retort. Dr. Chung does not give the appearance of someone with whom it would be easy to argue. Besides, I was not at all sure that she had given a negative answer to my question. Rather, what she was saying with her cryptic scriptural reference was that I might not be asking the right question. Whatever she meant, it was only later that I remembered that this same verse about new wine in old skins had been a the favorite of the early pentecostals. They sensed that the power they had encountered was not going to be contained by the old church structures, that the vessels were going to split and the seams were going to burst. The same thing may be happening on the Asian Rim today.

CHAPTER 12

Healers and Ecologists: Primal Spirituality in Black Africa

In each of us the Spirit is seen to be
working for some useful purpose.
One, through the Spirit, has the
gift of wise speech,
While another, by the same Spirit,
can put the deepest knowledge into words.
Another, by the same Spirit,
is granted faith,
Another, by the one Spirit,
gifts of healing.
2 Corinthians 12:8–10

*I*N A HUGE OPEN FIELD in a rural area of Zimbabwe thousands of people have gathered around gigantic stacks of wood and brush which at nightfall will be lit into towering pillars of fire. They have come a long way, so they spend the first few hours greeting each other. They have traveled from Gwelo and Bulawayo, from Kalamo and Lusaka, from the large and middle-sized cities of Zimbabwe, the country that Europeans once called Rhodesia, after Cecil Rhodes. They embrace and gossip. The children scamper and wrestle. Laughter rolls across the brush and stubble. Eventually all sit on the ground and share pieces of roast chicken and yams from the woven cloth bags and plastic sacks they have brought along. After the meal, the children snuggle into blanket rolls, and the conversations assume a more serious tone. Then, at first very quietly, but then more and more volubly, the adults begin to pray, both singly and in little knots of four or five. Some of the prayers are sobs and groans. As the evening wears on toward midnight people begin to walk around the fires, then to run and jump, shouting out their prayers in resounding cries and wails. As the orange flames leap and crackle the praying builds in intensity, subsiding only as the eastern horizon begins to appear and the fires turn into stacks of smoldering blue coals.

This gathering constitutes the preparatory phase of the annual Holy Communion service of the African Apostolic Church, one of the many thousands of independent Christian churches of Africa. What these worshippers are doing is searching their souls for whatever unworthy actions or thoughts they need to confess in order to prepare themselves to take part in the eucharistic meal with a clear conscience. Their prayers and cries express their efforts to search their hearts for whatever failings might stand in the way of their entering into the spirit of the communion. They are engaged in a more energetic version of what some Christians call the "prayer of general confession."

As the sun rises, the crowd becomes quiet. With great dignity and composure they line up to pass through what they call the "gates of heaven." Each of these gates consists of twelve "prophets," the title given to the ministering priests of the church, standing in pairs to form corridors. As the worshippers pass through these "gates," each makes his or her confession. When they get to the inside, they are symbolically entering the Kingdom of God. There they can share the messianic feast with God and with each other, sing, and offer prayers of thanksgiving before they pack their blankets and pots together and start the long trip home.

Like conscientious believers everywhere they confess a wide range of sins of omission and commission. Many of the misdeeds they mention—jealousy, anger, harboring a grudge—are common to all human beings. But there is a particular trespass they are encouraged to mention to the prophets that would not occur to most western Christians. It is the sin of *uroyi*, which is usually translated as "wizardry." In years past, this meant slipping back into the practice of placating the evil spirits and demons which, according to many African traditional religions, are the sources of illness, bad luck, and family discord. More recently, however, under the influence of a younger generation of leaders in these new Christian churches, of which the Apostolic Church is an example, wizardry has come to have a larger meaning. It now includes offenses against "the Earthkeeping Spirit," which is itself an African understanding of the Christian Holy Spirit. Violations of the Earthkeeping Spirit encompass any activities that lead to soil erosion, fouling the water supply, or chopping down trees without replacing them. In other words, on a continent plagued by the loss of woodlands and arable land, a religiously based ecological ethic is appearing. More specifically, this ethic is based on a spirituality that mixes ancient African religious sensibilities with modern environmental awareness, and it is taking place within a movement that has arisen as Christian pentecostal impulses have interacted with the throbbing universe of African primal religion. The prohibition against the wanton destruction of trees, for example, is not the result of importing an idea from modern western forestry. It is the extension of an age-old sanction against cutting the trees in a sacred grove, one that was inhabited by spirits. Now, however, the whole earth and all the trees are understood to be sacred.

The Apostolic Church, which was founded in 1932 by a prophet named John Maranke, who died in 1963, is part of the fastest growing Christian movement in sub-Saharan Africa. In most areas of this vast region these independent churches are expanding faster than Islam, at about twice the rate of the Roman Catholic Church and at roughly three times that of other non-Catholic groups. There are now over 5,000 independent Christian denominations, all born in the twentieth century, and all bearing the familiar marks of pentecostal spirituality, plus many distinctive qualities of their own. In South Africa they embrace about 40 percent of the black population. In Zimbabwe 50 percent of all

Christians belong to such African independent churches as the Zion Christian Church, founded by Bishop Mutendi, the Ndaza or "Holy Cord" Zionist Church, or the African Apostolic Church. In Zaire, the Church of the Lord Jesus Christ on Earth of the Prophet Simon Kimbangu, founded by Kimbangu in 1921, and the first such denomination to affiliate with the World Council of Churches, has more than 8 million members, making it the largest independent church on the continent. These churches go by a bewildering variety of names, but the words "Apostolic" or "Zion" or "Prophet'" appear in many of their titles. In addition to the several thousand denominations, ranging in size from a few thousand to millions of members, there are also innumerable unaffiliated congregations. At present rates of growth, by the year 2000 these churches will include more members in Africa than either the Roman Catholic Church or all the Protestant denominations put together.

The African independent churches constitute the African expression of the worldwide pentecostal movement. As the early pentecostal leaders insisted, pentecostalism is not a denomination or a creed, but a movement, a cluster of religious practices and attitudes that transcends ecclesiastical boundaries. These churches qualify as pentecostal for two reasons; their *style* and their *origins*. First, they are, as scholars of religion would say, "phenomenologically" pentecostal. Their worship exhibits all the features of pentecostal spirituality we have found from Boston to Seoul to Rio de Janeiro. Second, they were influenced by the high-impact spread of the American pentecostal movement, both within the major denominations and outside them, in the first decades of this century.

Let us look first at their *pentecostal style*. Like most pentecostal churches elsewhere, the majority of African independent churches do not bear the term "Pentecostal" in their titles. In this respect they are like similar congregations in other places, which call themselves "Full Gospel," or "Assemblies of God," as well as "Apostolic'" or "Zion" churches. What is important is that they display the same characteristics we have observed elsewhere and that would be recognized immediately as pentecostal by anyone familiar with those qualities. People dance and clap and testify. The preachers rely more on stories than on sermons to carry the message. The worship incorporates dreams, healing, trances, and a high degree of lay participation. The churches also assimilate a wide variety of indigenous religious practices—in this case African ones—into the fabric of Christian prayer and praise, so much so that like pentecostal churches elsewhere they are often accused of "syncretism." But unlike what happens in Korea, where the leaders often angrily deny suggestions that they have absorbed indigenous religious elements, African independent Christians seem proud that they have not forsaken the spiritual customs their ancestors passed on to them before the whites came, even though the first missionaries urged them to abandon these "remnants of superstition." They believe that God was already present in Africa before the Europeans arrived and that many of the ways Africans worshipped then are better than the ways the missionaries taught them. The result is a thoroughly "Africanized" version of Christianity.

Kofi Appiah-Kubi is a Ghanaian who has written extensively on the new Christian churches of Africa. But he does not like to call them "independent," which he says carries a condescending undertone and implies some outside point of reference by which they should be judged. He prefers the term "African indigenous churches" to suggest their rootedness in the local culture and their responsiveness to the spiritual hunger of African peoples. His theory is that these churches represent a "Christian answer" to the specific religious needs of the African soul. In particular, they provide their followers with the weapons of the Spirit they need to fight back against the forces of evil as they manifest themselves in disease and discord, and they encourage them to reverence the departed ancestors, who are viewed in Africa as the custodians of ethics and morality. Most of all, these indigenous Christian churches provide a setting in which the African conviction that spirituality and healing belong together is dramatically enacted. The typical disciple comes to such a church for the first time in search of healing, usually for a malady that has resisted either traditional or modern medicine or both.

But Appiah-Kubi also believes that the indigenous Christian churches are growing because they respond effectively to the particular temperament of Africans. "In contrast to a cold, frigid, professionally-aired Christianity that is mainly interested in form," Appiah-Kubi says, "these churches are free, emotional . . . and several are charismatic, lay, egalitarian and voluntaristic." He contrasts these qualities with the more hierarchical and professional organization of the "missionary churches." He adds that the indigenous churches—again unlike the European- and American-derived ones—have been led by women from the beginning. Thus Alice Lushina established the Lumpa Church of Zambia and Alice Tania founded the Church of the Twelve Apostles in Ghana. Further, like churches of a pentecostal stamp everywhere, indigenous congregations insist—against the teaching of the so-called mainline churches—that the gifts of the Spirit that were so evident in early Christianity—prophecy, tongue speaking, the discerning of spirits, and healing—are still available today. In all of these respects the African indigenous churches are thoroughly pentecostal in the most important meaning of the term. In fact they present a vivid example of how what I have called the "pentecostal impulse" overflows denominational labels and makes itself felt on a much broader scale.

It should be remembered, of course, that the idiom Appiah-Kubi uses to describe the worship patterns of the indigenous Christian churches of Africa is not the language the adherents of those churches use themselves. When they speak about playing drums and other African instruments in their liturgies, for example, the worshippers point out that Psalms 149 and 150 command Christians to praise God "with timbrel and lyre," which they freely translate into the rhythm, string, and wind instruments of their continent. As for dancing in church, which nearly all the other denominations discourage, they argue that the Psalms also endorse "dancing before the Lord," and that King David danced before the Ark of the Covenant. As they do in many other places in the world, pentecostals often succeed in *being* highly syncretistic while their leaders *preach* against syncretism. If what I call "primal spirituality" underlies all faith traditions, including the one recorded in the Bible, then what pentecostals are doing is reaching deep into the foundation of a common human religiosity which also underlies biblical faith.

But the African indigenous Christian churches are not pentecostal just because their worship incorporates a free-wheeling, Spirit-filled style. They were also touched at their *origins* by the sparks that blew from Azusa Street. It is true that even before the turn of the century there had already been some secessions from European-based missionary churches, mainly in South Africa, which resulted in what came to be called "independent" churches. One of these was founded by a black African Methodist, Nehemiah Tile, mainly as a protest against the mistreatment of Africans in his church. In 1882, another African Methodist, Moses Mokone, founded the Ethiopian Church, also in resistance to the racist policies of the white churches. The name "Ethiopian" is significant because it reminded the whites that the Christian church we now call the Ethiopian Orthodox Church existed in Africa for many centuries before European and American missionaries arrived.

These protest-based denominations were already present before any pentecostal missionaries from America arrived. But the real burst of growth for the African independent churches came later, and there can be little doubt that it was catalyzed by the worldwide chain reaction that started at Azusa Street. As early as 1907, within a year after the "fire fell" on Los Angeles, people who had visited William Seymour's swept-out stable found their way to Africa with tidings of the new outpouring of the Spirit. That year, two preachers, John Lake and Thomas Hezmalhalch, held pentecostal meetings in a black church in Doorfontein, South Africa. A new pentecostal denomination, the Apostolic Faith Mission, was founded in 1908. Another, the Full Gospel Church of God, was organized two years later. As it had in America, the word spread rapidly through the existing churches of Africa. But, as was also happening in America, preachers and lay Christians who responded to the new message were often rejected and ridiculed, and had to start churches of their own. For example, the founders of the two major independent Christian churches in

Zimbabwe, John Maranke who established the African Apostolic Church, and Bishop Mutendi who pioneered the Zion Christian Church, both started out as ministers in European-based churches. Maranke began in the Dutch Reformed and Mutendi in the Methodist church. But both came into contact with the pentecostal currents soon after the outset of their ministries, and both experienced classical pentecostal conversions, with tongue speaking and visions. They also picked up other elements of the pentecostal message, so the Holy Spirit came to play a larger and larger role in their teaching and preaching. Thus, echoing western pentecostal preaching, the leaders of the new African movements urged people to change their lives and convert soon, since God's judgment was imminent.

Pentecost is everywhere in the history and theology of the African indigenous churches. The author of one of the more or less official versions of the early history of Bishop Mutendi's church describes one of his early sermons, delivered in 1923, in words that were obviously meant to recall the original Pentecost. "He stood and preached with great power," the historian says, "as he was told to do by the prophets. . . . Many believers were possessed by the Holy Spirit." But then comes the familiar theme of misunderstanding, rejection, and persistence. "The people present got frightened and some of them ran away, saying, 'That man arouses the *zvitebwe* (the vengeful spirits which destroy cattle).' Some people laughed when they saw others getting possessed by the Spirit." Clearly Mutendi met with some of the same mixed reviews that greeted the disciples in Jerusalem at the first Pentecost and that rained down on the first American pentecostals. But, like Peter in Jerusalem and Seymour in Los Angeles, he was not disheartened. The Spirit, we are told, strengthened him, and "he never stopped preaching."

The special emphasis on baptism by the Holy Spirit, a common thread found among pentecostals everywhere, even appears among the prophets whose connection to the American movement are not so clearly traceable. Simon Kimbangu, for example, taught his followers to put on white garments for the "baptism of fire" which had to take place in the woods at night because his movement had been banned in what was then the Belgian Congo. Further, he instructed one of the prophets to read during the Spirit baptism from the account in the nineteenth chapter of the Acts of the Apostles which describes how Apostle Paul baptized twelve men at Ephesus on whom the Holy Spirit then descended. This is a favorite passage of pentecostals in all corners of the globe. They love to preach about it and I have often heard it played out with a comic twist. The text lends itself to a little slapstick. It says that when Paul arrived in Ephesus he met some disciples there and asked them if they had received the Holy Spirit. They told him, "No, we were not even told that there is a Holy Spirit." So Paul baptizes them in the name of Jesus, the Spirit descends, and the grateful recipients "spoke in tongues of ecstasy and prophesied." The passage has an additional significance for many Africans who, as we shall see in a moment, believe that the missionaries purposely hid from them any teaching about the Holy Spirit, and that it is now their special task to recover it.

The idea of pentecost is everywhere in the indigenous churches, but the emphasis on it assumes its own uniquely African flavor. For example, Maranke made the annual celebration of the Day of Pentecost, which is a fairly minor holiday in most western churches and virtually unknown to American pentecostals, into the major feast day of the year. Perhaps he did so because the religious context out of which the indigenous movement arose in Africa was more influenced by Anglican and Roman Catholic calendars in which Pentecost Sunday ("Whitsun") is a recognized holiday. If so, this once again suggests the remarkable capacity of pentecostalism to absorb both pre-Christian indigenous traditions and previous layers of Christian practice, and this in turn helps us understand its profound appeal.

I can understand Appiah-Kubi's objection to the term "independent" for the African indigenous churches. But no one can read their early history without noticing a certain element of rebelliousness against European expressions of the faith, for the founders of these churches were rebels as well as prophets. Like Luther, they wanted to reform the church, but they were ready to break away if they needed to. Take John Maranke for example. His call came to him in a mode reminiscent of what Americans have heard about Joseph Smith, the founder of Mormonism. God gave Maranke two books of revealed instructions. But, significantly, Maranke says he was unable to read them with the education he had received at the European mission school. He was puzzled at first. But then the Holy Spirit came upon him and enabled him to do what his European education could not: showed him how to read the books. The message in the books conveyed both a revolutionary and a prophetic summons. It called Maranke to become a Moses figure—an analogy also favored by Martin Luther King, Jr.—and to lead his people from the political and religious oppression enforced on them by Europeans. His church is often credited with preparing the people of Zimbabwe for their long and painful battle for independence, the struggle they now refer to as the *chimurenga*.

The theme of liberation by the power and guidance of the Holy Spirit from European domination is central to many of the African independent churches. In fact, in some the conviction emerged that the Europeans had purposely not told Africans about the Holy Spirit, but had brought them instead a trimmed-down edition of the faith; and it was now the responsibility of the Africans to restore the full Gospel. As we have seen, this suspicion was strengthened by reading about the puzzled disciples at Ephesus described in Acts 19 who had never been told about the Holy Spirit. Soon the Africans began to express the idea of a spiritual liberation from this European chicanery with a kind of exodus motif: just as God had led the Israelites out of their religious and political bondage in Egypt, so now the Holy Spirit was leading Africans out of their spiritual and social imprisonment by Europeans. So thoroughly did these indigenous prophets identify with the Israelites that when colonial governments outlawed them, some tried to gain entrance to the new state of Israel. Israeli immigration officials, undoubtedly a little puzzled by their request, turned them down, but the prophets remained convinced that they were reenacting the confrontation between Moses and Pharaoh.

As I read the accounts of the early founders of the indigenous churches of Africa, many of them available only in volumes that are hard to find in America, I could not help being mightily impressed. Indeed any reader of these narratives would have to be touched by the deep conviction and utter fearlessness of these extraordinary men and women. Kimbangu's story is one of the most poignant. A follower of the Baptist mission in what was then the Belgian Congo, he was called by God in a road-to-Damascus experience in 1921. But he had hardly begun his ministry when, six months later, he was arrested and imprisoned by the Belgian authorities, abetted, sad to say, by the local Roman Catholic hierarchy. It was a strange case. Kimbangu, himself a gentle and soft-spoken man, had instructed his followers to eschew all violence, but by 1921 African colonial governments were already becoming panicky about any black-led movement, so Kimbangu—standing in chains before the magistrate—was sentenced to death. On being petitioned for clemency by the Baptist missionaries, King Albert of Belgium, probably not wanting the blood of a martyr on his hands, finally commuted the sentence to penal servitude for life.

Kimbangu in a cell, however, was an even stronger presence for his followers than he had been on the outside. Like Nelson Mandela later, he became a symbol and a rallying point. His church continued to expand even faster than it had before. It spread out of the Congo and into adjacent countries while Kimbangu, locked behind the walls of the prison in Elizabethville, was denied any visits from family members or the services of a Protestant pastor. Unlike Mandela, however, Kimbangu was never released. Through thirty years of continuous incarceration he remained, according to penitentiary officials, a model prisoner. Toward the end of his life he was allowed to work in the prison kitchen, a duty he performed with a calm cheerfulness that impressed everyone who met him. He died in October 1951. One of the members of the church he had founded remarked that while Jesus had lived for thirty years before his ministry, Kimbangu had lived for thirty years after his.

Simon Kimbangu's story is not unique. No one has ever been able to count the number of leaders and followers of the indigenous Christian churches who were imprisoned or banished. But neither persecution by the state nor condemnation from their fellow Christians stopped them. Like the earliest pentecostals immediately following the Azusa revival, these Africans were certain that God had called them despite—or maybe even *because*—they were poor and unlettered, to carry the true and full story of the Gospel to their whole continent and to the world. Like their pentecostal sisters and brothers elsewhere, they set off to spread the news. Their churches have been expanding ever since.

From the outset, as it was with Azusa Street and with Aimee Semple McPherson, healing played an important role in the first years of the African independent churches. But during the 1950s and 1960s, according to M. L. Daneel, one of the historians of these movements, this emphasis on healing assumed its own unique African style. The difference from western pentecostal precedents was twofold. First, healing became a much more *central* activity, with much of the liturgy and preaching revolving around it. Bishop Mutendi even founded a residential community which he named Zion City, to which sick and helpless people were invited to come for help. But second, the *concept* of what was included in healing broadened. "Healing" now came to include not just bodily recuperation, but finding remedies for unemployment, family disputes, racism, marital discord, and controversies between factions in a tribe or village. This new and broadened definition of healing sometimes put these African pentecostal churches in direct tension with their white American brothers and sisters, who, bending under the criticism of both the liberals (who did not believe in divine healing) and fundamentalists (who insisted that the healing miracles had ceased with the New Testament), began to deemphasize healing as perhaps too spectacular. At the same time the earlier interest of the American pentecostals in the social infirmities that caused their people to suffer waned. They were concerned lest making an effort to address such structural sicknesses might appear too much like the Social Gospel, or some other suspect liberal scheme.

I am convinced that healing is the area in which the African indigenous churches have most to offer to other Christians and to the world at large. But one must move very carefully when trying to understand the healing practices of these churches, because healing is also the activity in which they are most often accused of "syncretism" or of relapsing back into pre-Christian tribal practices. But this is just the point. If one of the major strengths of the pentecostal movement is its capacity to absorb pre-Christian and extra-Christian practices into an explicitly Christian vehicle, then healing may be the key. It is the key both because it lays open the extreme intricacy of this absorption process and also because it provides a valuable insight into why the pentecostal impulse succeeds so well in bringing both premodern and postmodern cultures together.

Healing in the African indigenous churches is a complex affair. One can see how a superficial observer might conclude that it represents a "reversion to paganism," since, on the surface, the modus operandi of the indigenous Christian prophet/healer who undertakes it often appears to be very similar to that of the *nganga*, the traditional healer who is sometimes referred to by outsiders as a "medicine man." Both the prophet and the *nganga*, for example, first try to ascertain the cause of the patient's malady, and they often locate it in malevolent spirits, or sometimes—as is the case in Korean pentecostal churches—in dissatisfied ancestral spirits. This is what causes many western Christians, including many pentecostals, to recoil and to fault the African prophets for reverting to animism or paganism, or to the worship of the *emadloti*, the ancestral spirits.

But it is just here that the Christian prophet and the traditional *nganga* begin to differ, and the difference is an enormous one with far-reaching implications, not only for African Christianity, but—I believe—for the role of religion in the twenty-first century. The divergence is that while the *nganga* tries to *placate* the evil spirit, or attempts to counter its claim with divinations, the Christian prophet simply prays to the Holy Spirit to defeat and expel the intruder. While the *nganga* attempts to find out what the malignant spirits want, and then to satisfy them so they will go away, the prophet banishes them in the name of the Spirit of God, and assures the sick person that he or she need no longer fear the spirits' powers since God's Spirit is mightier. The similarity is that both healers recognize the real power—at least in the African context—of malevolent spirits. But there the resemblance ends, for instead of trying to mollify the bad spirits, the Christian prophet calls upon a higher power. A prophet assures the patient that the Holy Spirit has the capacity to vanquish whatever it is that is causing the disorder.

The distinction is important. Using the language of spirits, both kinds of healers seem to recognize that in coping with illness in an individual, larger collective powers and distorted relationships also come into play. This is an insight that western medicine has only recently begun to acknowledge. But the *nganga's* strategy, even if successful, often leaves the client fearful and apprehensive, afraid that he or she is surrounded by a universe of almost equally matched salubrious and toxic powers. If the prophet's healing succeeds, on the other hand, the patient catches a glimpse of a world that surely has its chaotic and disruptive elements, but in which he or she can confidently call upon a powerful and benevolent higher Spirit. This makes for an enormous difference.

At first this difference may seem trivial to those who live outside Africa and may still regard it as at least somewhat "primitive." But for persons who live their lives in terror of harmful wizardry and malevolent magic, the assurance that there is a powerful Spirit who is stronger than all the evil forces comes as very good news. The therapy practiced by the prophets of the African indigenous churches corresponds to the biblical conviction that in the ongoing conflict between good and evil, evil is real—not illusory—but that God has already triumphed in principle and will ultimately disclose that victory everywhere. In the New Testament this belief is dramatized by the Gospel stories about Jesus Christ casting out demons as a sign of the coming Kingdom; and by the somewhat more sophisticated concept found in the writings of Paul which proclaims the victory of Christ over the "principalities and powers," the collective and superindividual forces that impact human destiny.

But does this picture of the world have anything to offer to the "secular" west? Most recent western theologians have stayed very far away from the language of "principalities and powers," dismissing the idea of spirits or nonempirical powers, or "the demonic" as embarrassing holdovers from prescientific times. There are some evangelicals and pentecostals who do concern themselves with the demonic and who therefore comprise an exception to the current western mindset. The trouble is, as we shall see in chapter 15, they have often become so obsessed with the demons that they have forgotten the message of liberation. On balance, the African Christians seem to have gotten it right. They constitute another example of how the premodern melds with the postmodern, and of how the current upsurge of primal spirituality is more in tune with newly emerging scientific paradigms than western critical theology is.

Just as I was puzzling over the fascinating but enigmatic worldview of the African indigenous churches, with its vibrant sense of the vitality of the human ecosphere, I made a fortuitous discovery. I ran across this description of Margaret Wheatley's observations in her book *Leadership and the New Science*:

> Space is the basic ingredient of the universe; there is more of it than anything else. Even at the microscopic level of atoms . . . there is mostly space. . . . In Newton's universe, the emptiness of space created a sense of unspeakable loneliness. [But] Something strange has happened to space in the quantum world. No longer is there a lonely void. Space everywhere is now thought to be filled with fields, invisible, nonmaterial structures that are the basic structures of the universe.

Wheatley is a professor of Business Administration at Brigham Young University, and as I read these words it seemed a little humorous to me that even though many western Christians and certainly most academic theologians would find the primal cosmos of the African indigenous churches "primitive" or even "superstitious," the real situation is very different. We may be the ones

who are behind the times. Perhaps modern, liberal western theology—the kind I learned as a graduate student—has been vainly
striving to reconcile religion to an allegedly scientific worldview
which is actually becoming more outdated every day. Paradoxically, the traditional African cosmology, which the indigenous
Christian churches incorporate so inventively, may be more in
tune with the "quantum world" than western theology is. But, as
we have seen, this is not the only matter in which the African
indigenous churches may be a vanguard rather than a rearguard
in Christian history. While the western churches still seemed mired
in a theology that separates man from nature and grants him
"dominion" over the beasts and the plants, Africans are evolving
theology that locates human life within the web of nature and
views violations of the natural order—which is the domain of the
"Earthkeeping Spirit"—as a serious sin. While western medicine
has just begun to scramble for a new understanding of the place
of altered states of consciousness in curing human diseases, and
the mysterious link between mind and body, the indigenous
African churches have never given up the powerful bond between
prayer and healing.

It is instructive to study the extraordinary emergence and subsequent history of the indigenous Christian churches of Africa not
because the setting in which they have emerged is so beguilingly
exotic, but precisely because it is not. Africa may present us with
a picture of the future, not of the past. It is the home of a human
population that is living through many of the awful crises we in
the west have only begun to sense. The black plague of our era,
AIDS, is felling far larger proportions of Africa's inhabitants than it
is here—so far. Poverty and despair have rendered Africa's great
cities unliveable for a decade; ours are on the brink. Africa's grim
experience of famine, anarchy, racial turmoil, and religious strife
may be advance warning signals of what we will all have to contend with soon.

But at the same time, a new and powerful expression of human
spirituality and morality is also appearing in Africa. The indigenous churches draw on the past to prepare people for the future.
They are not burgeoning just because they help people to reclaim

ancient spiritual resources that seemed to be lost. They are growing because they help people apply those resources in a new and bewildering context. The pastor of an African indigenous church once told me, with a broad wink, that one reason his church was gaining new members was that instead of wasting their money on expensive nightclubs and cheap gin, the young people could dance and vent their pains and frustration at church, and that the music was even better. He was being facetious, at least in part. But he could also have pointed out that these churches give people a sense of dignity, a place in a community of friends which often stands as a surrogate for an extended family fractured by mobility and change, and the conviction that human beings are important and that whatever the sinister powers may try to do to them, they have a powerful cosmic ally and a secure standing in God's eyes. The fact that the indigenous churches, borne by the same wave pentecostals are so skillfully riding elsewhere, have done this by combining the old and the new, the pagan and the Christian, the pious with the pragmatic, is all to their credit. It is what we will all have to do eventually, perhaps quite soon. Instead of being a backwater, they may in fact be an avant-garde.

On the other hand, of course, they may not be. The great strength of the pentecostal impulse is its power to combine, its aptitude for adopting the language, the music, the cultural artifacts, the religious tropes, even the demigods and wraiths of the setting in which it lives. But this very flexibility can also be, at times, its most dangerous quality as well. Sadly, in South Africa there is just such an example of pentecostalism's failure to exorcise an evil demon because of its proclivity to absorb preexisting religious customs and make them its own.

The demon is race. One of the main reasons indigenous churches appeared in Africa, most particularly in South Africa, is that almost from the beginning, the pentecostal churches initiated by Americans and Europeans accepted apartheid with remarkably little hesitation. It was the way things were done, and furthermore racial separation had a carefully constructed religious basis in the theology of the Dutch Reformed Church, with its teaching about the orders of creation (which defined the separation of

racial communities as the will of God), and its twisted interpretation of the Covenant (which designated the Dutch settlers as the
chosen people who were entitled to the land of the pagans). The
white pentecostals, often so pleased with themselves because God
had given them the power to cast out devils, failed to exorcise
the evil of racism. That failure made it inevitable that the genuine
pentecostal impetus would leave the western-sponsored denominations behind and move into what have become the indigenous
Christian churches.

It is a disheartening history to read. Within months after its
founding, the executive board of the Apostolic Faith Mission—the
first pentecostal church—decreed that the nonracial policy with
which it began should be changed. Henceforth "the baptism of
natives shall in future take place after the baptism of white people." But apparently even that was not enough for the racial
purists, so a year later the same executive board decided that "the
baptism of whites, colored and natives shall be separate." Thus,
with a stroke of the pen, what Seymour had considered to be the
central miracle of Azusa Street, the erasure of the color line, was
conveniently disposed of. Instead of the miraculous reversal of
the curse of Babel, South Africa now reinstituted the confounding
of the nations, under pentecostal auspices.

It got even worse. By 1948, when the question of whether
apartheid could be Christian was just beginning to become a matter of debate, and when the South African government was decid-
ing whether to enact draconian new racial laws, the executive of
the Apostolic Faith Mission made its position unequivocal. It stood
squarely and publicly on the side of segregation. "The fact that
the Native, Indian or colored is saved," the church declared, "does
not render him a European." A decade later, when the Nationalist
prime minister, J. Styrdom, succeeded in removing all the so-called
Colored voters from the electoral roll, G. R. Wessels, a prominent
pentecostal minister and the vice-president of the Apostolic Faith
Mission was serving as a senator. He firmly upheld the government's racist policy.

At this point, of course, the early history of their movement
became a severe embarrassment for the South African pentecostal

churches. The more segregationist they became, the more embarrassed they were about their origins in a revival that occurred in a black church in Los Angeles. Obviously some "revisionist" history was called for, and a white pentecostal historian quickly obliged. F. P. Moller argued in a more or less official history of the church that it was really Charles Parham, the white man, not Seymour, to whom the movement should trace its beginnings. He acknowledged that Seymour had indeed played a certain role in the early days at Azusa Street, but contended that "Later Seymour was replaced by more able people and the different races ceased worship together." In the 1980s, when the Reverend Frank Chikane, the pastor of a black pentecostal congregation that was affiliated with the Apostolic Faith Mission began to oppose apartheid publicly he was removed from his ministry. It was not until 1986 that the first church document to question apartheid bearing the signatures of any pentecostal leaders appeared, hardly a pioneering act by then.

Finally, in 1988, a group of South African pentecostals issued a statement titled "A Relevant Pentecostal Witness." Though it arrived very late in the game, it is an eloquent and powerful indictment of apartheid. Furthermore, rather than borrowing theological concepts from other traditions, it draws on pentecostal theology and history, including the black American origins of the movement, to make its case. Speaking of the "spiritual gifts" so dear to pentecostal preaching, it proclaims that "when there is a separation and division then we can say that these spiritual gifts have been subverted and made of no effect."

These are stern words. But what seems even more significant to me is that the authors of the "Relevant Pentecostal Witness" found religious and theological meaning in the *constituency* of early pentecostalism. They did not regard what is clearly evident historically—that the people who first responded to the pentecostal message were poor and black—as a mere sociological detail. R. M. Anderson, in his classic social history of pentecostalism in America, once wrote that the membership of the early movement was made up of indigent urbanized whites and displaced blacks, and was drawn "almost exclusively from among these ethnically heterogenous, struggling working classes and impoverished unemployed . . . in the urban areas of the nation." This is now a well-established fact of historical scholarship. The question that at least some pentecostals are now asking themselves is, what does it *mean?* Were these beginnings among the outcasts, the pariahs, and the misfits merely accidental? Are they a source of embarrassment to be swept under the rug or "revised"? Or do the facts about who those early saints *were* have a spiritual meaning for the future of the movement?

I believe that the question of where and how, and among whom, the modern pentecostal movement came to birth has enormous religious meaning. Like the story of the ancient Israelites and the life of Jesus of Nazareth, it is another example of the way God uses unlikely vessels, at least unlikely in the eyes of the age, to accomplish the divine purpose. Pouring the new blessing on a one-eyed black preacher and a gaggle of social outcasts is like choosing a nation of slaves and the son of an unwed mother to begin new chapters in history. The great temptation facing pentecostals today is to forget or to minimize the circumstances of their birth, to try to blend into the religious and social atmosphere around them. But, as I have noticed time and time again, when they blend in—as they frequently do—they inevitably lose their essence, perhaps one should even say their souls. They become just one more denomination, one more creed, a slightly noisier crowd of religious hucksters trying to outshout the others. When they deny their origins they also deprive themselves of a future. They relinquish their extraordinary capacity to dig into the spiritual treasures below the religious crust. They forfeit their promise of shaping a flourishing faith that, because it once proved it could live in this fallen age without being seduced by it, might still provide a thriving spirituality for the century to come.

CHAPTER 13

Pentecostalism in America: "Whose Report Do You Believe?"

Run to the young man there and tell him
that Jerusalem will be without walls,
so numerous will be the people and cattle in it.
I myself shall be a wall of fire around it,
says the Lord, and a glorious presence within it.

Zechariah 2:4–5

*P*ENTECOSTALISM HAS encircled the world, but it was born in America. I knew very well that in order to write about it honestly, I would eventually have to come to terms with my mixed feelings about what was happening to it in the land of its birth. For five years I had tried to become familiar with as many different varieties of the American wing of the movement as possible. I visited tiny congregations in rented halls so poorly heated my teeth chattered until the singing warmed me up; and colossal congregations meeting in glistening air-conditioned ultra-modern temples where off-duty police directed the traffic into the parking lots. I sang and prayed with pentecostal people in the urban ghettoes of Los Angeles, Chicago, New York, and Boston; and in remote mountain hamlets in West Virginia and Kentucky. Within the United States alone I attended services in seven different languages. I worshipped with black, Latino, anglo, and Asian congregations and started to sense a special closeness and affection for pentecostal people. I even began to catch on to some of their inside jokes and esoteric references. I often found that I forgot my original status as an interested academic observer and began to feel completely at home in pentecostal churches.

But there was something that had not changed. Just as when I attended the "little church" with Lois nearly fifty years ago, I felt close to the people around me, but I still had plenty of mental reservations about many of the things the preachers said. Also I could not help noticing the deep divisions within the movement itself. I knew that arguments over theology, personality clashes, racial and ethnic tensions, regional differences, and denominational labels still prevented pentecostals from being the united people the promise of the first Pentecost held out. I also became aware that there are some very unattractive political and theological currents running through American pentecostalism today, features that most of my pentecostal friends hoped I would not notice, or—if I did—would not attach too much significance to when I wrote about their churches. I could understand their feelings. Pentecostals have endured more than their share of dismissive scholarship, condescending analysis, and popular disdain. They have been repudiated as semiliterate, spurned as psychologically deranged, or scorned as the hapless and pathetic victims of religious charlatans. They know what it feels like to be laughed at as "holy rollers," to bear the stigma of both religious and social banishment, and to be contemptuously ignored by the world of theological scholarship. I did not want to perpetuate any of these injuries on people I had come to love and respect.

As I came closer to the actual writing of this book, however, I realized that I could not ultimately avoid dealing with the unappealing side of pentecostalism, not just elements that I found unattractive, but the parts that are an embarrassment to the pentecostals themselves, at least to the ones I had come to know. Still, I did not savor the prospect. I had gotten so much of value from my association with pentecostals that I did not want to cause them any grief. The last thing I wanted was to relapse into the role of a patronizing objective observer. Then, just as I was wondering how I was going to undertake this more cheerless part of my journey, an opportunity came to plunge into it in a way I had not expected. I was grateful to get the chance, but the result was unsettling, and even alarming at times. Still, it gave me a way to say what needed to be said and still maintain the bonds of trust that had developed between me and the people I was learning from.

I had flown to a small college in Kansas to give a commencement address in May of 1993. After I had assured the graduates that they were the future leaders of America, and they had driven off with their diplomas and their happy families, I relaxed at the college president's home with some of the faculty members. The conversation eventually came around to what I was currently working on. When I told them I was writing a book about pentecostalism, at first they seemed a little surprised; but then the president told me there was a spectacularly successful pentecostal church in a nearby city that I simply had to visit, if only to help them all understand its astonishing appeal and rapid expansion. A quick phone call determined that there was a service that very evening, so within an hour, I set out, accompanied by the college psychotherapist and a professor of philosophy, both of them impelled in part by curiosity and in part by a reluctance to have their guest get lost in a strange city. We were off to visit the Sheffield Family Life Center in Kansas City, Missouri.

Although its name makes it sound like a counseling clinic, the Family Life Center is actually a pentecostal congregation affiliated with the Assemblies of God, the largest predominantly white pentecostal denomination in America. Like many other pentecostal congregations recently, however, the building it meets in is called a "family life center," in part because it provides the space for many of the church's other programs in addition to worship, and also because—I was beginning to learn—many pentecostals have attached themselves so enthusiastically to the recent religious celebration of "traditional family values" that the words have even found their way into the names of their churches.

We lost our way briefly while looking for the address, stopped at a gas station, and were informed by a friendly attendant that we were close and that if we continued on this road we would see it, but "it doesn't look like a church, it looks like a warehouse." After a couple of more inquiries, we found it, and saw that it would indeed have been easy to miss. The church is located in what can charitably be called an "unpromising section" of Kansas City. It stands in the midst of unmowed vacant lots, rutted roads, freight yards, a couple of service stations, and some nondescript, apparently unused buildings. Here and there a partial car skeleton peeped out of encroaching weeds, giving the neighborhood a certain Appalachian ambience. It was obviously an area in which real estate values are not particularly high.

My companions glanced around skeptically at the desolate location. But as far as I was concerned the forlorn surroundings did nothing to diminish the church's promise. After all, the pentecostal revival began in a warehouse, and the less-than-upscale people the movement draws often live near districts like this. Also, given the need for a large building and the meager resources many pentecostal people command—to say nothing of the need for parking spaces—this venue seemed quite appropriate.

We had arrived about ten minutes before the 6:00 P.M. service was scheduled to begin, but already both the parking lot next to the church and the larger one across the street were filling up rapidly with Fords, Chevies, pickup trucks, and an occasional Honda or Volkswagen. We parked in the larger lot, and I noticed that one of my companions, the psychologist who had driven us here, not only locked all the doors, but circled the car to test that each one was secure.

Inside, the building seemed utterly cavernous. Rows of metal folding seats, about 600 of them by my estimate, faced a wide stage on which an immense off-white curtain was presently drawn. From behind it we could hear the chirps and roars of invisible clarinets and trombones tuning up. There was an air of expectation in the crowd. We sat down about halfway back and looked around. People nodded pleasantly, but—as in most pentecostal churches—no one handed us a bulletin or a hymn book, not because they were not glad to see us but because the order of service is supposed to be spontaneous and the songs are flashed on a screen. I noticed that to our right there was a large balcony equipped with facilities for preparing and serving food. The railing of the balcony was decked with dozens of flags representing—as we learned later—the countries where the Assemblies of God has missionaries.

The auditorium was filling up rapidly but people were still arriving. Our earlier phone call, answered by a recorded voice, had informed us that there were 9 o'clock and 11 o'clock services in the morning as well as this one. I asked the smiling woman in the pew in front of me who welcomed us if she had been present that morning and she said she had. "And it was terrific," she added, "we really had *church*." From behind the curtain the tuning-up sounds, trumpet runs, and flute trills, were becoming more clamorous. The people seated around us did not appear well to do. Their clothes might have come from discount stores or rummage sales. Some of the young people sported bright message t-shirts. Many of the men wore no ties. The women seemed to favor print dresses and pants suits.

Most of the people were white, and—listening carefully to the accents I heard around me—I speculated that many had found their way to Kansas City from Appalachia and the Ozarks. But there was a scattering of blacks and Latinos, and a few Asians. Only slightly more than half those in attendance were women. Two seats to my right, with an empty chair intervening, sat a young black woman who appeared to be about eighteen years old. She was dressed poorly in a tattered knit sweater and a shapeless skirt. She wore sneakers and droopy yellow socks. I knew that poor people often save their best clothes, sometimes their only respectable apparel, for churchgoing. But when I saw her I was reminded that some people are so poor they don't even have Sunday-go-to-meeting clothes. She looked nervous, and was fingering a large black leather-covered Bible. Even though I knew what time the service was supposed to begin, I asked her anyway in an effort to start a conversation. She told me, but then quickly looked away. She was not interested in socializing, at least not with an unfamiliar white man wearing a suit and tie.

But there was a lot of socializing going on. A tall white woman adorned with a towering black bouffant hairdo strolled from pew to pew welcoming people. A tall, lean man with thick glasses and a slight squint, who later turned out to be the pastor, was sidling along between the rows of chairs shaking hands, beaming, and clapping people on the shoulder. He was dressed as I had never seen any Baptist or Lutheran minister attired, in a cream sport jacket, flamboyant red and blue tie, crimson suspenders, dark-blue trousers, and white shoes. It occurred to me that he could easily have played one of the Broadway gamblers—say Harry the Horse—in "Guys and Dolls."

The curtain was still closed when a very friendly middle-aged woman in purple slacks, green blouse, and yellow sweater leaned over from the row of seats behind us and laughed heartily as she shook our hands and welcomed us. The hue of her hair suggested a less-than-successful tinting. She spoke with a broad midwestern accent. It turned out she had accidentally bumped the philosopher's elbow while finding her seat and said she didn't want him to think she was trying to hug him. "That comes later on in the service," she said, and laughed again. The philosopher, who had told me earlier he was a back-sliding Episcopalian, glanced at me apprehensively. I seized the opportunity, however, to ask her some questions. No, she had not been here this morning, she had had to work, cleaning an office building. But she had certainly been here last week, she said, "and we really *got down* here. I mean we really *had church*."

It was the second time I had heard that expression in ten minutes. I had heard it previously among African Americans but not among whites, so I asked her what "really having church" meant. "You'll see," she said smiling, "in just a minute." She told me she had been coming to this church for three years, ever since she moved here from a small town in southern Missouri. When I asked her if most of the people in the church had recently moved to town she said, "No, everybody's coming here," adding with what seemed a note of pride that this was a new building because the congregation had overflowed the last one. As she was talking a man in olive-drab slacks and an open-necked flannel shirt joined her. He nodded to me, but our conversation was cut off as the lights dimmed and the curtain parted dramatically on a towering swell of music to reveal about fifty people on stage producing an eruption of joyous sounds.

Now all eyes were directed to the wide stage, bathed in spots and footlights. On the left sat five ministers, including the one in the crimson suspenders. In the middle a good-sized band perched on risers between two choirs, one on either side of a magnificent set of gleaming drums and cymbals. There were two lead singers. One was a very pretty, slim young white woman in her early twenties, wearing a semiclinging vivid red dress that reached just below her knees, with a stylish gold chain around her waist. She moved and swayed as she sang, and led a song called "Whose Report Do You Believe?" Her brown hair fell well below the shoulders and swirled as she turned back and forth, first pointing up to the ceiling on "whose," then to the congregation on "you."

Next to her, also leading the singing, stood a handsome black woman, a little older, adorned in a longer, somewhat more subdued but expensive-looking dark-patterned dress. Her hair was cut a bit shorter than her white companion's and carefully coiffed. Her gestures were lively, almost like those of her partner but perhaps a shade more muted, not quite as buoyant. There were other blacks on the stage too, in the choirs and in the band. The congregation was singing along vigorously and clapping. I glanced at the young black woman beside me. She was singing too, but still seemed a little reticent. I wondered what this splashy display of interracial haute couture meant to her.

I turned back to watch the band. Pentecostal churches almost always have them, but they are usually four- or five-piece affairs. This was the biggest one I had ever seen: flute, two trumpets, a trombone, three saxophones, a violin equipped with an amplifying device, a clarinet, keyboard, piano guitar, electric bass, and drums. A dark-skinned man dressed in a carefully tailored light-blue suit and a canary necktie seemed to be actually leading the singing. At least he was waving his arms while holding a cordless mike now in one hand, now in the other. I later learned he was a Filipino. The racial and ethnic mix of both the congregation and leadership seemed very impressive to me; and yet I would not hear the word "multicultural" all night.

After five minutes the same song was still going on. "Whose report do *you* believe?" the lead singers asked, pointing to the congregation. The message was: we don't believe "the world's" report. We believe *God's* report, the report that he loves us and sustains us, and that he "has given us the victory." As one song bounced quickly to another, the words flashed onto two large screens placed on either side of the stage. I used to wonder why pentecostals use this device so often, rather than simply photocopying the lyrics. When I asked a minister he told me it keeps people "from sticking their noses in books." It is also true that the words tend to be repetitious, and many congregations seem to know them by heart anyway.

After perhaps fifteen or twenty minutes of singing, the house lights went down even more and the Filipino man sang a poignant solo. It was about feeling lonely in the city, seeing homeless people, and asking, Why am I Here? It was a little schmaltzy, accompanied by a full orchestra on a tape instead of by the stage band. But everyone seemed to be listening intently, and I could well imagine that for many of the newcomers to this city from rural areas and small towns, the ballad carried very personal and painful connotations.

After the solo, we sang another song, with the same glamorous lead singers and the arm waver in the canary tie back in action. Then, just as the song ended, I heard a staccato burst of glossolalia. I looked around but then saw that it was coming from the drummer and was amplified by the clip-on microphone on his jacket. He went on for only about twenty seconds in a high monotone. As soon as he had finished, the pastor said through his own microphone, "That was speaking in tongues. Just as we read about it in Acts 2." Then the service proceeded apace.

I was bothered. I had heard tongue speaking in pentecostal churches many times before, and had never been annoyed. It can show how close the worshippers feel to God, and can provide a

way of praying that goes beyond normal linguistic
there was something about this instance that disturb
not come from the heart of the congregation, but
the footlights. It had been followed so quickly by
smoothly packaged explanation. This was not glossolal   protest
or as prophecy. It was glossolalia as performance, and—at least
to me—it sounded counterfeit.

Next the pastor came to the microphone and made announcements in an off-handed, jocular, manner. In the same humorous
vein he referred to the morning service in which a visiting preacher
had apparently made a sustained plea for money. Obviously the
guest's prolonged importuning had caused some complaints to
the host pastor. So now he was telling the congregation that Jesus
had talked about money more than any other single subject.

His remark reminded me that I had, in fact, noticed a lot of
talk about money in pentecostal sermons, and not just to raise
funds. They seem to talk about it much more than in the more
established churches where the mention of filthy lucre seems a
little gauche, and is usually restricted to Pledge Sunday. I have
often wondered why. After all, money is something that is on
people's minds a lot. My guess is that pentecostals talk about it
more because they usually don't have as much of it, therefore
they do not feel so guilty about it and can talk about wanting it
with fewer qualms. It is also possible that in a society where
everyone is told that not having enough money is one's own fault,
money becomes a source of anxiety and fantasy. The people who
attend pentecostal churches tend to be from the same population
that plays the lottery.

Money—why you don't have enough and how to get more—
has come to play such a central role in many pentecostal churches
that recently a whole new theology has grown up around it. It is
premised on the belief that God not only wills eternal life for all
believers, but robust health and material prosperity as well. They
call it "the-health-and-wealth gospel," and one of its best-known
practitioners, Kenneth Hagin, has explained it in a book aptly
entitled *Redeemed from Poverty, Sickness and Death*. The idea is
that through the crucifixion of Christ, Christians have inherited all

e promises God made to Abraham, and these include both spiritual and material well-being. The only problem is that Christians have too little faith to appropriate what is rightly theirs. What they need to do is to state that claim loud and clear. This so called name-it-and-claim-it, or positive confession theology has become very popular—and very controversial—in pentecostal circles recently. In 1990 an Assemblies of God professor at the denomination's Southeastern College in Lakeland, Florida, published a scalding condemnation of it as a serious deviation from the Christian Gospel, derived from such cultic sources as New Thought, which was a nineteenth-century mind-healing movement. He also correctly added that it owed much to the "positive thinking" philosophy of the late Norman Vincent Peale and to the upbeat religious boosterism that televangelist Robert Schuller purveys from his Crystal Cathedral. Still, few pentecostals will deny that despite such condemnations, the gospel of health and wealth has many adherents among their people and their ministers.

I did not hear any name-it-and-claim-it theology at Sheffield Family Life Center that night. But was it somehow implicit in the spectacle, the spotlights, and the theatrical production values? Aimee Semple McPherson's colorful "illustrated sermons" had introduced this theatrical style into pentecostalism: but they had been straightforward parables, often presented with a redeeming element of self-parody. Here, however, the genre had been carried to excess. The glitz and glamour had defaced the Gospel. What message was the poor young black woman beside me actually getting from all of this? Whose report *should* she believe? The message of the Gospels (which were not read and hardly even alluded to that night), or the "report" that was conveyed with such luster by the beautiful people behind the footlights who seemed so happy, so chic, and so at ease in their elegant attire, and yet so much closer than the people she saw on television. When, later in the service, she went forward to accept the Lord, what did she think she was accepting? If it is true that in most religion, and in pentecostalism in particular, the medium is the message, exactly what *was* the message of this throbbing display of youthful energy and opulent beauty, especially to an auditorium filled with people who clean office buildings and shop at yard sales?

As soon as the minister's peroration on money was over, something else happened that only deepened my already uneasy mood. He started talking excitedly about how *big* the Assemblies of God denomination was and how fast it was growing. Why, the Lord was adding *thousands* and *thousands* of souls every day. "Just *look* at the flags from all over the world. It's the biggest thing going!" I glanced at the people around me. They were looking at the flags, but they did not seem all that impressed. My hunch is that they had much more immediate problems, and that whether or not the church they were attending tonight was part of a worldwide religious bandwagon was not of pressing interest to them. I had heard a lot of boasting from pentecostals about their staggering growth statistics and it was beginning to irritate me: it sounded like more health-and-wealth theology. They seemed to be saying, in effect, "God must be on our side." But this is a somewhat ironic claim to be made by a movement that early in its life maintained that the proof that God was with them was that they were so small and so despised.

I could feel my attitude souring by the minute. But I caught myself, decided not to make premature judgments, and tried to listen as sympathetically as I could. We sang another song. Then something surprising happened. The pastor came back to the microphone and, while the band played softly and the choirs hummed, he issued what both pentecostals and evangelicals call "the invitation" or "altar call." It is a plea for anyone present who is unsaved to come forward, accept Christ, and be redeemed. I was familiar with the practice, of course, but I was surprised because I had never seen it come so early in a service. It is usually reserved for the grand finale, after the singing and preaching have induced a receptive mood. Later on I was to learn why it came at this point on that night. The guest preacher was still present. He was going to preach again tonight. And he still wanted money to support his hospital in Calcutta. Consequently, the peak moment of this service was not going to be an entreaty to accept Jesus but an appeal for cash.

The preacher dragged the altar call out for several minutes. While he was pleading I noticed the young black woman was becoming agitated. Finally she left her seat and went forward to accept the Lord, leaving her Bible on the seat. A couple of other people also made their way to the front of the auditorium—there was no altar of any kind there—and counselors led them all off to a side room. I noticed that, as the pastor had said while he was repeating the invitation, men counselors accompanied the men and women counselors the women. The heated excitation of their worship has made pentecostals especially sensitive to accusations of sexual impropriety, and the widely publicized indiscretions of such televangelists as Jimmy Swaggart and Jim Bakker have made them even touchier.

Finally the minister introduced the visiting preacher. This was not a typical night at the church that I had hoped for, and I was disappointed that we would not hear the regular preacher in the crimson suspenders speak, since I had been told of his reputation as a riveting orator. But once more I stilled my disappointment and sat back to listen to the guest as the house lights dimmed again. The visiting missionary started by talking about his family, and how he had consulted with them before making this trip back to America. They had all prayed about it together, he said, and they had finally granted him permission to fly from Calcutta for this week of missionary emphasis. He asked the ushers to hand out little calling cards with a color photo of himself with his smiling wife and two small children. Like many pentecostal preachers he was an accomplished raconteur. He warmed his listeners up with some piquant stories and jokes, then effected a careful transition into an attack on possessiveness in family affairs and in life in general. Then he lampooned the self-righteous folks who think they'll be the only ones in heaven. To do so he told the oft-repeated story about the people who had to be walled off in the celestial city because they thought they were the only ones the   ought as I listened that however hackneyed this old   was not a story a fundamentalist would ever tell.   sts believe that they *will* be the only ones saved,   ntecostals do not. Pentecostals do insist they have something other believers lack, but they usually concede they are not the only passengers on the ship of salvation.

I still felt grumpy, but as the preacher got going I also discovered that somehow I *wanted* him to do well. I wondered why. Of course, I had put myself on the spot by persuading the philosopher and the psychotherapist to give up an evening to come with me, and at this point I was not so sure they were glad they had come. But there was something else. I became aware that throughout my travels around the realms of pentecostalism I had been keeping a kind of mental ledger, entering positive and negative points about what I observed. And I knew that for some reason I wanted the positive side to prevail at the end. So I found I was trying to help this preacher, chuckling at the jokes even when I had heard them many times before, nodding at the sentimental stories.

After ten minutes of banter the preacher announced his text. My hopes rose again. It was from the book of the Old Testament prophet Zechariah. The text, quoted in the epigraph to this chapter, foresees the reestablishment of a renewed and glorious Jerusalem. It says that "Jerusalem will be without walls," that people and cattle will be "numerous," and God promises, "I myself shall be a wall of fire around it . . . and a glorious presence within it." I was pleased because this is a perfect text for a pentecostal sermon: it predicts the New Jerusalem. It describes the lushness and abundance of the coming millennium. It promises the immediate presence of God with his people. And it has *fire* in it, this time the Lord Himself *is* the wall of fire that protects the inhabitants from danger. I was prepared to witness a spirited presentation, if not reenactment of this explosive text.

But he let me down. After making a compelling start at what could have been a strong, engaging, almost completely narrative sermon, he skidded like a truck on the ice into a totally different style. He started in on what in his mental file must be labeled "the missionary sermon." Now his manner changed abruptly. A well-rehearsed catch came into his voice at the end of nearly every phrase, as though he could hardly fight back the sobs: "Her little legs were so thin [sob] that they were no thicker than my

[sob] finger." Then he recounted a personal story he must have repeated a hundred times before. It told of how his parents had seen a vision that instructed them to pray for him while he lay sick in a rude hut on a distant island in the Indian ocean. They had called people together in New Jersey, prayed, then telegraphed him. He was cured, got to his feet, and preached at a revival in which many souls were saved. He had had other visions, lots of them, and he had also been blessed time and time again by the miraculous appearances of complete strangers who mysteriously handed him money just when he needed it.

Now I was getting downright edgy. Of course I had heard about signs and wonders and miracles and visions before in pentecostal churches, but this preacher claimed to be an ambulatory lightning rod for supernatural interventions. As I looked around me I noticed that some of the regular worshippers appeared edgy too. They seemed to *want* to believe this courageous emissary from a city so far away, but did they feel some of the creeping incredulity I did? When does testimony turn into bragging? At what point does reliance on God's grace curdle into an infantile dependency on just plain magic? When do insight and discernment slip over into clairvoyance and telepathy? I knew that we were now traversing one of the perilous edges of pentecostal spirituality, the indistinct border it shares with crystal reading, channeling, and other New Age nostrums.

My mind began to wander. As I watched the preacher pace the stage and heard his breath reverberate through the microphone, I was carried back to a visit I had made five years earlier to another pentecostal family life center, the one located on the 279-acre headquarters estate of Jimmy Swaggart Ministries in Baton Rouge, Louisiana. What was it that had called forth the mental association? Maybe it was the flags. That was the last time I had seen so many of them in a church setting. Only there they represented not the mission fields of a denomination, but the 195 nations reached by Swaggart's own sprawling world ministry. I remembered that I had been shown a state-of-the-art television production center, a private Christian elementary school, and an impressive printing plant. Swaggart's Family Worship Center itself is a modern eight-sided building whose lobbies are decorated with gigantic world maps showing where his television evangelism is carried. At that time the statistics were spectacular, even for a pentecostal televangelist. At the height of his fame, before his widely publicized "fall," it is estimated that Swaggart was reaching 500 million people, the largest television audience ever to watch a regularly scheduled program of any kind. His preaching was carried on more than 3,000 stations not counting cable. Contributions poured into his office, which had its own ZIP code and handled more mail than any other single address in the state. It is estimated that in 1986 the money flowed in at the rate of about half a million dollars a day. It was an impressive set-up.

But, sitting in the Sheffield Family Life Center in 1993, I also remembered being disappointed by Swaggart himself. I don't know what I was expecting. Like many people I had seen him frequently on television—weeping, scolding, dancing, singing along with his choir, sometimes picking out tunes on the piano. Also like many others who did not like his theology I found him a little frightening, but strangely compelling, a voice from some hidden dimension of myself perhaps. I had often puzzled over just what it was that kept me from switching him off right away when I happened upon his familiar face while grazing the channels. I continued to be puzzled until I read Lawrence Wright's candid description, in his book *Saints and Sinners*, of why he felt the same fascination. "I felt an unhappy kinship with this man," he writes, "I could sense the raw and sometimes dangerous expansiveness of the human spirit. His was not a religion I could believe in—but then mere belief was not what he was after: it was surrender, total abject surrender of the spirit. And of course a part of me longed for exactly that, the ecstatic abandonment of my own busy, judgmental, ironic mentality."

That was it. On television at least, Swaggart was something of a shaman. By putting himself into an ecstatic state of consciousness, with hundreds of millions of people watching, he conveyed a wildly dissonant note from a register that is somewhere within us, but that we do not hear from very often. As Wright puts it, he was beguiled by Swaggart in part because of fear, a fear that the man was on to something, "that the whole point of life was to plunge into the wilderness and joyfully throw aside the resistance and anxiety that characterize the skeptic." He confesses that when he watched a Swaggart program he was both drawn to and terrified of the possibility of becoming himself a person "bursting with spiritual power."

I had also sensed some of that power on television. But at Swaggart's church it was diluted. He seemed almost puny. It was clearly one of those instances in which the power of the television medium transforms and magnifies the ordinary. Kathleen Reid, a professor of Communications at Lee College, a pentecostal institution in Cleveland, Tennessee, has suggested that Swaggart—and the kind of primitive pentecostalism he represents—is extraordinarily well suited to television. Television is a modern technology that has a curious similarity to the magic of shamanism. The shrinking of distance, the larger-than-life presence, the compression of time, the sense of belonging suggested by the congregation's response, the appeal to emotion rather than logic—all integral to the topography of television—are also elements of shamanism. The problem is that when the shaman is pacing a stage 200 feet away, when the contortions of his face and the glint in his eyes—so visible on the screen—cannot be seen, then something of the magic evaporates.

I have not seen Jimmy Swaggart on television for a long time now. After his tearful confession of his various rendezvous with prostitutes, and his defrocking by the Assemblies of God, many stations stopped carrying his program. He is also—along with Jim and Tammy Faye Bakker—a severe embarrassment to many pentecostals who wish they could have been spared the shoddy saga of the rise and fall of such celebrities. But Swaggart remains an important figure for anyone who seeks to understand the appeal of the pentecostal impulse. For me he represented not only the unprocessed harshness of primal spirituality, but also how easily it can be manipulated and misused in the hands of a skilled practitioner.

I think that Wright is correct that Swaggart was in touch with something fearsome but real in all of us. But Swaggart was also an unprincipled megalomaniac, a cruel and mean-tempered man whose rambling sermons attacked "faggots" and Catholics and the leadership of his own denomination with equal ferocity. I do not believe, however, that in saying no to Swaggart's version of pentecostal Christianity, as many pentecostals do, one can deny the reality of the spiritual forces he was able to conjure. Denying them does not make them go away. Nor does exploiting them for sordid purposes mean that they cannot also inspire generosity and compassion. I think that Swaggart is a warning signal to the tired mainline churches, pointing to genuine spiritual energies most of them have forgotten. But to pentecostals he is *also* a warning signal, a reminder that the fire from heaven can burn and destroy as well as purify and inspire. Both the unprecedented fame and the unparalleled nosedive of Jimmy Swaggart remind us that reemergence of rudimentary spirituality at the end of the twentieth century can be both good news and bad news.

When I snapped out of my reverie about Jimmy Swaggart and glanced at my watch I was startled to find that although my mind had been wandering for nearly ten minutes, the preacher was still going on unabated. Now I just wanted to leave, and I hoped the he would wind it up or at least move on to something else soon. He did move on: he started to rage about the U.S. government, which he declared was at this very moment being taken over by a satanic conspiracy. Now my disquietude turned to revulsion. I had heard that some pentecostals have become ardent believers in satanic plot theories, and that some were even devotees of accounts of the alleged recovery of memories of satanic ritual abuse. I glanced toward the doors and wondered how obvious it would be if my companions and I left. Would this make us part of the conspiracy?

I was relieved when the service finally ended, though only after twenty-five more grueling minutes of the visiting preacher's sobs, stagey sniffles, and pleas for money. Other worshippers seemed relieved too. After the benediction, people pushed toward the doors quickly and there was not much socializing. The woman in the purple slacks with the tinted hair who had greeted me so merrily before barely glanced at me as we sidled out between the rows of chairs. I thought maybe she was sorry I had picked this night to come to a church she obviously loved, because now I might go away with a bad impression. I wanted to assure her that I understood, that not even the worst excesses of a guest preacher's histrionics could dampen my affection for pentecostal people and for their way of worshipping God. I knew that as far as she was concerned, tonight we had *not* "had church," but I also knew there would be other nights when we would. Moving toward the doors, I even felt a little protective toward the people around me. Uprooted, neglected, the also-rans in the fierce American battle for success and security, it was they and not the melodramatic evangelist who brought the real pain and the longing—the sense of the reality of God—to pentecostal worship. Suddenly, as we returned to the car I realized that despite my anger and discomfort, the Spirit had been telling me something that evening after all. I was going to have to write about the disagreeable underside of pentecostalism not because I disliked the woman with the tinted hair but because I liked her very much. She deserved something better than she had gotten that evening, and if what I wrote could tilt the current battle within pentecostalism even a little in her direction, it would be worth the effort.

CHAPTER 14

Pentecostalism in America: Body Snatchers and Spiritual Warriors

I saw three foul spirits like frogs
coming from the mouths of the dragon,
the beast, and the false prophet. These
are demonic spirits with power to work
miracles, sent out to muster all the
kings of the world for the battle on
the great day of God, the sovereign Lord.
Revelation 16: 13–14

*T*HERE ARE MANY pentecostals in America today who are fascinated to the point of obsession with demonic spirits and the powers of darkness. This preoccupation has been developing for some time, but it reached a critical point in 1986 when a previously unknown writer named Frank Peretti published his novel *This Present Darkness*. I had occasionally heard about this book and about the enormously wide readership it has gained, especially among a group of evangelical Christians and pentecostals who sometimes refer to themselves as the "Third Wave." These people see classical pentecostalism as the first modern outpouring of the Spirit; the charismatic movement in the "mainline" churches as the second; and themselves as the third. For various reasons these Third Wavers do not like to be identified with either of the previous two "waves," and they do not want to be called "pentecostals," but since their teachings are having a widespread impact on pentecostalism I wanted to find out about them. I asked a pentecostal scholar where I should start to explore what was for me an exotic terrain, and he suggested that I begin with Peretti. He told me the novel had already sold nearly 2 million copies and was such a hot item among satanic conspiracy buffs that it has been called the "bible" of the Third Wave.

I am glad it was the beginning of my summer vacation when I began reading *This Present Darkness* because, though it is not by a long shot Dostoyevsky's *The Possessed*, it is an absorbing yarn. At times it reminded me of the old movie *The Invasion of the Body Snatchers* with a few themes from *The Exorcist* and Bram Stoker's *Dracula* thrown in. It did not take me very long to read the book itself, but reading it propelled me into another body of literature, including a collection of essays entitled *Wrestling with Dark Angels: Toward A Deeper Understanding of the Supernatural Forces in Spiritual Warfare*. I soon discovered that the Third Wave material is virtually limitless. I needed all summer not just to read the material but to blink, look again, and try to make sense out of what these writers were saying.

This Present Darkness unfolds in a small college town which sounded to me at first like Oberlin, Ohio, where I started out my life as a teacher and minister after I finished seminary thirty-five years ago. But there the similarity ends. For in this town, which in Peretti's novel is meant to represent the whole world, a horrifying war is going on. The battle is between no less than the demonic powers of darkness and the angelic hosts of light. The objective of both sides is to gain control of the town (read "world"). But what brought the bodysnatchers and similar celluloid classics to mind is that this cosmic shoot-out between opposing battalions of "spiritual forces" is taking place in and through the bodies of living men and women. In fact, one sometimes gets the impression that the human beings are little more than puppets tugged and jerked by transcendental forces.

The characters are not drawn with particular subtlety. The hero is the laudably devout pastor of a small church, which is obviously not affiliated with one of the established mainline denominations. He is aided by the courageous local newspaper editor and a retired missionary woman. Arrayed on the other side are the minister of a mainline church, a psychology professor, the town's chief of police and—to thicken the plot—the courageous editor's own daughter. The hosts of heaven are conveniently headquartered in the small church. The demonic forces have their command post in the basement offices of the psychology department.

The storyline lumbers on, with a few frisky twists, involving embezzlement, satanic ritual abuse, and murder; but it soon becomes evident that plot is not what this book is about. It is about cosmology. It is a geography and gazetteer of the angelic and demonic domains. As I read it I had the curious impression that I was back in graduate school studying some of the Jewish apocalyptic documents we analyzed to help us understand the prehistory of the New Testament, such as First Enoch or Baruch or some of the scrolls from the Dead Sea. The difference was that in Peretti's book the angelology and demonology are even more complex. Among the angelic forces, the good guys, one finds such figures as a silver-haired angel called The General, the captain of the host whose name is Tal, and other seraphim who are called Triskal and Guilo. In the opposite corner lurk the dark forces under the direct command of Satan and his lieutenant, Ba-al Rafar, and who go by such unattractive names as the Prince of Babylon, Lucius, and Strongman. They want to enthrone a spurious New Age Christ, and the evil rule they are intent on establishing is called, oddly enough, the "New World Order." When I read that, I wondered whether former president George Bush's speechwriters might have been better advised to avoid this term to designate the objectives of Operation Desert Storm.

What intrigued me most was the way these supernatural personages, both benevolent and diabolic, make use of human beings to get their respective jobs done. Indeed human beings appeared to have little to do with it. Sometimes the good ones could open themselves to the angelic beings through prayer, but they were also likely to be thwarted by the bad ones conniving with the minions of darkness. But the spiritual agents were not restricted only to people to do their work. The pestilential forces could foul car motors as well, and sometimes did. But mainly they came to their human partners in seances or visions. The scariest element was that the demons could also materialize themselves in the form of human beings. The book ends somewhat ambiguously. Although the dark forces have been banished, at least temporarily, from the town, we are sure that they will strike again elsewhere. Indeed on the last pages the angelic host heads off for another location where yet another clash in the unending battle is about to begin.

As hammock fare, *This Present Darkness* can keep a vacationer from nodding off. But as theology I found it distressing and, given the number of readers it has found, somewhat ominous. I wanted to dismiss it as an eerie but harmless genre of religious science fiction. But when I started to read the more formal theological sources on which Peretti drew, and which apparently inform the Third Wave mentality, I could not.

Wrestling with Dark Angels is not fiction. It is a collection of papers presented at a conference convened in 1988 by C. Peter Wagner, one of the founders of the Third Wave, at Fuller Theological Seminary in Pasadena, California. Wagner's own article takes off from a statement made by one of his own mentors, Timothy Warner, who once suggested that "Satan does indeed assign a demon or corps of demons to every geopolitical unit in the world, and they are the principalities and powers against whom we wrestle." Wagner himself asserts that "Satan delegates high ranking members of the hierarchy of evil spirits to control nations, regions, cities, tribes, peoples, groups, neighborhoods and other significant networks of human beings throughout the world." These higher-ranked demons have the responsibility of directing the work of the lower ranking ones. Another Third Wave writer, Dick Bernal, has taken this geographical specialization of the diabolic forces a step further. He instructs his readers and listeners about the evil specialization of each cluster of demons. Thus, according to a report in the *San Francisco Examiner*, he says that San Francisco is ruled by the Spirit of Perversion, Oakland by the Spirit of Murder, San Jose by the Spirit of Greed. The whole of Marin County, he says, is ruled by the New Age Spirit, which most of the Third Wave writers seem to think is the worst villain of all. But even Bernal's demonology is not as labyrinthine as the one set forth in Frank and Ida Mae Hammond's *Pigs in the Parlor: A Practical Guide to Deliverance*. They catalog 53 "common demon groupings," and more than 200 different types of demons. But they modestly assure the reader that their registry is not complete.

By the time I had read my little pile of Third Wave books, a mere sampling of what has become a torrent, I wondered what had happened to the whimsical but spiritually insightful ideas of the great Christian intellectual and science fiction writer C. S. Lewis, the favorite of many evangelical Christians. As a youngster I had relished his *Screwtape Letters* which are written in the form of a senior demon's letters to his small-fry helper. I still think the musings of that book are profound. But as I read the Third Wave material I had the sinking feeling that a metaphor had somehow become a metaphysic, a story had been turned into an ideology. Later, in a very informative article by the late Robert Guelich, a professor at Fuller Theological Seminary who has carefully studied the Third Wave movement and shares many of my misgivings, I found a quotation from *The Screwtape Letters* that seemed to put the whole matter in just the right perspective. "There are two equal and opposite errors," Lewis writes, "into which our race can fall about the devils. One is to disbelieve in their existence. The other is to believe and to feel an excessive and unhealthy interest in them. They themselves are equally pleased by both errors, and hail a materialist and a magician with the same delight."

One of the reasons why I was upset by the "excessive and unhealthy" fixation on demons that holds so many pentecostals in thrall is that I am afraid their fetishism on the subject will drive many people toward the opposite danger that C. S. Lewis identified. As a student of Paul Tillich, who was brave enough to use the idea of "the demonic" in his theology, I am convinced that modern liberal theologians have too easily discarded the idea of transpersonal forces of evil. Instead of trying to fathom what references to evil spirits in the Bible point us to in our own age—which I believe is something quite real—they have dismissed the whole notion of the demonic as implausible. But in my opinion a century that has witnessed Auschwitz and Hiroshima and the Gulag is in no position to laugh off the ugly reality of diabolical forces that seem capable of sweeping people up in their energies. I also believe, however, that we must ponder these destructive currents that surge through our psyches without pretending we know much about them and, most of all, without locating them in the people we oppose. Tillich knew there were "principalities and powers" of darkness because he was hounded out of Nazi Germany. Despite many criticisms directed against him, he continued to insist throughout his life that evil in the world has a structural and not just an individual quality. What annoys me about the experts who catalog and chart the different devils today, and who are sure the demons are at work in their opponents, is that they are making a very serious religious question seem trivial and ridiculous.

As the summer waned I tried to extricate myself from the spell-binding world this new demonology weaves, to lay it aside as a bizarre but harmless fantasy. But a couple of things happened that jolted me into the realization that I had to take it more seriously. One was a lead story in one of the newspapers that sits there with the *National Enquirer* on the rack next to the cash register at my local supermarket. This one is called *Weekly World News*, and the week I noticed it, the cover carried an arresting picture of what appeared to be the faces of Jesus Christ and Satan, formed by clouds, and facing each other. The headline read: "FACES OF JESUS AND SATAN SEEN OVER TEXAS." With some embarrassment I bought it and tucked the paper discreetly in the bag with the orange juice and breakfast cereal. The story inside, which I read when I got to my car, reported that "some two dozen stunned witnesses" had indeed seen this cumulus epiphany, and that "noted Bible scholars" were of the opinion that it signaled "the final earth-shattering battle between good and evil." One of these noted scholars, a Dr. Anthony Padula, identified by the paper only as a "prominent Dallas theologian," told the reporter Laurel Bowie that the "face-off" could only mean one thing: "Judgment Day as foretold in the book of Revelation is upon us, or at least very near."

I admit that I harbor a few reservations about the veracity of the *Weekly World News*, but I have no doubt whatever that a vivid strain of apocalyptic inventiveness runs through the popular imagination of millions of Americans. And it frequently draws on familiar, if sometimes vague, images from the Bible. Maybe what Frank Peretti and the pentecostals who promote satanic conspiracy theories are doing is analogous to what we have observed among pentecostals in Asia, Africa, and Latin America: absorbing the flotsam and shards of popular piety into their theology. But, as we have also seen elsewhere, this is pentecostalism's most serious weakness as well as the source of its greatest strength. Still, this "excessive and unhealthy interest" in demonology can not be dismissed as a harmless fascination. It has become a dangerous obsession, especially when it is combined with the newly awakened commitment of American pentecostals' participation in politics.

This commitment is something new. In the early years of their movement pentecostals did not have much time for the politics of this fallen world. Since Jesus was coming again soon it didn't matter much who was mayor or governor or even president. In the past two decades, however, American pentecostals have put aside their reluctance to participate in politics and in some instances have plunged in with high energy. The political figure who has tried the hardest to harness this newfound enthusiasm is Pat Robertson. Robertson's book *The New World Order: It Will Change the Way You Live* is neither fiction, nor a collection of theological speculations, nor a tall tale churned out for a pulp journal. It is an analysis of American society by a man who was once a serious candidate for a presidential nomination and might well be one again. In this book Robertson suggests that the leaders of the world financial community and the bosses of the world

communist movement have joined hands with certain occult forces
to bring in a "New World Order." It seems less than accidental
that what the demons are up to in Robertson's book is given the
same name as the evil scheme of the dark forces in Peretti's novel.
Also involved in the conspiracy with various degrees of awareness are Jimmy Carter, Lenin, Shirley MacLaine, the Masonic Order,
the Council on Foreign Relations, and even the hapless George
Bush. Since Bush was still in the White House when Robertson
was producing this work, the author allows that the president
may have been "unknowingly and unwittingly carrying out the
mission and mouthing the phrases of a tightly knit cabal whose
goal is nothing less than a new order for the human race under
the dominion of Lucifer and his followers."

It should be said immediately that Robertson does not belong
to a pentecostal church. He is a Baptist and was an ordained minister in that denomination before resigning his ordination to seek
the Republican nomination for president in 1988. But he clearly
belongs to what is sometimes referred to as the "pentecostal-
charismatic movement," that amorphous grouping of pentecostal
churches and congregations—some in the established denominations and some independent—that encourage a pentecostal style
of worship. Robertson's following among members of pentecostal
churches is considerable. His popularity is a little hard to understand given the theological differences that separate the "classical" pentecostal, those who trace their heritage back to Azusa
Street, and Robertson. The most important disparity hinges on
precisely the teaching that set the early pentecostals so clearly
against most of their fellow Christians, namely the question of
when Jesus will return. For the black and white believers who
gathered at Azusa Street, the answer was simple: any day now.
Therefore they were not interested in reshaping civil society or
running for public office.

Robertson seems to have started out with the same "*premil-
lennial*" view about the imminent approach of the Last Days. This
is also the belief of most fundamentalists, who hold that Christ
will actually return *before* the establishment of his Kingdom, and
in the meantime things will get progressively worse. It is opposed

to the *post*millennial idea that righteousness and justice will gradually spread and increase so that when Christ comes again the earth will be purified for his appearance. The distinction may seem to be a fine one to outsiders, but the two perspectives generate contradictory convictions about the proper role of Christians in society. If the End Times are indeed near and conditions are sure to worsen no matter what we do, then there is little point to running for president or even for the local school board. But if the reign of God might come gradually, and if Christians can help it along, then there is some reason to sign petitions or write to senators and representatives.

It is clear, however, that in recent years Robertson has modified his opinions on eschatology. He now believes that Christians—at least the ones who share his views—are called upon to try to assume positions of power wherever they can in order to build a more righteous and god-fearing society. This would seem to make him a *post*millennialist, and it puts him closer to what is now called "dominion theology" than to what pentecostals have traditionally taught. Dominion theology is based on a particular reading of the first chapter of the biblical book of Genesis in which God, having created Adam and Eve, says to them:

> Be fruitful and multiply, and fill the earth and subdue it; and have dominion over the fish of the sea and over the birds of the air and over *every living thing that moves upon the face of the earth*. (Genesis 1:27, emphasis added)

According to this reading, "every living thing" means not only animals but institutions, and since—as the health-and-wealth theology also teaches—Christians have inherited all these Old Testament mandates, this clearly means that Christians (and Robertson would add religious Jews) should rule on earth. They should "take dominion" over all the major institutions and run them until Christ comes again, which might be soon but could be a very long time. This vision of a nation whose courts and legislatures and schools and corporations are all run by believers may suggest the reason why Robertson changed the name of the university he heads in Virginia Beach from Christian Broadcast

Network University to Regent University. A "regent," says Robertson in explaining the name change, "is one who governs in the absence of a sovereign." The purpose of Regent University, which has 700 graduate students in education, communications, religion, and law, is to prepare its graduates to rule until Jesus, the absent sovereign, returns. Fred Clarkson, who discussed Regent University in an article in a journal called *Church and State* in January 1991, quotes Robertson as saying: "One day, if we read the Bible correctly, we will rule and reign along with our sovereign, Jesus Christ. So this is a kingdom institution to teach people how they may enter into the privilege they have as God's representatives on earth."

What flusters Robertson's liberal opponents is that for years Christians in the more ecumenical churches have criticized pentecostals and evangelicals for "being so concerned about heaven they are no earthly good" as a familiar saying used to put it. They were derided for promising people pie in the sky while turning their backs on the suffering and injustice of this present world. But this is no longer the case, and now that such movements as Jerry Falwell's fundamentalist Moral Majority of the 1980s and Robertson's Christian Coalition are actively at work in the political realm, liberals seem hoist on their own petard. They can hardly criticize Robertson or the dominion theologians for jumping into the political mix. But if they differ with their goals and methods, they have to argue the case on theological grounds and come up with a different interpretation of what the dominionists claim to find in the Bible.

Still, the shift in theology this long-term rather than short-term eschatology required in order to get so many pentecostals away from the mourning bench and into the precinct meetings was a momentous one. What has surprised me is how easily so many people seem to have made the transition. I have only met Mr. Robertson once. It was when he visited Harvard in 1988 during his unsuccessful quest for the Republican presidential nomination. I asked him about a passage in his book *The Hidden Kingdom* in which he wrote that the Bible teaches that the Soviet Union would be destroyed by earthquakes and volcanic eruptions. This sounded to me like distinctly *pre*millennial theology, since the holders of this position frequently interpret natural catastrophes as signs of the approach of the Last Days, just as the Azusa Street preachers interpreted the San Francisco earthquake of 1906. I asked Robertson why, if this were the case, we needed such a large defense budget.

He was not put off even for a moment by my somewhat impertinent question. Shrugging boyishly and flashing his famous smile, he said he certainly did believe that eventually God's kingdom of peace and justice would be established, but he did not know when, and in the meantime he hoped to work as hard as he could toward its realization. I wish I had known more at the time not just about Robertson's somewhat flexible views on eschatology, but about his ideas on governance. These only became clear to the public at large as the campaign proceeded, and even then he was sometimes a little less than forthright. Later, however, he made his views very clear indeed. In his book on the "New World Order" he wrote a paragraph in which he vigorously defended his belief that only those "who believe in Judeo-Christian values" are qualified to rule. His closed this section with a ringing summation of his political theology:

> There will never be world peace until God's house and God's people are given their rightful place of leadership at the top of the world. How can there be peace when drunkards, communists, atheists, New Age worshipers of Satan, secular humanists, oppressivedictators, greedy moneychangers, revolutionary assassins, adulterers, and homosexuals are on top?

This statement is a classic not only because it articulates the nub of dominion, or "Kingdom Now" theology so succinctly, but also because it so graphically catalogs the kinds of people Mr. Robertson's Christian Coalition—with its 450,000 members and its $12 million-a-year budget—consider to be their enemies, and the enemies of God. Admittedly, homosexuals and adulterers may be shocked at first to find themselves lumped with dictators and assassins, but dominion theology holds that *all* of the Old Testament laws are currently applicable, and not only to so-called

Christian nations but to all nations and to every institution within all those nations.

I have tried to take some small comfort in the reassurances I have heard from several people who know Robertson and Regent University better than I do, that he does not represent anything like the hard-core dominion theology position. In an excellent book on the subject entitled *Heaven on Earth,* for example, the American historian Bruce Barron suggests that the faculty members of Regent University take a much more pragmatic view, accept religious pluralism, and do not believe that every aspect of Old Testament law is immediately applicable today. They argue, rather, that the founding fathers, the U.S. Constitution, and the Declaration of Independence were strongly shaped by biblical concepts of law, but that current legal practice has drifted away from these foundations. They prefer to be called "constitutionalists" and are viewed by Barron as a moderating influence in the broader dominion theology movement.

At first I was not fully persuaded of Robertson's or Regent's "moderating" stance. The more I perused the fascinating but disconcerting literature of the dominion theology movement, however, the more I could see that it included thinkers who made me much more nervous. For example, I kept running into the name of a theologian who has influenced dominion thought in a very fundamental way but with whom, despite years of study in the field of theology, I was completely unfamiliar. The more I learned about him, however, the more I could see why some people are not only concerned but terrified by the prospect of his disciples gaining governmental powers. He is Rousas John Rushdoony, an American of Armenian background. According to one reference to his thought I ran across, Rushdoony insists that the Old Testament laws mandating the death penalty for adulterers, homosexuals, blasphemers, astrologers, witches, and teachers of false doctrine should still be enforced today. As one who, at least in the opinion of Mr. Rushdoony's adepts, is probably a teacher of false doctrine, I am not entirely at ease with this idea.

When I eventually found some of Rushdoony's books, including his 1,124-page *Roots of Christian Reconstruction,* I became even more uneasy, and also even more surprised that his ideas have won such a wide acceptance among some pentecostals and charismatics. Rushdoony, although he does not mention them very frequently, obviously does not have a high regard for pentecostals. In fact, in his book *The Institutes of Christian Law*, he issues them a direct slap in the face. Arguing as he does time and again for the *present validity* of Old Testament law, he says, "If the law is denied as the means of sanctification, then, logically, the only alternative [for believers] is Pentecostalism, with its antinomian and unbiblical doctrine of the Spirit."

On its face, this sharp reproach might seem to make Rushdoony and his ideas anathema to pentecostals. Paradoxically, however, the man who is trying harder than anyone else—albeit with mixed success—to bring all the different dominion, Kingdom Now, and reconstructionist groups together under a single canopy organization called the Coalition of Revival (cor) is Dr. Jay Grimstead, a member of a Pentecostal Holiness congregation in San Jose, California (a city which, it will be remembered, is currently ruled—according to Dick Bernal—by the Spirit of Greed). One of the first difficulties Grimstead had to confront in his ambitious effort to bring these highly opinionated groups together was of course the burning question of eschatology. What could be done about the long war of attrition that had been fought for decades between the premilliennalists and the postmilliennalists? Grimstead's answer was a simple one: we will just not argue about it anymore. Instead, we will get on with the task of remolding American society on the basis of biblical law. Not surprisingly, Rousas Rushdoony is a member of the steering committee of cor, and it has been reported that when the organization opens the doors of its new Kingdom College, he will teach the most important courses, the ones on biblical law.

At first I was merely puzzled about how so many pentecostals, whose battle-cry for years was the imminent return of Christ, could have fallen in love with dominion theology. When I discovered what some historians of the movement think the answer is, I was astounded. These historians believe that the turning point came with the same "Latter Rain" movement of the 1950s, one of whose massive revivals I had attended some forty years ago with my college friend in Philadelphia and witnessed speaking in tongues for the first time. Although I did not realize it then, the leaders of this movement were so convinced that the Spirit was at work in their spectacular displays of healings and prophecies that they believed a worldwide revival was at hand. They quietly set aside the idea that Jesus would return soon which, according to one of Latter Rain's leader's George Hawkin, may once have "served a useful purpose" but that was really "a false hope." In 1948 Hawkin wrote these words, which are remarkably prophetic of present-day Kingdom Now theology:

> We are entering into the Kingdom Age in a sense now, for the *Kingdom is being formed in us* and when it is completed . . . all judicial as well as religious authority will be vested in the church of Christ.

So it turns out that the boisterous demonstration of "praying through" and glossolalia I had witnessed from the balcony in that auditorium in Philadelphia was really part of a revolution within the pentecostal movement itself. It is true that the Latter Rain preachers did not advocate political action. They believed the spiritual purification and renewal of the church itself would accomplish the transformation of the world. In any case the Latter Rain revival did not last long, perhaps a decade, but it laid the *theological* groundwork for what has now become the Kingdom Now movement with its passionate activism and its intention to reestablish civil society along biblically mandated lines.

One of the features of dominion theology that rankled me more than any other is the uncanny similarity of some of its rhetoric to liberation theology. The big difference is that liberation theology produces a more progressive expression of religious activism, whereas dominion theology almost always engenders very conservative public policy. Both, for example, put a heavy emphasis on the idea that Christians are responsible for *continuing* the ministry and work of Jesus. Both place the concept of the Kingdom of God, albeit interpreted quite differently, at the center of their respective theologies. Both insist that believers can and should strive to change the *institutional* patterns of earthly societies and not just convert individuals.

The crucial difference between the two, of course, is that liberation theology begins with what is called the "preferential option for the poor" and attempts to read the Bible from the perspective of the suffering and the disinherited. Its goal is not, like dominion theology, to place Christians in positions of power, but to shape institutions that are more responsive to the weakest members of any society. Still, it can be a little unnerving to find both Archbishop Desmond Tutu and Pat Robertson talking about using "kingdom principles" in politics, or to realize that both Bishop Oscar Romero and Rousas Rushdoony urge the application of biblical values to the society.

The growing influence of dominion theology within American pentecostalism has motivated some pentecostal theologians to mount an impressive counterattack and to formulate what might be called a pentecostal liberation theology. Eldin Villafañe, a Puerto Rican professor at Gordon Conwell Theological School, in Beverly, Massachusetts, in *The Liberating Spirit* argues for a "pneumatic" social ethic, and urges pentecostals to move beyond preaching individual sin and salvation in order to address such systemic issues as housing, human rights, unemployment and racism. By a "pneumatic" social ethic, Villafañe means one that is based on a belief in the presence and power of the Spirit, a central pentecostal conviction. Murray Dempster who teaches at Southern California College in Costa Mesa, affiliated with the Assemblies of God, is one of the clearest voices in the attempt to formulate a pentecostal social ethic that avoids the triumphalism of dominion theology. Dempster was the president of the Society for Pentecostal Studies in 1991, and he devoted his presidential address to the subject. His ideas sound to me like a pentecostal liberation theology:

> The mission of the church is to witness to the truth that the Kingdom of God which still belongs to the future has already broken into the present age in Jesus Christ and continues in the world through the power of the Holy Spirit.

So far, many dominionist pentecostals might agree with this statement. But the outcome of Dempster's emphasis on the Kingdom is a very different one. Basing his description on the Gospel accounts of the ministry of Jesus, Dempster writes:

> Strangers are incorporated into the circle of neighbor love; peace is made with enemies; injustices are rectified; the poor experience solidarity with the human family and the creation; generous sharing results in the just satisfaction of human needs in which no one suffers ·deprivation . . . social practices that embody love, justice and shalom constitute the normative moral structure in a social ethic reflective of God's kingly rule.

Dempster and Villafañe represent encouraging signs on the current pentecostal scene in America, and there are others. Even so, the overall picture does not look hopeful.

I did not enjoy my brief sojourn through the pentecostal netherworld with its legions of reconstructionists, Kingdom Now organizers, satanic conspiracy buffs, name-it-and-claim-it preachers, health-and-wealth theologians, and advanced demonologists. I was genuinely sorry that the engrossing dialogues between God and the devil I had watched being acted out at the "little church" with Lois fifty years ago had distended into a macabre distortion of what I believed the Bible teaches. I was disillusioned to find that some believers in the movement that had been born in a stable were now being seduced by preachers who told them that God wanted them to have dominion over everything. I was infuriated by preachers who were telling trusting and vulnerable listeners that if they were poor or not in perfect health it was their own fault for not having enough faith. I was exasperated at the way the sleazy values of the rich and the famous had seeped into pentecostal worship. And I was genuinely fearful about what might happen to America if people with the ideas I had read in some of the reconstructionist theology ever really came to power.

Most of the pentecostals I knew personally were as outraged by all this as I was. But I was not at all sure that even the most courageous of them could put up the kind of battle that seemed to be needed in their churches. I began to harbor the sad suspicion

that the pentecostal movement I had come t⁄
ing of its history and in my visits to othe⁄
destined for an endless splintering into⁄
headed by power-obsessed egotists in t⁄
feared that it might loose touch completely w⁄
gins and become the righteous spiritual ideology oʼ
middle class. But then it occurred to me that almost all the ⌣
tling experiences I had had in the pentecostal world had been in
largely white settings. I also remembered that although the right-
wing Christian groups I had encountered always placed a few
African Americans and other minority people in positions of high
visibility, the groups themselves cater largely to whites. It began
to appear more and more certain to me that American pentecostalism has paid a very high price for its racial divisions. In
1907 William J. Seymour, the moving spirit of the Azusa Street
revival, wrote in the mission's newspaper *The Apostolic Faith:*

> Tongues are one of the signs that go with every baptized person,
> but it is not the real evidence of baptism in everyday life. . . . The
> secret is: one accord, one place, one heart, one prayer, one soul,
> believing in this great power. Pentecost . . . brings us all into one
> common family.

But this ideal faded quickly. The revival that one visitor said
was a demonstration of the power of the Spirit to "wash away
the color line with the blood of the cross," and to purge the
church of the sin of racism, had resegregated itself very quickly.
Today pentecostalism stands in grave danger of losing the invaluable message it could bring to the other churches and to the rest
of the world. What had happened to the spirit of Azusa Street?

CHAPTER 15

The Liberating Spirit

You could say I lost my faith
in science and progress.
You could say I lost my belief
in the holy church.
You could say I lost my sense
of direction.

British rock singer Sting
"If I Ever Lose My Faith in You"

*A*S THE FIRST DAYS of the new millennium draw closer, the prospects for the human spirit seem both promising and chilling. For the past three centuries, two principal contenders—scientific modernity and traditional religion—have clashed over the privilege of being the ultimate source of meaning and value. Now, like tired boxers who have slugged away too long, the two have reached an exhausted stalemate. As British rock singer Sting laments in one of his most popular songs, many have now lost faith *both* in "science and progress" *and* in "the holy church." People are still willing to rely on science for the limited things it has proven it can do, but they no longer believe it will answer their deepest questions. They remain vaguely intrigued with the traditional religions, but not with conventional churches. They want to pick and choose and are less willing to accept religions either as systems of truth or as institutions. But the loss of direction Sting sings about also has a positive side. Increasing numbers of people appear ready to move on, and are on the lookout for a more promising map of the life-world.

There is no shortage of cartographers marketing their guide-books. Rarely in history have so many models of reality and so many metaphors of what human life is intended to be, made their cases with such vigor and in such jarring proximity to each other. To some observers the religious bazaar of our age resembles the riotous confusion and heady potential that enlivened the first axial age, some 2500 years ago, when the archaic gods were already in retreat but the classical religions had not yet taken hold. To others it seems more like the Hellenistic period, when the first generations of Christians competed both with the decaying pagan-ism of the Roman pantheon and with the exuberant cults of Cybele, Isis, and Mithra, streaming into the Mediterranean basin from the Middle East. To some it seems that today our shrunken world is heading for spiritual chaos, but others hope that out of the churning a new and unifying style of sanctity and a fresh planetary awareness may well appear.

As both scientific modernity and conventional religion pro-gressively lose their ability to provide a source of spiritual mean-ing, two new contenders are stepping forward—"fundamentalism" and, for lack of a more precise word, "experientialism." Both pre-sent themselves as authentic links to the sacred past. Both embody efforts to reclaim what is valuable from previous ages in order to apply it to the present and future. Which of these two rivals even-tually prevails will be decided in large measure by which one grasps the nature of the change we are living through. Philosophers, theologians, poets, and many others—both famous and not so famous—have tried their hand at comprehending that change. Forty years ago the Roman Catholic philosopher Romano Guardini became the first to refer to "the end of the modern age." Then the British historian Arnold Toynbee wrote that western civ-ilization had entered a period of decline and that only a spiritual renewal could save it from destruction. The Russian Orthodox philosopher Nicholas Berdyaev thought that we might be on the threshold of a "new age of the Spirit," but T. S. Eliot foresaw only a dessicated wasteland peopled by hollow men. Others spoke of the decline of the west, or the death throes of patriarchy, or the twilight of either capitalism or socialism.

There is an underlying thread that connects many of these diverse portrayals of the emerging Zeitgeist. Most agree that we are entering a period in which we will see the world and ourselves less cerebrally and more intuitively, less analytically and more immediately, less literally and more analogically. Most depict the self and the world as moving beyond subject-over-against-object. The great Asian religious sages have always sensed this, but they have sometimes lost the self altogether in an undifferentiated whole, a drop of water merging with the boundless ocean. Perhaps it has taken the very recent and unprecedented meeting of east and west to produce this new stage of consciousness. In any case, these thinkers find evidence for a new phase of history in virtually every field of human endeavor—in atonal and improvisational music, in the environmental movement, in new styles of painting and sculpture, in experimental architecture, and especially in poetry. I think one can also find it in pentecostalism.

I believe that these thinkers, although they differ on the details, have discerned the broad outlines of the vast historical metamorphosis we are living through. But sometimes their descriptions seem too ethereal to me. They write as though changes in consciousness take place with no connection to markets, elections, revolutions, technological innovations, population growth, or social upheavals. They seem to forget that modes of human consciousness and forms of human community shape each other. Still, they have had their fingers on something real. The proof for me is that there are so many ordinary people who echo the sentiment of Sting's song, who are no longer content with either one-dimensional modernity or with stagnant religious practices. Though they might not use the words, they are more trustful of intuition and immediacy, and they are looking for ways to participate instead of observing. They are attracted to archaic and mystical modes of perception but do not want to surrender the more inductive ways of thinking recent history has evolved. Their worlds include both acupuncture and open-heart surgery, both meditation and international e-mail. They are fumbling for a new consciousness, but they do not want to live in a monk's cave. They appreciate a measure of material well-being but they envision a more equitable and inclusive society too. Which of the two challengers—fundamentalism or experientialism—seems more likely to touch their inmost aspirations?

Although there appear at first to be certain parallels between fundamentalism and experientialism, their differences are much more important. The fundamentalists are the most visible. Zealous, unswerving, and impassioned, the devotees of the new fundamentalist movements, although they confess a variety of convictions and creeds, and are frequently at each others throats, seem curiously similar in many respects. The word "fundamentalist," which was originally used in the early twentieth century to characterize a particular tendency within American Protestantism, is now applied to the Hindus who tore down the Muslim mosque in Ayodya, India, the Buddhists who harass the Hindu minority in Sri Lanka, the Jewish members of Gush Enumin who insist that God has granted them the land of their Arab neighbors, and the Muslims who want to enforce Islamic law on everyone through state power, along with those Christians who believe in the verbal inerrancy of the Bible.

The use of the label "fundamentalist" to describe such a heterogenous miscellany of movements and sects may stretch the word. But there is no denying that these diverse legions of resolute believers all bear what Martin E. Marty and Scott Appleby, who have written about them at some length, call a "family resemblance" to each other. Each presents itself as a revival, drawing upon what its leaders insist are the "fundamentals," the non-negotiable bedrock beliefs of a religious tradition which have undergone cultural erosion or direct attack by secular forces in the modern age. Furthermore, each fundamentalist movement claims to be the sole authentic representative of the religion it speaks for, and fundamentalists often treat fellow believers who do not grant them this prerogative with more venom than they do outsiders. Inquisitors are always quicker to stoke the fires for heretics than for mere unbelievers.

There is one important feature to be pointed out immediately about fundamentalists. Though they insist they are "traditional" in one way or another, these movements are really what the British historian Eric Hobsbawn calls "invented traditions." In their own distinctive ways they are all modern by-products of the religious crisis of the twentieth century. As Marty and Appleby put it, "Fundamentalists do not simply reaffirm the old doctrines; they subtly lift them from their original context, embellish and institutionalize them, and employ them as ideological weapons against a hostile world." The great irony of Christian fundamentalism, for example, is that it shares the same disability that plagues and cripples the modern rational mind—literalism. In their frantic effort to oppose modernity, Christian fundamentalists have inadvertently embraced its fatal flaw. Their prosaic view of the Bible and their cognitive conception of faith—epitomized by a shrill defense of scriptural "inerrancy"—place fundamentalists squarely in the modern camp. Fundamentalism is not a retrieval of the religious tradition at all, but a distortion of it. The fundamentalist voice speaks to us not of the wisdom of the past but of a desperate attempt to fend off modernity by using modernity's weapons.

The various "fundamentalisms" abroad in the world today are recent reactions to different forms of modernity and, however much they claim to be the original article, they differ in essential respects from the classical historical expressions of their traditions. At first this might seem to undermine their plausibility. But their claim to have a firm grip on absolute truth attracts those who have become weary in their searches or who are afraid even to begin the quest. The problem with such hermetic certainty, however, is that while it might work in an isolated ghetto where one religion predominates, it is very difficult to maintain when one is surrounded by other people who are also making absolute claims. The increasing religious diversity of today's world pits different kinds of fundamentalists against each other in a no-holds-barred conflict. The dissension is especially volatile when some variety of religious fundamentalism combines, as often happens, with some form of nationalism. The emergence of an assortment of fundamentalists in recent decades, and the inevitable discord between them, raises the awful specter that instead of a new beginning for the spirit, we may be heading for an ugly replay of something like the Thirty Years War between the Catholics and Protestants in Europe—only this time on a global scale.

The other contender for spiritual ascendancy in the next century is "experientialism." By its nature, however, it is more disparate and inchoate, harder to describe than fundamentalism. It also assumes different forms, but is unified by a common effort to restore "experience," albeit defined in different ways, as the key dimension of faith. In recent years liberation theologies and feminist theologies—among many others—have shared this penchant for experience. Like fundamentalism, this bent toward experientialism is also appearing within a variety of different religious traditions. Also, just as the various fundamentalisms in different religions bear a striking family resemblance to each other, the experientialist tendencies in different religions are more like each other than like the fundamentalist wings in their own households of faith. Thomas Merton once claimed he felt closer to Buddhist monks and Hindu mystics than to certain people in his own Catholic Church.

Like the fundamentalists, the experientialists also try to reach back past current distortions to the sources of the faith and to make these sources freshly available in the present. Unlike fundamentalists, however, they do not always claim to be the single authoritative voice of their tradition, and—like Merton—they often find much in common with people on other paths. In a troubled time, these two prevalent tendencies—fundamentalism and experientialism—stand like mirror opposites of each other, our benign and the malignant angels.

No one sketches the features of what I have called "experientialism" better than the French scholar of religion Danièle Hervieu-Léger. An heir of the great tradition of Emile Durkheim, Hervieu-Léger once during a visit to America accompanied me to a black pentecostal church in Boston. When we talked about the service afterward, she told me she believes that what millions of people are doing today is turning to the historic religious traditions not as prepackaged answer to their quests, but as what she calls "tool-boxes." Rather than complete worldviews, they see these religions as invaluable depositories from which they can freely draw the symbolic sustenance they need to make sense of the world and of their own lives. They do so, however, as she says, "without this necessarily meaning that they identify them-selves with the comprehensive view of the world that was histor-ically part of the . . . traditions concerned." This emerging mode of spirituality, therefore, finds its cohesion not in the system but in the person, not in the institution itself but in the people who draw on its resources to illuminate their daily lives.

It is immediately evident, however, that this experiential spir-ituality places an enormous load of responsibility on the individ-ual, and this in turn requires a different form of religious affiliation; so the new pattern of church is more network than hierarchy. The traditional authority of the clergy is displaced by a company of seekers who support each other and provide a setting in which they can mine and reassemble the religious tradition's treasures. With a deft Gallic sense of the right word, Hervieu-Léger calls this collecting and compiling of resources "spiritual bricolage." It is a radically personal style of piety in which, as it were, each person is constantly compiling his or her own collage of symbols and practices in the light of what coheres with their own chang-ing experiences in the tortuous passage through life in a world where the old, allegedly comprehensive charts no longer com-mand confidence.

Hervieu-Léger's description of what is happening to religion is based mainly on her observations in Europe. But I think it is also true in a growing measure for the rest of the world as well. She believes that what she calls "the extraordinary power of fas-cination still exerted by the great religious traditions within mod-ern societies" is due to the fact that these societies, whether in Europe, Asia, South America, or elsewhere, are still "prey to anx-iety and uncertainty" and presumably always will be. People need coherence, some grasp of how their own lives fit into the big pic-ture, but modern secular societies—by their very nature—have been unable to provide a "culturally plausible response" to this need. Indeed, where such societies have tried to invent some overall meaning, the result was a disaster as both the communist and fascist attempts to devise pseudoreligions proved.

This new environment puts religious authorities in an uncomfortable position. The traditional clergy plays a much less privileged role. Neither ecclesiastical ordination nor theological education guarantees that anyone will pay any attention to them. At worst, certified religious leaders are sometimes viewed as obstacles to a genuine personal appropriation of the faith. At best they are seen as useful, but not indispensable counselors and guides who help other people reach into the reservoirs of archetypal symbols and exemplary stories. Consequently it is not surprising that many religious functionaries staunchly oppose the experiential current. I often hear priests and ministers complain about what they call "cafeteria-style spirituality" or "religion à la carte." Professional theologians insist on maintaining the elegant intricacy of the whole doctrinal system and resist any effort to adopt part of it without accepting the entire bundle. Theologically trained and ordained religious leaders often feel that their authority derives from the fact that they represent *the* tradition in its fullness, and they resent the nonspecialists who are not impressed by their credentials. Hervieu-Léger compares this situation among religious institutions to "deregulation" in the economic sphere.

The other feature of "experiential" spirituality that religious professionals resent is that today's seeker is often looking for some very practical results. The postmodern pilgrims are more attuned to a faith that helps them find the way through life here and now. There is something quite pragmatic about their religious search. Truths are not accepted because someone says they are true, no matter what that leader's religious authority may be, but because people find that they connect, they "click" with their own quotidian existence.

No one seems more dramatically caught by this seismic shift in religious sensibility than the most visible Christian in the world, Pope John Paul II. During the summer in which I started to write this book, the pope flew to Colorado and was warmly received by thousands of young people, many of them not Catholics, who thronged to an outdoor mass. There could be little doubt that the pope *meant* something to these sun-burned young hikers, most of whom had known him previously only as a television celebrity. But just what did he mean? When the TV crews interviewed the vacationing high school and college students who attended the event it was clear that few of them knew anything at all about his teaching. Most could not identify a single papal encyclical, and when it came to the church's prohibition of contraception, something the pontiff has accentuated with increasing emphasis recently, most of them shrugged and politely disagreed with his position. They liked the songs, the fellowship, the feeling of being with a huge group of compatriots who were serious about spiritual matters. They sported t-shirts with the pope's photograph on them. But it was obvious that he was not winning many of them to the uncompromising version of Catholic doctrine he has been teaching for his entire pontificate. They liked the salesman, but they were not buying the package.

After the pope left I pondered what had gone on. It seemed to me that many if not most of the young people who had come to Colorado are excellent examples of just what Hervieu-Léger says is transpiring in the religious world today. The pope, with his cope and mitre, and wearing his ancient colorful vestments, is a living symbol of something they long for, an alternative to the vacancy and monotony of their sped-up consumer culture. The young people loved the pageantry, but not the catechism. They were more like those growing millions of people who find their way to the pilgrimage shrines of Europe, but who rarely attend mass at home. They were like the hundreds of thousands of Europeans and Americans who in 1994 stunned the recording industry by buying so many copies of the serene Gregorian chants sung by the Benedictine monks of Santa Domingo de Silos, an eleventh-century monastery in Spain, that the disc became a platinum best-seller. They did not come to embrace the entire Roman Catholic doctrinal and moral system, or to make it their atlas and gazetteer for negotiating the tricky byways of post-adolescence. They were taking from that occasion what made sense to them, what reached them at their cores, and there is little doubt that what resulted was a "collage," a more or less coherent set of values, beliefs, and practices that those young people will hold on to so long as it helps them along the way. Even the pope is not exempt from deregulation and bricolage.

The contest between the fundamentalist and the experiential-ist impulses has barely begun. The question of which one will eventually supersede the spent and weary forces of scientific modernity and conventional religion as the principal source of coherence and value in tomorrow's world is still undecided. The stakes are very high, and the battle is raging on several fronts at once. In fact, as soon as I discerned the fault lines of this world-wide controversy, I began to see that it has erupted in virtually every religious tradition. Writing about the role of mystical expe-rience in Judaism, Rabbi Arthur E. Green says, "We are living through one of those ages in history . . . when the traditional sources of culture are not succeeding in satisfying the spiritual cravings of our most sensitive individuals." "Clearly," he contin-ues, "it will be the mystical aspects of our tradition to which young people will turn, insofar as they turn to Judaism at all." Green calls for the Jewish equivalent of an experiential revival. "Where," he asks, "are the angels who used to people our prayer-book? . . . Where are the *ushpizin* for our Sukkah or our dancing in the moonlight at *kiddush levanah?*"

Since Green wrote that article in 1976, some of what he asked for has begun to return to synagogue worship in America. When I visited Temple B'Nai Jeshrun on Manhattan's Upper West Side, I saw both old and young people dance through the aisles hand in hand as they began the Sabbath celebration. Last fall I joined dozens of students and townspeople who were dancing with the Torah in front of a synagogue right in my hometown on the Jewish holiday of Simhat Torah. Whenever I participate in such festive events, I agree with Rabbi Green that the most vigorous alterna-tive to such Jewish "fundamentalist" groups as the Gush Enumin is this renascent mystical and celebrative current in contemporary Judaism. It is also an invaluable ally for analogous movements in other faiths.

There are similar experiential stirrings in still other religious traditions as well. Consider a recent book edited by Seyyed Hossein Nasr, perhaps the most preeminent Muslim scholar in the world today. In *Islamic Spirituality: Manifestations*, the editor defines spirituality as that place in each person which "is open to the transcendent dimension" and where the person "experiences ultimate reality." The book is almost entirely devoted to Sufism, the most experientially intense current in Islam. Arising in the late tenth and early eleventh centuries, it has always emphasized the immediate personal union of the soul with God. Sufism has produced some of Islam's finest lyric poets, including Omar Khayyam and Jalal ed-Din Rumi. At a time when the popular press often conveys the impression that Islam is little but a nest of terrorists and fanatics, it is important to realize that there are powerful and deeply rooted countertendencies.

Parallel experiential impulses are also occurring in Hinduism and Buddhism. The features of Asian spirituality that most attracts young people today, not only in the west but in Asia itself, are not their theologies but their practical disciplines such as meditation, yoga, and the various styles of martial art. One of the most fascinating qualities about the so-called new religions of Japan, which are mostly updated expressions of Buddhism, is their emphasis on personal practice and their no-nonsense, pragmatic attitude. For every fervid preacher of fundamentalist versions of these different world faiths, there are others who are trying to help people uncover—within their own lives—the original vision that brought the tradition to birth. In this connection it is important to recall that the Buddha himself was born into an age of religious contention and rival schools of metaphysics. His advice was to accept nothing on the authority of someone else, not even himself, but to test out every claim in one's own experience.

So the battle between fundamentalists and experientialists rages on. Which way will it eventually go? As I returned to my writing desk after all my reading, conversation, and travel through the many worlds of pentecostalism, I found myself asking not only this question, but also another one: how will pentecostalism itself weigh into this struggle for the soul of humankind? The question is important because the people who are attracted to pentecostalism around the world, although many critics dismiss them as an anachronism, are actually more of an avant-garde. They are the

very people who are already bearing the brunt of the same numbing social dislocation and cultural upheaval that is in store for all
of us. Despite themselves they are the pioneers of the vertiginous
world the rest of us will also be trying to negotiate in the decades
to come. So the question of how pentecostalism will influence
them is a critical one. Will it stoke the fires of xenophobia and
hostility? Will it channel the emotions it releases into perpetuating
and deepening the ruptures that divide us? Or will it open people
to new outpourings of the divine spirit and a fresh recognition of
the motley oneness of the human family and its multitudinous fellow dwellers on our frail planet?

A part of me wishes I could be more reassuring about pentecostalism's role in all of this. I wish it were true that the movement's persistent accent on personal experience as the *sine qua
non* of spirituality and the indispensable touchstone of faith would
place it squarely in the experientialist camp, and make it a potent
alternative to the authoritarianism and anxious closemindedness
of the fundamentalist temptation. I wish I could say this because
I have grown very fond of the pentecostal people I have come to
know over the course of writing this book. But I also know that
if I painted such a sanguine picture, they would be the first to
recognize that I had not told the truth.

The truth is that the larger struggle between fundamentalists
and experientialists is being played out even within the parameters of pentecostalism. The movement is not on the side of the
experientialists. Nor is it on the side of the fundamentalists. Rather,
it is itself a battlefield, and an exceedingly crucial one. Within the
churches, denominations, associations, schools, and publications
of the pentecostal movement a sharp clash is under way between
those who would like to capture it for the fundamentalist party
and for the religious-political right, and those who insist that its
authentic purpose is to cut through creeds and canons and bring
the Gospel of God's justice and the Spirit's nearness to everyone.

Some pentecostals want to cooperate with ecumenical groups.
Others do not. Some feel at home in the evangelical or even fundamentalist household. Others want to dissociate themselves from

those groups. When I attended a service at the church associated with the international headquarters of the Assemblies of God in Springfield, Missouri, a couple of years ago during a meeting of the Society for Pentecostal Studies, some of the denomination's leaders seemed upset when the president of the society suggested that pentecostals had their own history and a particular message of their own for the world and should not be subsumed under an evangelical or fundamentalist umbrella. When a woman teacher from a pentecostal college excitedly told about representing their tradition at the National Council of Churches, some in the audience looked skeptical. Wasn't the National Council that "liberal superchurch" their evangelical friends had warned them about?

The divisions between third world pentecostals and their North American brethren are more political in nature. For instance, when I talked with some Mexican pentecostal leaders in Guadalajara, they complained that their North American brothers and sisters had gotten so carried away by the health-and-wealth gospel and were so much under the sway of the right-wing group known as the Christian Coalition that they had forgotten their original mission to the downtrodden. And even within North America there is little cooperation between white pentecostals and their black fellow pentecostals, some of whom contend that The Assemblies of God was founded at least in part to take the leadership out of the hands of blacks.

The divisions are not just trivial. While perhaps a majority of white pentecostals in the United States strongly supported American aid to the Contras in Nicaragua's civil war and the effort to eradicate the guerilla rebels in Guatemala, many pentecostals in both these Latin American countries were actually fighting on the other side. A missionary to Guatemala told me that in that country alone seventeen pentecostal pastors had been killed by the army in its effort to root out insurrectionaries. Few white American pentecostals welcomed the news that many of their brothers in Chiapas joined their Catholic neighbors in the Zapatista uprising that surprised both the Mexican government and the world in January 1994. Meanwhile the leaders of the Christian Coalition's strategists are making every effort to enlist the pentecostal churches in their efforts to take power in every institution in the land. The political split in pentecostalism is deep and—it seems—widening.

Because the organizational pattern of pentecostalism is so anarchic, or so lacking, it is not easy to discern the battlelines. Relations between the large black pentecostal denominations such as the Church of God in Christ and the predominantly white ones such as the Church of God and the Assemblies of God are often tense and edgy. Black and Latino pentecostals within all of these different denominations often find themselves closer to each other than to their fellow denominationalists. Almost everyone is embarrassed about Jimmy Swaggart and Jim Bakker, but no one knows whom to blame. The pastors of the small, struggling pentecostal churches that are still serving the lower-class people with whom the movement started out often feel overshadowed and ignored by the pastors of the new "megachurches" who have achieved splashy celebrity status. Tensions among the "classical" pentecostals who date back to Azusa Street, the "charismatics" who appeared in the established churches in the 1970s, and the Third Wavers who emerged in the 1980s and claimed the gifts of healing and prophecy but did not want to bear the onus of the "pentecostal" label, continue to simmer. Meanwhile, the growth of pentecostalism among white people has slowed considerably, while its expansion among minorities and in the third world continues to accelerate.

These internal struggles will go on for a long time and may never be fully resolved. But the answer to the larger question of whether pentecostalism will contribute more to fundamentalism or to experientialism will depend on two key features of pentecostal life and theology. The first is the problematical term "experience" itself, and the second is the idea of the "Spirit." Both of these concepts are utterly central to pentecostal self-understanding; consequently, to raise questions about them is to go to the core of what the movement is.

Pentecostals talk about *experience* a lot. The old tent-meeting adage that "a man with a doctrine doesn't stand a chance against a man with an experience" is still frequently quoted. But if pentecostalism is to become a strong ally in what I have called the "experientialist" side of the attempt to shape a spirituality for the next century, then pentecostals will have to be much clearer about what they mean by "experience." Otherwise a vacuous "cult of experience," too much in keeping with the contemporary celebration of "feelings" and the endless search for new sources of arousal and exhilaration, could undermine its authenticity. Pentecostalism could disappear into the vogue of New Age self-absorption. The popularity of health-and-wealth theology shows how quickly this could happen. Some pentecostal preachers I have heard and watched are so fascinated by sensational displays of rapture that they appear to have forgotten the original meaning of the "signs and wonders" which were seen as tokens that a new day was coming, that the reign of God was breaking into history. Speaking in tongues, especially, which became so important for the early pentecostals, was not just an "experience" that one sought for its own sake; it was the "initial evidence" of the Spirit's baptism, a sign that God was about to "do a new thing in the world."

Pentecostals often talk about experience without being very precise about what they mean. In fact, they sometimes claim, like the mystics from whom they have descended, that the experience they are referring to defies verbal expression: "When it happens to you, you'll know, and you won't have to ask." There is some truth in this. However, virtually anyone can claim anything in the name of experience. The results are often exciting but confusing. For instance, liberation theologians insist that the Bible must be read and Christian theology worked out anew in the light of the experience of poor and oppressed people. Feminist theologians base their work on the experience of women, and one feminist theologian, Paula Cooey, identifies pentecostals as among the forerunners of this experiential approach. It seems that pentecostals, though some of them might feel uncomfortable in the company of liberationists and feminists, are actually making a very similar claim, and were making it long before these others did. But each of these approaches has its own take on what "experience" means.

What they actually mean by "experience" is the keystone on which the pentecostal enterprise depends, and the answer is not all that clear. But it would be wrong to single out pentecostals for their lack of precision. Some years ago the German philosopher Hans-Georg Gadamer wrote, "However paradoxical it may seem, the concept of experience seems to me one of the most obscure we have." The great American thinker Alfred North Whitehead was even more forthcoming. "The word 'experience,'" he remarked, "is one of the most deceitful in philosophy." Nonetheless, whether it is obscure or even deceitful, most Christian theologians have included experience—sometimes precisely defined, most often not—as one of the authoritative bases for religion and theology, along with scripture and reason (and tradition among Catholics). But just how much relative weight should be assigned to each of these has never been settled, and a kind of low-intensity skirmishing has gone on for a very long time. Periodically one or the other—sometimes reason, sometimes tradition, sometimes experience—emerges from the pack to insist that it has been wrongly denied its rightful place.

The argument seems to come in waves. During the Protestant Reformation, Luther and Calvin stressed scripture against tradition. During the Methodist revivals, Wesley and his followers accented experience over both. During my boyhood, the emphasis on religious experience in my own Baptist denomination was being sharply challenged by fundamentalists who were insisting on doctrinal purity. When I was in seminary, the "neo-orthodox" theologians such as Karl Barth and Emil Brunner were once again stressing the Bible against what they feared was a wave of hazy subjectivity. Later, when I went to Harvard to study for my doctorate, the spirits of Jonathan Edwards, William James, and Ralph Waldo Emerson, all of whom stressed religous experience, were still very influential. More recently, as we have seen, experience has made another comeback via liberation theologies. But no sooner had that happened than a new anti-experientialism once again became the rage among academic theologians. Highly influenced by current anthropology, these "post-liberals" such as Professor George Lindbeck at Yale argue that religious experience, is not primary at all. They believe that religions are cultural and linguistic systems that shape and define the kinds of religious experiences the individuals within them have. Thus, "religion" comes first, and experience is secondary. So the argument goes on. It seems that once again, as Gadamer and Whitehead warned, "experience" is proving to be a slippery concept.

For pentecostals the crux of this renewed debate between the primacy of belief systems and that of personal experience may lie in precisely that feature of their life which has sometimes brought upon them the most reproach and caused them the most embarrassment: ecstatic worship—which I believe is a kind of populist mysticism. What pentecostals call "speaking in tongues," or praying in the Spirit, has appeared in history before, and it is always a sure signal that the available religious idiom has become inadequate. Glossolalia is a mystical-experiential protest against an existing religious language that has turned stagnant or been corrupted. But glossolalia does not occur in a vacuum. It almost always takes place among people who are themselves culturally displaced, and often politically or socially disinherited as well. It is a form of cultural subversion, a liberating energy that frees people to praise God in a language of the Spirit that is not controlled by dominant modes of religious discourse. Furthermore, glossolalia helps to create a new religious subculture, one that in turn amplifies and affirms personal experience.

There is one thing the critics of experience-based theologies overlook when they claim that culture and language always precede and shape experience. They overlook pain. They forget that some human experiences are so intense that they defy words and compel us to create new words, sometimes whole new worlds. Of these world-creating experiences, perhaps the principal ones are spiritual and physical suffering. Pentecostals, unlike feminists and liberation theologians, usually like to stress the more joyful dimension of their meeting with the Spirit. But, as the pentecostal theologian Steve Land has pointed out, this encounter also involves anguish and yearning. I think this is the key. Anyone who has felt real pain knows that not all moans of distress are culturally patterned. Suffering is som~~'
in available cultural motifs, but sometimes it
reconstruct our worlds. Pain changes us. It con

out of our normal modes of thinking and to see life in a different way.

The final word has not yet been said about what the oh-so-simple-sounding but "obscure" and "deceitful" concept of "experience" means. The debate is sure to go on, and if the past is any guide, professional theologians and ecclesiastical leaders will usually be skeptical of "experience," while lay people will tend to trust their experiences more than they trust theology. For me the question ultimately is not whether experience should be important. I agree with Paul Tillich—who was surely not a pentecostal—but who maintained that all religious belief *must* be subject to what he called "experiential verification." Experience, after all, is the experience *of something.* Even in the most "experientially" oriented spiritual movements, experience itself is not the Source, it is the means by which the Source is known. Experience does not create the spiritual reality. It makes something real *for me* which was not so real before. If the pentecostals can clarify this, they could become a major ally of the experientialist against the fundamentalist party in today's battle. But in order to grasp what the spiritual experience they talk about is an experience *of,* pentecostals will have to become more precise about the meaning of the second key term in their vocabulary, "Spirit."

A special encounter with the "Holy Spirit" (which they called the "Holy Ghost") was at the heart of the early pentecostal movement. But they were not talking about just any spirit. They said it was the same Spirit who hovered over the primal chaos when God created the world, who spoke through the prophets, who dwelt in Jesus Christ and—most important—who had begun to fulfill all the biblical promises by creating a new heaven and a new earth where justice and compassion would reign. The early pentecostals saw themselves positioned "between the already and the not-yet," witnesses to the "first fruits of the Kingdom" but not yet to its fullness, living in the light that precedes the dawn. In other words, the *experience* they testified to was an encounter with a Spirit who has a purpose not just for them but for the whole world. And for the unemployed janitors and domestic servants who gathered at Azusa Street, this purpose was no less than the coming of the Kingdom of God as it had been taught and demonstrated by Jesus. Therefore they believed that when it came, the poor would be lifted up, the hungry fed, and the broken-hearted comforted; while the mighty would be brought low and the rich sent away empty. It is hard to imagine a more radical vision of the future than the one this life-changing experience of the Spirit awakened in them.

Not only did the early pentecostals believe that the Kingdom of God was coming soon, they also believed they themselves were the evidence of its arrival. The future was already breaking into present. What theologians call "eschatology" was not merely one conviction among others. It was their escutcheon, their trademark, their rallying point. It was utterly focal to the other features of the movement. Healings and tongues and prophecies were seen as certain signs of the imminent arrival of the reign of Christ the King. This vivid millennial expectation continued for decades. When Aimee Semple McPherson set out across the country in her "Gospel Car," the words emblazoned on the side read "Jesus Is Coming Soon: Get Ready."

But now things have changed. My impression, after visiting churches on four different continents, is that today pentecostals are even more uneasy about this radical vision of the future than they are about speaking in tongues. In most churches today the message centers on the immediate presence and compassionate availability of the Spirit of Jesus Christ as helper, healer, and companion. The expectation that the Lord will come again soon, though it is voiced now and then, seems muted. It surely does not to hold anything like the pivotal place it once did.

I have a very ambivalent attitude about this change. As one who has imbibed at least some of the liberation theology's practice of rethinking theology from the vantage point of the poor, I regret in some measure that pentecostals seem to have dampened their early eschatological fire. The confident hope that God's judgment and blessing were on their way soon has both comforted and catalyzed oppressed peoples for centuries. But today many middle-class pentecostal congregations appear very much at ease with the status quo. Now they seem confident not that Jesus is coming soon, but that He probably isn't, and that therefore nothing will interrupt their pursuit of success and self-indulgence. The Kingdom Now movement and the "name-it-and-claim-it" preachers have elevated this complacency into a theology.

On the other hand, I frankly hope that pentecostals do not try to reclaim the *literal* End Time urgency that swept the world in the early years after the Azusa Street revival. But they *are* faced with a difficult dilemma. The disappearance of eschatology produces stagnation, comfort, and the consumer religion of the Kingdom Now preachers; a short-term apocalyptic vision, on the other hand, makes it impossible to address the long-term issues that Christians, along with all human beings, must confront, particularly the environmental crisis. When a former Secretary of the Interior said that he saw little purpose in trying to preserve rainforests since Jesus was coming soon anyway, he did not speak for all pentecostals. But clearly any theology that allows Christians to ignore the threats of water and air pollution, resource exhaustion, and the destruction of the atmosphere, all because they believe our delicate orb is only the "late great planet earth," is both morally irresponsible and patently unbiblical. If pentecostalists do not reformulate their eschatological vision of what the Spirit is doing in world history, they end up supporting the fundamentalist party, and telling us not to fret about the ruination of the environment since Daniel and Revelation teach that we are in the Last Days and there will be no future generations anyway.

I am heartened to find among the younger generation of pentecostal ministers a serious effort to rethink pentecostal eschatology. They teach their congregations that what the Bible envisions is not the fiery dissolution of this world, but its transformation into the promised Kingdom, and that the scripture strictly warns against setting dates and timetables. These same young pentecostal leaders also believe that the fact that their movement started among the disowned and dispossessed is not a mere historical memento, but a decisive indication of what the Spirit wants them to be doing today. Unlike the Kingdom Now preachers who court the well-to-do and advocate the takeover of worldly institutions, these leaders recognize that Jesus promised His kingdom to the poor and to those who suffer for righteousness sake.

Much to the chagrin of the political right-wingers, a kind of pentecostal liberation theology is now emerging. The Puerto Rican theologian Eldin Villafañe, a pentecostal himself, believes that the genius of pentecostalism is an encounter with the power of the "liberating Spirit," and he believes that this Spirit has a "project" that is being worked out within human history. His sketch of a pentecostal liberation theology is an exciting prospect, and it is not a passing chimera. Sociologist Cecilia Maritz, who studies the small Catholic "base communities" in Brazil, the local study and action groups from which liberation theology arose, has noticed that in some places these groups function very much like pentecostal communities. Father Pablo Richard, a Costa Rican Catholic who spends most of his time teaching Bible courses for the lay leaders of these base communities all over Latin America, claims that the difference between them and pentecostal congregations is diminishing rapidly. If these two powerful movements, both of them on the "experientialist" side of the ledger, were somehow to combine their strengths in the coming decades, the result would be extraordinarily potent. If the pentecostals, following Villafañe's lead, absorb something of the social vision of liberation theology, and the Catholic base communities shed the residual elements of vertical authority they still sometimes retain, the offspring could be more powerful than either of its parents.

Whether pentecostals will come down on the side of the fundamentalists or on the side of the experientialists is an open question since vigorous forces are pulling both ways. Whether such core ideas as "experience" and "Spirit" are interpreted in ways that push the movement—against the grain of its history—in the fundamentalist direction, remains to be seen. But whatever happens, given the nature of the pentecostal impulse, I doubt that it will be settled through theological debate. Pentecostal theology is found in the viscera of pentecostal spirituality. It is emotional, communal, narrational, hopeful, and radically embodied. Furthermore, whatever changes occur in pentecostalism will begin in the lives of its hundreds of thousands of congregations. Answers to the questions about what experience is and what the Spirit is doing in the world will not appear first in journals but in the ways that these little outposts of the Kingdom *live* in a world that is both hostile and hungry. The reason I am hopeful that pentecostalism will emerge from the current fray on the side of the angels comes not principally from what I have read, but from what some of these outposts, especially a very small but very symbolic one, are actually doing.

The Grove Hall area in Dorchester is one of the most neglected and crime-ridden sections of Boston. Many of the stores are boarded up, and commuters who drive through lock their doors. The police call it "Beirut West." In the middle of this desolation there is a tiny congregation of young black pentecostals, many of them graduates of the elite universities of the Boston area, who have chosen to return to live in the ghetto as an expression of their Christian faith. They do not own a building, but meet to pray and sing and study in a rented hall. They attend court, monitor the police station, train young people in work skills, and encourage them to stay in school. Amid continuing setbacks and great discouragement they try to include people who live in the neighborhood in their fellowship and to build a basis for hope in an atmosphere of anger and corrosive cynicism. They know about early pentecostalism, and with a finely honed sense of history they call themselves the "Azusa Christian Community."

The day I visited the regular Sunday worship of the Azusa Christian Community in Dorchester the members sang with gusto, shook tambourines, and worshipped with infectious jubilation. But what impressed me most was the intensity of their prayers. A shooting had taken place just outside the apartment of one of the members, so they prayed for the victim and his family. They prayed that God would touch the hearts of the drug dealers who pandered their wares openly just down the street so they would see the error of their ways. They prayed for the sick, including, when I requested it, my sister-in-law who was suffering from leukemia. But they also prayed for help in getting through their exams, finishing their lab projects, and finding a job. I was touched. Here were people who had chosen to be actual witnesses to the kind of community their pentecostal ancestors foresaw. But they know they cannot do it without each other's support or without prayer. The Reverend Eugene Rivers, who leads the congregation, makes the rounds of the Massachusetts Institute of Technology, Harvard, and Boston University, challenging young graduates to forego moving to the suburbs and to join the Azusa community on the urban frontier. "But if you don't pray," he warns them, "don't come."

The service at the Azusa Christian Community lasted longer than I anticipated, so I had to slip out a bit early. The streets were glum and the sky was gray. Orange peels, cigarette butts, and dented cans littered the gutter. Three children played on the hood of an abandoned car. As I climbed behind my steering wheel I heard a siren. A police van raced by, followed by a fire engine. I waited until they turned the corner onto Blue Hill Avenue and the sound of the siren grew dimmer as it moved south toward Mattapan. But then, just as I put my key in the ignition, I heard the congregation inside start to sing again, and when I looked back I saw that one of the young men had come to the door to smile and wave goodbye.

My visit to the Azusa Christian Community in Dorchester brought me full circle. The fire from heaven had first fallen on a tiny handful of people at a place called Azusa Street. It crackled and hissed, then caught on and leaped across continents and oceans. Eventually it reached around the world. I had seen the evidence of its effects in many, many places. But never had I felt closer to the original spirit of Azusa Street than when I visited its namesake, in a rented hall forty minutes from my doorstep.

BIBLIOGRAPHICAL NOTES

Introduction

For the early Quakers' noisiness, see Clarke Garnett, *Spiritual Possession and Popular Religion: From the Camisards to the Shakers* (Baltimore: Johns Hopkins University Press, 1987). I base the statistical description of pentecostalism on the figures cited in Steven J. Land's *Pentecostal Spirituality: A Passion for the Kingdom* (Sheffield, Engl.: Sheffield Academic Press, 1993), and in Vinson Synan, *The Spirit Said "Grow,"* published by MARC, a division of World Vision International, Monrovia, Calif., 1992. See also David Barrett, *World Christian Encyclopedia* (New York: Oxford University Press, 1982) See also Cheryl Bridges Johns, *Pentecostal Formation: A Pedagogy Among the Oppressed* (Sheffield, Engl.: Sheffield Academic Press, 1993).

Chapter 1

I am grateful to the librarians in charge of the rare books at the Frances Loeb Library of the Graduate School of Design at Harvard University for allowing me to read the precious old books and catalogs relating to the great Chicago Fair of 1893 and for providing the white gloves to wear while I paged through these brittle old volumes. I especially enjoyed *The Dream City: A Portfolio of Views of the World's Columbian Exposition* (St. Louis: N. D. Thompson, 1893). The introduction is by Professor Halsey C. Ives, and the frontispiece carries the quotation from Revelation 21:26. I also relied heavily on David Burg's *Chicago's White City of 1893* (Lexington: University Press of Kentucky, 1976). Norman Bolotin and Christine Lang, both devoted world's fair buffs, published *The World's Columbian Exposition* (Washington, D.C.:Preservation Press) in 1992. Its splendid photographs complement a highly informative text. For the connection between the beaux-arts tradition and the philosophy of technical utopianism, see Paul Rabinow, *French Modern: Norms and Forms of the Social Environment* (Cambridge: MIT Press, 1989). Louis Sullivan's testy remarks on the White City appear in his *The Autobiography of an Idea* (New York: n.p., 1924), p. 316. Christine Boyer's book is entitled *Dreaming the Rational City: The Myth of American City Planning* (Cambridge: MIT Press, 1983). The most valuable source for the World's Parliament of Religions is *The Dawn of Religious Pluralism: Voices from the World's Parliament of Religions, 1893* edited by Richard Hughes Seager (LaSalle, Ill.: Open Court, 1993). Dr. Seager also generously permitted me to read the manuscript of his *A Gathering of the Tribes* to be published in 1994 by the University of Indiana Press, Bloomington, Indiana.

Chapter 2

For Los Angeles at the turn of the century, I relied on Mike Davis's wonderfully readable *City of Quartz: Evoking the Future of Los Angeles* (London: Verso, 1990). On William J. Seymour and Azusa Street, see Iain MacRobert's *The Black Roots and White Racism of Early Pentecostalism* (New York: St. Martin's Press, 1988). Cecil Robeck has an informative essay titled "The Social Concern of Early Pentecostalism" in Jan A. B. Jongeneel, ed., *Pentecost, Mission and Ecumenism: Essays on Intercultural Theology* (New York: Peter Lang, 1992). This book is a "Festschrift" in Honor of Professor Walter Hollenweger, whose helpful personal encouragement to me as I began my work on this subject was very supportive. Robert Mapes Anderson's *Vision of the Disinherited* (New York: Oxford University Press, 1979), Donald Dayton's *Theological Roots of Pentecostalism*, (Metuchen, N.J.: Scarecrow, 1987) and Walter Hollenweger's magisterial *The Pentecostals* (London: Student Christian Movement Press, 1972) were also indispensable. See also the chapter "Restoration as Revival: Early American Pentecostalism" by Edith Blumhofer in the book she edited with Randall Balmer, *Modern Christian Revivals* (Urbana: University of Illinois Press, 1993). *Witness to Pentecost: The Life of Frank J. Bartleman* edited by Cecil M. Robeck, Jr. (New York: Garland Publishing, 1985) contains some firsthand accounts of the Azusa Street revival. My most valuable source was Douglas J. Nelson's unpublished doctoral dissertation, University of Birmingham, England, "For Such a Time as This—The Story of Bishop William J. Seymour and the Azusa Street Revival" (1981). See also Edith Blumhofer, *The Assemblies of God: A Chapter in the Story of American Pentecostalism* (Springfield, Mo.: Gospel Publishing House, 1989); and Grant Wacker, "The Functions of Faith in Primitive Pentecostalism," *Harvard Theological Review* 77:3–4 (July–October 1994), pp. 353–375.

Chapter 3

By far the most important source for this chapter is "The Everlasting Gospel" by D. William Faupel, unpublished dissertation, University of Birmingham, England, 1989. Some books that helped me pick my way through the fascinating labyrinth of early pentecostal history are James L. Tyson, *The Early Pentecostal Revival* (Hazelwood, Mo.: Word Aflame Press, 1992), which features the story of the branch called "The Pentecostal Assemblies of the World"; Walter Hollenweger's *The Pentecostals* (London: Student Christian Movement Press, 1972); Charles Conn, *Our First Hundred Years 1886–1986*, which rehearses the story of the Church of God, the one with headquarters in Cleveland, Tennessee, where the book was published by Pathway Press in 1986; Both scholarly and readable is Vinson Synan's *The Holiness-Pentecostal Movement in the United States*, (Grand Rapids, Mich.: Eerdmans,1971). My favorite, however, was *Witness to Pentecost: The Life of Frank Bartleman*, an absorbing collection of autobiographical essays and journals, edited by Cecil Robeck, Jr. (New York: Garland Publishing, 1985). See also Stephen Webb, *Blessed Excess: Religion and the Hyperbolic Imagination* (Ithaca, N.Y.: State University of New York Press, 1994).

Chapter 4

See Emile Durkheim, *The Elementary Forms of Religious Life* (London: Allen and Unwin, 1976); Noam Chomsky, *Language and Problems of Knowledge: The Managua Lectures* (Cambridge: MIT Press, 1988) Ernst Bloch, *The Principle of Hope* (Cambridge: MIT Press, 1986). Wesley's observations are quoted in George Williams and Edith Waldvogel, "History of Speaking in Tongues and Related Gifts," in *The Charismatic Movement*, edited by Michael Hamilton (Grand Rapids, Mich.: Eerdmans, 1975) p. 80.

For a description of what tongue speaking meant to the early pentecostals, see G. B. McGee, *Initial Evidence* (Peabody, Mass.: Hendrickson, 1991). For a very thoughtful modern pentecostal view of the significance of tongues, see Frank Macchia, "Tongues as a Sign: Towards a Sacramental Understanding of Pentecostal Experience," in *Pneuma* 15 (Spring 1993), pp. 61–76. See also Mortin Kelsey, *Tongue-Speaking: An Experiment in Spiritual Experience* (New York: Doubleday, 1964). Richard Baer's article "Quaker Silence, Catholic Liturgy, and Pentecostal Glossolalia: Some Functional Similarities" in *Perspectives on the New Pentecostalism*, edited by Russell Spittler (Grand Rapids, Mich.: Baker Book House, 1976), contains, as the title indicates, some fascinating comparisons. For description and analysis of tongue speaking outside pentecostalism, see L. Carlyle May, "A Survey of Glossolalia and Related Phenomena in Non-Christian Religions," *American Anthropologist* 58 (May 1956), pp. 75–96.

See also Amos Wilder, *The New Voice: Religion, Literature and Hermeneutics* (New York: Herder and Herder, 1969), p. 126; and Susan Sontag, *A Susan Sontag Reader*, (New York: Vintage Books, 1982), p. 195. The story of the boy in the synagogue is retold by David J. Wolpe in his fascinating book *In Speech and Silence: The Jewish Quest for God* (New York: Henry Holt, 1992), p. 123. This book is an invaluable source of insights about ecstatic utterance. See Frederick J. Ruf, *The Creation of Chaos*, which is about William James's thought (Ithaca, N.Y.: State University of New York Press, 1994).

Chapter 5

The following are some of the resources I made use of in this chapter. Albert J. Raboteau's *Slave Religion: The "Invisible Institution" in the Antebellum South* (New York: Oxford University Press, 1978) is the key source for African American spirituality; *Strange Gifts? A Guide to Charismatic Renewal*, edited by David Martin and Peter Mullen (Oxford: Basil Blackwell, 1984); and a fine collection of essays, *New Heaven? New Earth? An Encounter with Pentecostalism* (London: Darton, Longman and Todd, 1976), with articles by Simon Tugwell and John Orme Mills, both of whom are Dominican priests, and Peter Hocken (a Catholic priest) and George Every (a Catholic layman). A good short account of the revival of healing in Christianity can be found in an essay by Meredith Maguire, "Religion and Healing," in Phillip E. Hammond, ed., *The Sacred in a Secular Age: Toward a Revision in the*

Scientific Study of Religion (Berkeley and Los Angeles: University of California Press, 1985.) In this, as well as in other chapters, I often consulted S. M. Burgess, G. B. McGee, P. H. Alexander, eds., *Dictionary of Pentecostal and Charismatic Movements* (Grand Rapids, Mich.: Zondervan, 1988).

Chapter 6

One of the first documents to alert me to pentecostalism as an "alternative discourse" in the tradition of Christian utopian thinking was a senior thesis written at Harvard College by Cynthia Marie Silva in 1984, "Pentecostalism as Oppositional Culture: Some Socio-Political Implications of a Conservative Christian Faith." This superb example of original undergraduate writing helped me to see pentecostalism in an entirely new perspective. It is still unpublished. Most of the material on American black millennialism in this chapter first came to my attention in an article by Timothy E. Fulop of Princeton University, "'The Future Golden Day of the Race': Millennialism and Black Americans in the Nadir, 1877–1901," published in the *Harvard Theological Review* 84:1 (1991), pp. 75–99.

Chapter 7

For further information on the intriguing life of Aimee Semple McPherson, see Edith Blumhofer, *Aimee Semple McPherson: Everybody's Sister* (Grand Rapids, Mich.: W.B. Eeadmans, 1993). See also Daniel Mark Epstein's engaging biography, *Sister Aimee: The Life of Aimee Semple McPherson* (New York: Harcourt Brace Jovanovich, 1993). For an informative biography of another charismatic woman preacher, see *Kathryn Kuhlman: The Woman Behind the Miracles* by Wayne E. Warner (Ann Arbor, Mich.: Servant Publications, 1993). Elizabeth Brusco's research is found in "The Household Basis of Evangelical Religion and the Reformation of Machismo in Colombia," Ph.D. dissertation, City College of New York, 1986. Her book, *The Reformation of Machismo* will be published by the University of Texas Press in 1994. Elaine Lawless's study is titled *God's Peculiar People: Women's Voices and Folk Tradition in a Pentecostal Church*, (Lexington: University Press of Kentucky, 1988). See Northrop Frye, *The Great Code: The Bible and Literature* (New York: Harcourt Brace and Javonich, 1982). I was also helped in my interpretation of the Latin American women's testimonies by comparing my own observation with the field notes and an unpublished article by one of my students, Kathryn Tiede, and I am grateful to her. Charles H. Barfoot and Gerald T. Sheppard have a fine article on this subject, "Prophetic vs. Priestly Religion: The Changing Role of Women Clergy in Classical Pentecostal Churches," in *Review of Religious Research* 22, 1 (Sept. 1980), pp. 2–17. See also Edith Blumhofer's "Women in Evangelicalism and Pentecostalism," in *Women and Church*, edited by Melanie May (Grand Rapids, Mich.: Eerdmans, 1991), and "Beyond the Sound of Silence: Afro-American Women in History," in *Gender and History* 1, 1 (Spring 1989), pp. 50–67; as well as "'Together in Harness': Women's Traditions in the Sanctified Church" by Cheryl Townsend Gilkes in *Signs: Journal of Women in Culture and Society* 10, 4 (1985), pp. 678–699.

Chapter 8

Martin Williams's essay "Jazz Music—A Brief History," in *The Smithsonian Collection of Classic Jazz* New York: W.W. Norton, 1973) is a very useful source. See also Michael W. Harris, *The Rise of the Gospel Blues* (New York: Oxford University Press, 1992), and Clarke Garrett, *Spirit Possession and Popular Religion: From the Camisards to the Shakers* (Baltimore: Johns Hopkins University Press, 1987). *Sinful Tunes and Spirituals* (Evanston: University of Illinois Press, 1977) by Dana Epstein describes the acculturation of African music in the New World. Ronald Morris's *Wait Until Dark* (Bowling Green, Ohio: Bowling Green University Popular Press, 1980) describes the early New Orleans jazz scene. *Jazz, Myth and Religion* (New York: Oxford University Press, 1987) by Niel Leonard analyzes the connection between the elements of the title. Bill Cole's *John Coltrane* (New York: Schirmer Books, 1976) is a fascinating biography of one of the great figures in the history of jazz. See also Edward Strickland's article, "What Coltrane Wanted," in *The Atlantic Monthly*, December 1987, 260, 6, pp. 100–104. See Jaroslav Pelikan, *Bach Among the Theologians* (Philadelphia: Fortress Press, 1986).

Chapter 9

Tongues of Fire: The Explosion of Protestantism in Latin America by David Martin (Oxford: Basil Blackwell, 1990) is the best book yet on evangelicals and pentecostals in Latin America. See also *Rethinking Protestantism in Latin America* edited by Virginia Garrard-Burnett and David Stoll (Philadelphia: Temple University Press, 1993). See *Algo Mas Que Opio*, a collection of essays in Spanish on pentecostalism in Latin America which, as the title (*Something More than an Opiate*) indicates, takes sharp issue with the Marxist charge that religion is the "opiate of the masses." It was published by Editorial DEI in San Jose, Costa Rica, in 1991, edited by Barbara Boudewijuse. From the same press, see *Pentecostalismo y Liberacion* edited by Carmelo Alvarez, published in 1992. For a fascinating glimpse of the important role women are playing in Latin American pentecostalism, see the report of the first "Encuentro de Mujeres Pentecostales" held in Cartago, Costa Rica, in August 1992, attended by thirty-nine women leaders of pentecostal churches in fourteen Latin American countries. It is available from Post Office Box 136-7050, Cartago, C.R.

See also Jean-Pierre Bastian, "Religion y Cambio Social: Aspectos Teoricos" in *Cristianismo y Sociedad* 25, no. 1, pp. 7–109. Emilio Willems's book is *Followers of the New Faith* (Nashville: University of Tennessee Press, 1967). Christian Lalive d'Epinay's book is *Haven of the Masses* (London: Lutterworth Press, 1969). See also David Stoll, *Is Latin America Turning Protestant?*, (Berkeley and Los Angeles: University of California Press, 1990). I was also helpfully informed by two articles published in Portuguese in *MP Documento*, printed in Rio de Janeiro: "Catolicismo perde terreno no Brasil," and "O impacto social dos evangelicos," both of which appeared in June 1991. The census of recent pentecostal growth in Rio was reported in *Vermelho Brabco*

38, (April 1993), p. 8. See also Carlos Garma Navarro, *Protestantismo En Una Communidad Totonaca de Puebla, Mexico* (Mexico City: Instituto Nacional Indigenista, 1987) for a careful account of how pentecostalism and other evangelical groups interact with indigenous cultures. The interview with Benedita da Silva mentioned at the end of this chapter is reported by Ken Serbin in *The Christian Century*, May 5, 1993, p. 489–491.

Chapter 10

The Revenge of God (University Park: The Pennsylvania State University Press, 1994) is the translation by Alan Braley of the widely discussed *La Revanche de Dieu* by Gilles Kepel, originally published in France in 1991. Roswith I. H. Gerloff's *A Plea for British Black Theologies* (New York: Peter Lang, 1992) is yet another example of the excellent series *Studies in the Intercultural History of Christianity*. The only source I was able to find on the small charismatic movement in German churches is Uwe Birnstein's *Neuer Geist in Alter Kirche? Die Charismatische in die Offensive* (Stuttgart: Kreuz Verlag, 1987). Georgio Roschat of the University of Torino has collected documents dealing with Mussolini's repression of the non-Catholic churches of Italy in the 1920s. The volume is entitled *Reoime fascista e chiese-Evangeliche* (Turin: Claudiana, 1990).

Salvatore Cucchiari's best article is "Between Shame and Sanctification: Patriarchy and Its Transformation in Sicilian Pentecostalism" in *American Ethnologist* 17, (Nov. 1990), p. 687–707. Lucia Chiavola Birnbaum's book is *Black Madonnas, the Case of Italy* (Boston: Boston University Press, 1993). William C. Fletcher's *Soviet Charismatics: The Pentecostals in the USSR* (New York: Peter Lang, 1985) is an excellent history of the subject but has been, of course, outdated by recent changes in Russia. See also Sally McFague, *The Body of God: An Ecological Theology* (Minneapolis: Fortress Press, 1993).

In a carefully researched article "The Heretical Woman as Symbol in Athanasius, Epiphanius and Jerome" in *Harvard Theological Review* 84, 3 (1991), pp. 229–248, the historian Virginia Burrus shows that in early Christian history, a favorite tactic of the largely male custodians of what later came to be called "orthodoxy" (although at the time it was merely one theology among many) was to identify women with heresy and vice versa. The fourth-century figure of the "heretical woman" she says, "is almost invariably identified as sexually promiscuous" and "projects the threatening image of a community with uncontrolled boundaries."

Chapter 11

I benefited greatly from Boo-Woong Yoo's *Korean Pentecostalism: Its History and Theology* (New York: Peter Lang, 1988). Part of the *Studies in the Intercultural History of Christianity* series. I am also very grateful to Katie Crane, my student, for allowing me to make use of her unpublished paper, "What Happened at Canberra: Diversity and Dialogue or Dissent and Division?"

For shamanism, see Mircea Eliade, *Shamanism: Archaic Techniques of Ecstasy* (Princeton: Princeton University Press, 1964). I also made use of Tungshik Ryu's "Shamanism, the Dominant Folk Religion of Korea" in *Inter-religio Newsletter* 5 (1984), pp. 18–34. See also Kyoko Fuchigami, "Faith Healing in Korean Christianity, the Christian Church in Korea and Shamanism" in *Bulletin of the Nanzan Institute of Religion and Culture* 16 (1992), pp. 33–59. For a fascinating and splendidly researched account of the Jewish mystical influences on Paul, see two articles by C. R. A. Murray-Jones titled "Paradise Revisited" in *Harvard Theological Review* 86, 2 and 86, 3 (1993), pp. 177–217, 265–291.

The quotation from Max Weber is from the Charles Scribner's 1958 edition of the English translation of *The Protestant Ethic and the Spirit of Capitalism* published in 1930 by George Allen and Unwin (London), p. 175. Peter Drucker's *Managing for the Future: The 1990's and Beyond* was published by Dutton (New York) in 1992.

The principal sources for minjung theology are Kim Yong-Bock's *Messiah and Minjung* (1992), and David Kwang-sun Suh's *The Korean Minjung in Christ* (1991), both published by the Christian Conference of Asia (Hong Kong). See also James Cone's, *The Spirituals and the Blues: An Interpretation* (New York: Seabury Press, 1972).

Dr. Roger Walsh's book is called *The Spirit of Shamanism* (Los Angeles: Jeremy P. Tarcher, 1990). I am especially grateful to Kyriacos C. Markides who gave me a copy of his fine book just as I was pondering these questions: *Fire in the Heart: Healers, Sages and Mystics* (London: Penguin, 1990).

Chapter 12

The volume entitled *Southern Africa* edited by Marjorie Froise in the useful series *World Christianity* has several accounts of the independent/indigenous churches. The editor of the series is Edward R. Dayton (Monrovia, Calif.: Missions Research and Communications Center, 1989). The book I found most valuable was *Fambidzano* by M. L. Daneel. Subtitled *Ecumenical Movement of Zimbabwean Independent Churches* (Gweru Press, Zimbabwe: Mambo Press, 1989), it is a long work, full of careful descriptions of the organization, liturgies, and programs of these churches, and includes excellent photographs. *Empirical Studies of African Independent/Indigenous Churches*, edited by G. C. Oostguizen and Irving Hexham, brings together descriptions, histories, and commentaries by both outsiders and insiders. I also found the collection edited by Mercy Amba Oduyoye and Musimbi R. A. Kanyoro, *The Will to Arise: Women, Tradition and the Church in Africa* (Maryknoll, N.Y., Orbis Books, 1992), a useful source on such issues as polygamy, sexuality, family life, and women's rituals. The essay by Kofi Appiah-Kubi referred to in this chapter is "Indigenous African Christian Churches: Signs of Authenticity," in *African Theology En Route*, edited by Appiah-Kubi and Sergio Torres (Maryknoll, N.Y.: Orbis Books, 1979). Adrian

Hastings's *A History of African Christianity: 1950-1975* (Cambridge: Cambridge University Press, 1979) is a particularly rich source and contains the account of the imprisonment of Simon Kimbangu. *No Life of My Own* by Frank Chikane was published in 1988 by Orbis Books (Maryknoll, N.Y.). The paraphrase of Margaret Wheatley's *Leadership and the New Science* is quoted from the September 1993 *Center-Piece*, the newsletter of the Center for Psychology and Social Change, Harvard Medical School, Cambridge Hospital.

Chapter 13

Lawrence Wright's book *Saints and Sinners* was published in 1993 (New York: Alfred A. Knopf). See also Janice Peck, *The Gods of Televangelism: The Crisis of Meaning and the Appeal of Religious Television* (Cresskill, N.J.: Hampton Press, 1993). See also Steve Bruce, *Pray TV: Televangelism in America* (New York: Routledge, 1990); Stewart M. Hoover, *Mass Media Religion: The Social Services of the Electronic Church* (Newbury Park, N.J.: Sage Publications, 1988). For an inspired and prescient discussion of televangelism, see Walter J. Ong, *Orality and Literacy? The Technologizing of the Word* (London: Methuen, 1982).

Chapter 14

I am grateful for Margaret Paloma's fair and informative book *The Assemblies of God at the Crossroads: Charisma and Institutional Dilemmas* (Knoxville: University of Tennessee Press, 1989) for its balanced portrait of the issues now being faced by one of the main pentecostal denominations. An article by Thomas Pratt, "The Need to Dialogue: A Review of the Debate on Signs, Wonders, Miracles and Spiritual Warfare in the Literature of the Third Wave Movement," *Pneuma: The Journal for Pentecostal Studies* 13 (Spring 1991), pp 7–32), helped me understand the internal pentecostal struggle over these questions. *Wrestling with Dark Angels: Toward a Deeper Understanding of the Supernatural Forces in Spiritual Warfare* (Ventura, Calif.: Regal Books, 1990), was edited by C. Peter Wagner and F. Douglas Pennoyer. See also Don Williams, *Signs, Wonders and the Kingdom of God* (Ann Arbor, Mich.: Servant Books, 1989), and John P. Kildahl, *Miracles, Demons, and Spiritual Warfare* (Grand Rapids, Mich.: Baker Books, 1990). Frank Peretti's novel *This Present Darkness* was published by Regal Publishers of Ventura, Calif. in 1986. See also Pat Robertson, *The New World Order* (Dallas: Word Publishing, 1991).

Chapter 15

The title for this chapter is borrowed from my friend Eldin Villafañe's *The Liberating Spirit* (Grand Rapids, Mich.: Eerdmans, 1993). Martin E. Marty and Scott Appleby are the editors of *Fundamentalisms Observed*, volume 1 of a massive study conducted under their leadership by the American Academy of Arts and Sciences, published in 1991 by the University of Chicago Press. Robert Jay Lifton has also used the term "fundamentalist" in his fine book *The Protean Self* (New York: Basic Books, 1993), but he employs it to designate a personality type, while I use it in its more original religious sense.

Danièle Hervieu-Léger has written very widely on the subject of the new religious sensibility. The articles I refer to here are "Present-Day Emotional Renewals: The End of Secularization or the End of Religion?" in W. H. Swatos, ed., *A Future for Religion? A New Paradigm for Social Analysis* (London: Sage, 1992); and "Permanence et devenir du religieux dans les societeés Europeanes," in *Autres Temps* 38 (June 1993), pp. 33–44. Stephen Warner applies a paradigm similar to Hervieu-Léger's to America. See his "Work in Progress toward a New Paradigm for the Sociological Study of Religion in the United States" in *American Journal of Sociology* 98, 5 (March 1993), pp. 1044–1093. Arthur Green's "The Role of Jewish Mysticism in a Contemporary Theology of Judaism" was published in *Conservative Judaism* (Summer, 1976) pp. 12–22. *Islamic Spirituality: Manifestations,* edited by Seyyed Hossein Nasr, was published by Crossroads Publishing Company (New York: 1991). See also William James, *The Varieties of Religious Experience* (New York: Penguin, 1982).

The vigorous new discussion about the authority of experience in theology was launched by George Lindbeck's *The Nature of Doctrine: Religion and Theology in a Postliberal Age* (Philadelphia: Westminster, 1984). Relying heavily on the anthropologist Clifford Geertz and the British philosopher Ludwig Wittgenstein, Lindbeck, a Lutheran, argues very forcefully that religions are like languages. They are "cultural-linguistic systems," interpretative schemes with correlative forms of life. Lindbeck dismisses what he calls "experiential expressivism" as intellectually insupportable. His subtitle signals a critique of "liberal" theology, but given the penchant for experience shared by liberationists and pentecostals, his work is also an important critique of their use of "experience" as well. For a subtle and fair analysis of the various ways in which "experience" is used in theology, see Wayne Proudfoot, *Religious Experience* (Berkeley and Los Angeles: University of California Press, 1985). The comparison between pentecostalism and feminism can be found in Paula Cooey, "Experience, Body and Authority," *Harvard Theological Review* 82, 3 (1989), pp. 325–342. Theophus Smith, *Conjuring Culture: Biblical Formations of Black America* (New York: Oxford University Press, 1994) is a brilliant contribution to the ongoing discussion of the origins of ecstatic worship and the essential role it plays in the larger culture. See also Elaine Scarry, *The Body in Pain: The Making and Unmaking of the World* (New York: Oxford University Press, 1985). See also Owen Thomas, "Theology and Experience" in Harvard Theological Review 78, 1–2 (Jan.–Apr. 1985), pp 179–201

Steven J. Land's book is *Pentecostal Spirituality: A Passion for the Kingdom* (Sheffield, Engl.: Sheffield Academic Press, 1993) See also Murray Dempster,

"Christian Social Concern in Pentecostal Perspective: Reformulating Pentecostal Eschatology," in *Journal of Pentecostal Theology* 2, (1992), pp. 1–22. For a good comparison of pentecostalism and liberation theology see Miroslav Volf, "Materiality and Salvation" in *Journal of Ecumenical Studies* 26 (1989), pp. 447–67. For Cecilia Mariz on pentecostals and Catholic base communities in South America see her *Coping With Poverty: Pentecostals and Christian Base Communities in Brazil* (Philadelphia: Temple University Press, 1994).

INDEX